BLUE-RIBBON BABIES AND LABORS OF LOVE

Book Twenty-two
Louann Atkins Temple Women & Culture Series
Books about women and families, and their changing roles in society

BLUE-RIBBON BABIES
AND LABORS OF LOVE

*Race, Class, and Gender
in U.S. Adoption Practice*

CHRISTINE WARD GAILEY

UNIVERSITY OF TEXAS PRESS
Austin

The Louann Atkins Temple Women & Culture Series is supported by
Allison, Doug, Taylor, and Andy Bacon; Margaret, Lawrence, Will, John,
and Annie Temple; Larry Temple; the Temple-Inland Foundation; and
the National Endowment for the Humanities.

Requests for permission to reproduce material
from this work should be sent to:
Permissions
University of Texas Press
P.O. Box 7819
Austin, TX 78713-7819
www.utexas.edu/utpress/about/bpermission.html

∞ The paper used in this book meets the minimum requirements of
ANSI/NISO Z39.48-1992 (R1997) (Permanence of Paper).

Library of Congress Cataloging-in-Publication Data
Gailey, Christine Ward, 1950–
Blue-ribbon babies and labors of love : race, class, and gender in
U.S. adoption practice / Christine Ward Gailey.
p. cm. — (Louann Atkins Temple women & culture series ; bk. 22)
Includes bibliographical references and index.
ISBN 978-0-292-72127-2 (cloth : alk. paper)
1. Adoption—United States. 2. Interethnic adoption—United States.
3. Intercountry adoption—United States. 4. Families—United States.
5. Kinship—United States. I. Title.
HV875.55.G35 2010
362.73408'0973—dc22
2009031875

For Sarah, who followed the Drinking Gourd with transcendent courage

CONTENTS

ACKNOWLEDGMENTS

A project of this duration and complexity involves so many people who enabled, enriched, encouraged, and otherwise helped me in the process. I owe much to Jennifer Wells, adoption advocate and family counselor, who guided my first research into adoption and with whom I spent many a fruitful hour discussing the politics and dynamics of adoption. Rosemary Broadbent offered her insights and experience in looking at the adoption process itself. Rachel Port got involved in the adoption research from the outset, and we became friends as well as fellow travelers: I am grateful to her for our dozens of kitchen table talks and so much more. I thank the many participants in the research project, who have been more than generous with their time and experiences. Some of the interviews were painful, others thrilling, many poignant, all of which helped me reexperience the intensity that sometimes accompanies research. I hope that these adopters and their families find the results useful, even at points where they might disagree with my interpretation of the narratives.

Colleagues in the Association of Black Anthropologists gave me counsel and insight into child rearing in a racist society and the kinship dynamics of race identity in adolescence. The framing of the chapter on transracial adoption owes much to Lynn Bolles, Cheryl Mwaria, and Angela Gilliam, as well as Jennifer and Tim Welles, Ida Susser, Karen Brodkin, Ethan Nasreddin-Longo, and Enoch Page. Mary Anglin helped me realize the significance of the research on parenting older girls for feminist theorization of gendered violence. Heléna Ragoné pushed the argument regarding infertility and ideologies of adoptive motherhood in ways that were very productive. Ida Susser heard many of the arguments in the formative stages and helped me concentrate on the most salient issues; I deeply appreciate her editorial suggestions. My conversations with Lisa Edelsward on similarities and differences between adoption in the United States and Canada and about recent research on neurological changes after early trauma have informed my arguments on older child and transracial adoption.

I want to thank a number of Canadian colleagues for validating the research when it was not so widespread in the United States. Sally Cole buoyed me at a low point and introduced me to the stimulating research of Chantal Collard and Françoise Ouelette. Richard Lee, Michael Lambek, Harriet Rosenberg, Jackie Solway, and Gavin Smith helped me realize implications of adoption for kinship theory. I want to thank the Wenner-Gren Foundation and the organizers of the Symposium "New Directions in Kinship Studies: A Core Concept Revisited"; Pauline Turner Strong, Signe Howell, and Kath Weston were especially helpful in their comments regarding changing ideologies of kinship and maternity. I am particularly grateful to Signe and Anne-Lise Rygvold, Monica Dalen, and Babro Saetersdal of the PLUS "Yours, Mine, Ours — and Theirs" conference on international adoption, held in Oslo, Norway, for introducing me to one of the most congenial and intellectually exciting group of scholars I have ever encountered. I want to single out John Triseliotis, Peter Selman, Kathy Mason, and Jon Telfer for their insights into the political economy of international adoption. The chapter on international adoption owes a great deal to that extraordinary conference.

Audrey Aduama and Barbara Schram were generous in discussing their participant observation of adoptive and foster kinship and interracial family dynamics. I thank the graduate students in my family and kinship courses at both Northeastern University and the University of California, Riverside, for discussions of contemporary dynamics of reproduction and family formation. I have had a decade-long conversation about gender and kinship in the United States with my colleagues Gordana Rabrenovic, Debra Kaufman, Lynn Stephen, and Ellen Herman that shifted with our families' developments. Katherine Krohn and Susan Melito offered their insights into the politics of lesbian adoption, and I thank them for that and for sharing their delightful family during patches both rough and smooth.

Colleagues and staff in the Women's Studies Department at the University of California, Riverside, have shown steadfast encouragement during the writing process and an intellectual vitality unrivaled in my experience of the academy. Carlos Vélez-Ibáñez removed many obstacles and paved our pathway to the West Coast. Margie Waller has been especially generous with her time and critical commentaries on the arguments and early drafts of several chapters. Irma Kemp read drafts and made me laugh at foibles. Amalia Cabezas and Scott Coltrane have heard most of the arguments for the book and given their incisive evaluations, all valuable. The members of our Reproductive Ideologies and Technologies seminar at the Center for Ideas in

Society, part of a Ford Foundation Cloning Cultures grant headed by Piya Chatterjee, afforded me time to theorize the sections on class and parenting. Michael Kearney provided me with a forum for exploring the implications of adoption for American kinship, and Barbara Anderson gave me the opportunity to link the adoption work with wider implications of new ways of making family. I thank Carol Nagengast for our intense discussions of kinship and attachment theory, which occurred in a California hot tub that is the stuff of East Coast derision and envy. Not all research is grueling.

Wendy Ashmore has lent her wise and critical attention to my outlining arguments for each chapter. She and Tom Patterson took time out of their own coast-to-coast upheaval to "unpack" daily writing over suppers during the most intense period of writing. As a colleague and friend, Tom has heard me run through the roughest of drafts, patient and encouraging always.

Meg and Tim Gailey, my dear brother and sister (in- and far beyond law), provided a conversational lifeline, Scrabble and blueberries, and much-needed quiet and beauty during the writing phase. My nephew and niece, Adam and Clare Gailey, read drafts and kept me on task during the revisions. Louise Berndt edited the massive draft and drubbed me with great good humor into paring the manuscript as only a sister-friend can do without biting or being bitten. And I could never have finished this project without the understanding and Job-like patience of Theresa May of the University of Texas Press.

Most of all, I thank my daughter, Sarah, whose spirit I treasure, and from whom I have learned that trauma is never as strong as hard-headed courage, trust, and love.

Riverside, California
May 2008

BLUE-RIBBON BABIES AND LABORS OF LOVE

ONE

PROFILING ADOPTION IN THE UNITED STATES TODAY

Adoption, like motherhood, has always been a woman's issue.
It is women who give birth, and women have had their birth children
taken from them because of cultural, political or economic forces;
and it is women who sometimes feel they must relinquish their birth
child in order to protect that child. It is women who choose or
agree to take on the work of mothering.

—SUSAN WADIA-ELLS, *THE ADOPTION READER*

Race, class, and gender issues permeate and shape adoption in the United States. Adoption has always concerned race, from the first efforts by white settlers to adopt Native American children to the ongoing controversy surrounding interracial placement of children. It has an abiding location within a class hierarchy that draws children for adoption from the indigent or working-poor. Adoption today is also heavily gendered: women initiate the vast majority of adoptions; the preponderance of adoption social workers are women; and birth mothers are most often the sole parent for their vulnerable children. These hierarchies determine the structural risks facing children, the profiles of prospective adopters, and the institutions that operate foster care and adoption services.

PUBLIC AND PRIVATE ADOPTIONS

Adoptions in the United States today are arranged through three major mechanisms. Public agencies accounted for 40 percent of all adoptions in 2004. This represents a large increase from the 15.5 percent reported for 1992 (Child Welfare Information Gateway, 2004: 1; Stolley, 1993). These so-called public adoptions, or adoptions of children from domestic foster care, generally are accomplished through state agencies or the private agencies contracted to them for specific categories of children, especially those labeled as "hard to place" or "special needs." In public agency adoption, effects of gender and class are palpable: the economic conditions of adoption social workers, prospective adoptive mothers, and birth mothers are often not much more than two paychecks and medical insurance apart from one another. In international adoption, by contrast, the economic separation of adopters from their children's birth mothers and the social workers that sign off on the home studies tends to be extreme.

An increasing number of domestic adopters are sufficiently well off and legally connected to obtain children privately. They work through licensed businesses that often are no more than an individual known as a "facilitator," someone who brokers agreements between prospective adopters and pregnant women, mediated through lawyers. Although researchers know this form of adoption is increasing, particularly for infant adoptions, exact figures are elusive because states are not required to collect data on this arrangement. Another type of private adoption involves licensed local, regional, or national agencies that locate children with particular characteristics (typically age, sex, and/or race) either within the United States or elsewhere. Since many private agencies are faith-based, adopters pursuing this line of access often seek children of their own religion. Agencies associated with particular communities may contract with state child welfare departments for adoptions to and from that constituency. Other agencies maintain national networks or specialize in international adoption; some do both. Private agency adoptions account for most of the international adoptions today; the number of domestic adoptions through private agencies is less clear. Because of the way the Department of Health and Human Services collects and processes adoption data, about 40 percent of adoptions can no longer be separated statistically into private agency, kinship/stepparent adoptions, or adoptions through Native American tribal agencies (Child Welfare Information Gateway, 2004: 1).

ADOPTIVE KINSHIP IN THE CONTEXT
OF CLASS, RACE, AND GENDER

In the reassortment of children across space, economic stratification, and social hierarchies, what does kinship mean? How do adopters perceive their children? How do they conceive of kinship and family? How and why do they prefer some children rather than others placed for adoption? How do they build relationships with their children?

This study involved extensive interviews with 131 adopters from many walks of life. Some received their children through public adoption agencies, others from private ones. Some arranged adoptions using specialized lawyers' networks or contacted birth mothers via licensed "adoption facilitators" over the internet. Some adopted their children from the foster care system in the United States, and some adopted children from public or private institutions or networks in other countries.

These adopters' commentaries enable us to see the tensions between ideologies and practices of kinship in the United States today. We see how ideologies of gender, race, and class crosscut and interact as people create families. Examining how these adoptive parents speak about their families and the various participants involved in their particular adoption experiences provides a lens through which we can glimpse the impact of dramatic social changes on children: class mobility, interracial kinship, or international migration, in addition to early upheavals of foster care or placement in institutionalized care. In assessing the ways adoptive parents speak of issues regarding nature and nurture, and how they have brought their ideologies to bear on family formation, we can see how adoption has challenged, transformed, or reinforced their commitment to these beliefs. In how they discuss their children's integration into their new communities, we see how parents' commitment to their adopted children interacts with their (usually unspoken) commitment to reproduction within their socioeconomic class.

Although many adopters might disagree, adoption in the United States is not a private matter. As both policy and practice, adoption involves people with different degrees of social power in a society of ever-increasing wealth differences, racial and ethnic hierarchies, and uneven but persistent discrimination by gender and sexual orientation. The state is always an interested party, and in the case of international adoption more than one state is involved. It is a process that often brings people from different social classes into coordination or conflict about one of the most intimate arenas in adult life: reproduction. How adopters speak of birth mothers/parents, social workers, foster mothers/parents, and so on gives a sense of the anxieties of class in reproduction today.

In the ways adopters speak of their children's needs related to early disruption and even trauma, we can detect the weight the adopters give their received notions of kinship, gender, sexuality, race, ethnicity, and sometimes nationality and religion. The various responses of parents to their children reveals a great deal about some of the ways these families forge kinship that inadvertently or consciously subverts prevailing ideologies and practices. It also reveals how some of the parents subordinate the child's needs to their own desire for an idealized "American family."

To grasp the kinds of kinship that adoptive families in the United States construct, we must situate adoption practices in a national and global contexts: neoliberal policy shifts away from social services and social welfare in the last quarter of the twentieth century, the collapse of the Soviet bloc, the economic and social reforms in China, and the proliferation of capitalist markets throughout the world. Internationally, the desire for hard currency, whether on the part of the particular state, ill-paid bureaucrats, downwardly mobile workers, or underemployed professionals in regions newly opened to capitalist markets, episodically creates a practice of adoption that in effect trafficks in children.

Neoliberal reforms in the United States have diminished state regulation of major arenas of the economy, and this too has changed the face of adoption. Forms of adoption once considered to be a gray, if not completely illegal, market in children have now become the most prevalent types, excepting only stepparent adoption. So-called private and independent adoptions—arrangements between prospective adopters and pregnant women willing to relinquish their parental rights—are mediated through lawyers, private agencies, or individual brokers (called facilitators). In European countries where welfare state protections and regulations remain somewhat intact despite neoliberal pressures, such adoptions are illegal, considered to constitute a market in children. Public agency adoptions, drawing on a pool of children in foster care, once were second only to stepparent adoptions in frequency but are now a decided minority.

National policy shifts in welfare, foster care, health care, and reproductive rights have shaped today's demographics of adoption with regard to the social class and ethnic or racialized profiles of adopters, of those available for adoption, and of birth parents. The typical patterns of marital status and sexual orientation of public versus private agency adopters, private agency versus independent adopters, and domestic versus international adopters also have changed. On the state level, legal battles continue over how and when birth mothers and birth fathers can cede legal claims to children and when the state can terminate such rights. Guidelines for placing children in foster care vary from state to state, based on definitions of what constitutes child abuse or neglect. States also vary in the regulation of public and private adoption agencies and the requirements that individual adoption facilitators must meet. The greatest controversy surrounds whether adoptive parents or adult adoptees can have access to original birth certificates and other adoption records: this controversy is widely known as the "sealed records" or "open records" debates.

In this country, economic trends that have resulted in fewer jobs capable of sustaining a parent with children, scarce or prohibitively expensive infant and child care, and a steady rise in the number of families lacking medical insurance have affected the number, ethnicity, race, and age of children entering foster care or experiencing legal separation from their birth families. Legislative changes in social welfare, marriage, child custody, immigration, and child protection intersect with these economic effects and often compound their influence on children becoming available for adoption.

The situation is even more complex when we consider the 15 percent of U.S. adoptions that involve children from other countries. In addition to the economic processes and legal changes in this country, there is variation in the other country's state-run or private foster care policies and arrangements, the stability and extent of governmental regulation and social service supports, and the differential impact of trade and international lending practices that make hard currency scarce and disproportionately desirable in the global South.

To analyze such a complex set of issues and connections that span from political-economic processes to kinship formation requires interdisciplinary research. To approach the intersections of race and gender in adoption demands familiarity with critical race theory and feminist theory. To evaluate to what extent a "culture of adoption" exists, or how adoption practices vary, participant observation as a research technique needs to be informed by critical theories of culture and comparative ethnology. The following section outlines the project design and how the research process raised issues of informed consent, researcher-participant relations, the role of emotion in research, and other dimensions of the broader sense of methodology. Here it is sufficient to outline the number of people in the study, their social profiles, and the kinds of adoptions they undertook.

METHODS

Over a period of thirteen years, I interviewed 131 adopters of ninety children. In New York, Massachusetts, Vermont, and New Hampshire I developed a snowball sample of ninety-three parents of sixty-one children adopted between 1991 and 1997. In Southern California from 2000 to 2004 I interviewed a snowball sample of thirty-eight parents of twenty-nine children adopted between 2000 and 2004. I selected the California sample to delve into patterns that had emerged in the earlier research, so I made no attempt to model the numbers after the northeastern sample or on federal statistics.

Both samples included single mothers, heterosexual married couples, lesbian couples, and gay couples. In the Northeast there were six African American couples, twenty-nine white couples, four African American single mothers, eighteen white single mothers, and one white father. The father was part of a gay couple, and three of the aforementioned single mothers were actually from lesbian couples: one African American, one white, and one African American and white.

In the California sample there were eleven married couples: two African American couples, three Latino/Anglo-white couples, one African American/white couple, and five white couples. There were two single fathers (both white) and fourteen single mothers: nine whites, three Latinas, and two African Americans. Of the fourteen single mothers, eight adopters (listed first) in fact represented lesbian couples: one Latina/African American, two Latina/Anglo-white, two African American, one white/Asian American, and two white. The two single fathers represented gay couples, one white/Asian-American and one white. Where I talk of gay and lesbian couples in the adoption process and in the sample, I use only the legal adopters, since gays and lesbians cannot legally adopt as couples, but where I discuss parenting practices, I have included both partners.

Of the sixty-one children adopted by families in the northeastern sample, public agencies placed thirty-six, private agencies nineteen, and private, independent channels six. Among these adoptions, forty-seven were domestic and fourteen were international; in Southern California, sixteen were domestic and thirteen were international. Fourteen of the twenty-nine Southern California adoptions were through public agencies or private ones contracted to the state for special needs adoptions; thirteen were international adoptions through private agencies; and two were independent domestic, that is, arranged privately through adoption facilitators and lawyers.

All of the sixteen Southern California public adoptees and twenty-five of the northeastern children adopted domestically were "older child" adoptions, over three years old when placed. All but two of the northeastern international adoptees were infants or toddlers when placed. Because the Southern California international adoptions were disproportionately those by nongovernmental agency personnel or U.S. academics working internationally (eight of thirteen), more of the children were older than is typical of international adoptions in the United States. Six of these eight children were between four and ten years old. The five children not adopted by the NGO/ academic group were all infants or below the age of two.

In all likelihood I oversampled gay and lesbian adopters in Southern California, although the statistical situation is so poor that one cannot be certain. I did this because for ethical reasons I could not use extensive interviews I had done earlier with the northeastern lesbian and gay adopters; they had expressed fears that the channels through which they adopted would be shut to others if their stories were published. Southern California lesbian and gay adopters, partly because of regional attitudes and partly because of shifts in state adoption practices, were less fearful.

To acquire a sense of the dilemmas faced by adoption workers, I interviewed six adoption social workers active during the period in the Northeast and in Southern California, and three adoption social workers and two staff members from private agencies that dealt almost exclusively with international adoptions. I had the opportunity to interview two birth mothers who had relinquished children through private adoptions, but it was legally problematic to interview the adopters.

To construct the snowball samples, I began with adoptive acquaintances that knew other adopters and the sample ramified. Snowball sampling generally overrepresents or underrepresents participants by class, race, gender, or sexual orientation. To develop the snowball, then, I was careful to locate myself in urban arenas where diversity would be commonplace: churches, adoption conferences, post-adoption social groups, grocery stores, public swimming pools, and neighborhood playgrounds as starting points. For the international adopter groups I began interviewing acquaintances in university settings, but I became aware quite quickly that at least among international adopters, academics were decidedly at odds with the national patterns. To explore this more deeply, I developed a Southern California sample of professionals and academics that had adopted from countries where their ongoing work with non-governmental agencies or their research had provided long-term ties to local communities. I have used this NGO/academic group, then, to compare and contrast with the sociologically more typical international adopters.

Because African American children disproportionately staff the ranks of children in foster care waiting for adoption in the United States, and because young and unmarried black mothers run the highest risk of losing children to foster care, I thought it was necessary to get a better sense of how shifts in welfare laws over the last decade have affected young African American mothers. To better appreciate the conditions faced by such single mothers, I interviewed five women who were in the kinds of circumstances that could lead to relinquishment or removal of children. I also interviewed the sister of one mother known by one of these women to be a crack addict.

The northeastern and Southern California sites, the ways ethnicity and race articulate with public agency adoption recruitment, and the vagaries of snowball sampling led to my sample including black adopters (Americans of Afro-Caribbean heritage and African Americans) and whites of various ethnicities, but few Spanish-speaking, East Asian, or South Asian adopters. I attempted to remedy this with the Southern California materials, though with limited success because of the snowball technique. There is considerable effective outreach by Southern California state agencies to recruit Chicanos and other Latinos as adopters that is not reflected in the study. Outside the region, outreach to Spanish-speaking populations is minimal. Neither of the pre-adoptive training sessions in the Northeast that I was allowed to observe, for example, included any Spanish-speaking participants. There were no alternative sessions for people speaking other languages. The necessary resources for such outreach were not available in the social services sectors of the northeastern states I investigated.

With all this in mind, how representative is this study's sample? It is an important question, but no one can answer it with any certainty. We simply do not know exactly how many formal adoptions take place in the United States every year, let alone how many informal ones occur. The paucity and accuracy of available adoption statistics are lamentable; until the long-awaited census of 2000, there had not been even what could be called somewhat reliable figures since 1992 (see Stolley, 1993). In that year most adoptions were by stepparents or relatives (42 percent), followed closely by adoptions through private agencies or mediated through lawyers and privately arranged (37.5 percent). Only 15.5 percent of the 127,441 adoptions recorded that year were through public agencies, and only 5 percent of the total adoptions were international. We know that the number of international adoptions has increased from 1992 to about 15 percent of all (estimated) adoptions in 2006: those adoptions are tracked through the State Department issuance of visas, so the figures are reliable. But while we also know that privately arranged adoptions have increased a great deal, judging from internet facilitator and related sites, the figures are not tracked. Indeed, federal statistics merge adoptions arranged through Native American auspices, stepparent adoptions, and private domestic adoptions.

The proportion of public agency to international adopters within the sample is parallel to the 1992 figures. Gauging the relative representation of private agency and independent adoptions in the study sample vis-à-vis national patterns is difficult, but it is safe to assume that the study underrepresented independent adoptions.

My sample differs from national patterns for a number of reasons. First, I did not include stepparent and other forms of kin adoptions. My concern was how kinship is constructed in a context of race, class, and gender dynamics that shape adoption practices. The presence of birth-related relatives would cloud important issues of claiming. Second, while private agency and privately arranged adoptions are far more numerous today, they also are the forms least accessible to researchers. Indeed, the federal data obscures their numbers. I located some private adopters because I had permission to participate in and observe a training program for prospective adopters at a private agency; others I found through conferences on adoption. Third, because I wanted to investigate how parents whose children had been through early traumas constructed parenting "in the wake of history," as I termed it, I needed to concentrate on older child adoption and thus more than the usual number of public agency adoptions. Because I needed both class and racial diversity to inform the study, I had to develop the public agency end of the snowball more extensively. The amount of media attention paid to international adoption mandated a focus on that category beyond the 5 to 15 percent of adoptions during the study period.

Alongside the snowball sampling, I was opportunistic about initiating supplementary interviews. For example, while waiting for an hour with my daughter in line at a major theme park, I struck up a conversation with two men and their young son in front of us. They were interested in the project and agreed to be interviewed about their gay adoption experience. While they were not part of the snowball, their perceptions and experiences have been used as illustrations where the snowball was inadequate.

My efforts to locate birth mothers were not as successful as the other parts of the project: I managed to interview five women who either had relinquished a child to adoption or had had a child placed in foster care with little likelihood of retrieving the child. I also interviewed relatives of women who were similarly at risk of losing legal rights to their children. I include their stories to give a sense of the conditions faced by those birth mothers who are not the much sought-after unmarried white women from "good homes" who found themselves "in trouble" and did not believe in abortion. Since today virtually all white birth mothers who relinquish their children are involved in privately arranged adoptions, I gained access to only two such women, one of whom was a single woman of Vietnamese heritage; her Anglo-Vietnamese son had been adopted by a white married couple. The other birth mother was white, single, and a fundamentalist Christian: her white baby was adopted by a white, married, Christian couple.

In an effort to analyze privately arranged domestic and international adoptions, I contacted eight lawyers nationally whose practices focused on adoption. Three of those involved in international rather than domestic adoptions agreed to be interviewed; each of these interviews lasted under an hour and all lawyers insisted upon complete confidentiality. Only one lawyer working in domestic, privately arranged adoptions agreed to be interviewed.

Within the interview groups I tracked basic socioeconomic status information, such as occupation, educational attainment, approximate annual income, gender, marital status, number of birth and adopted children, whether either parent was an adoptee (none were), whether the parent(s) had experienced foster care themselves as children, and self-identified race or ethnicity of both parents and children. I did not ask directly about sexual orientation, although several single-parent informants informed me that they were heterosexual or lesbian.

I gave all married parents or those in a committed relationship the option of being interviewed alone, together, or both. The location for the interview was at the discretion of those interviewed; most opted for being interviewed at home in the evening, but a sizeable minority chose to be interviewed in a restaurant over lunch. Of those interviewed in the Northeast I re-interviewed about half of them five years after the first interviews (the others were either no longer in the area, had left no forwarding information when they moved, or declined follow-up). In these cases I interviewed the adopters under the same settings as previously. In the follow-up interview I asked questions about how they saw their children faring, whether they had adopted or otherwise acquired more children, what if any changes adopting had made in their familial relationships, whether they would do it again, and what advice or suggestions they would make to improve adoption in the United States.

The interviews covered the adopter's motivations to adopt, the decision-making process about when and where to adopt, the adopter's characterization of the home study and pre-adoptive training process (if any), how the adopter imagined the child, what the adopter wanted in a child, the story of how the parent(s) first met the child(ren), and how they "came home" and formalized the adoption. Beyond this, I asked the parents to characterize the child's adjustment to the new family, their own adjustments, how they characterized the process of bonding and attachment, what their arrangements were regarding child care and/or schooling, and how the extended family reacted to the adoption. I asked one intentionally very open-ended question: how did they think their child was doing after whatever amount of time had elapsed since "coming home."

In analyzing the narratives that flowed from the interviews, I paid particular attention to the language used to describe familial relations in general, the child in particular, silences, sighs, hesitations, and points of consensus or disagreement if two parents were involved. I noted where emotional tones involved in speaking of the child shifted (tears of joy or grief, anger, frustration, among others), facial expressions, and gestures. In drawing my interpretation of how parents related to children, all these factors were relevant.

PUBLIC AGENCY ADOPTERS

Of the sixty-one adoptions in the northeastern sample, thirty-six had taken place through public agencies or agencies subcontracted to public agencies for adoption purposes. In other words, at the time of adoption these children had spent some time in foster care. Of these, twenty-three were girls adopted over the age of four and one was a boy age seven; eleven of the children (six boys and five girls) were adopted under the age of four. These public agency children went to thirty-two families.

Twenty of these families had adopted twenty-three girls who were between ages four and twelve at the time of adoption. Their daughters were between five and fourteen years old at the time of the interviews. Ten families had adopted ten black girls; these families consisted of two single African American women, three single white women, three African American married couples, and two white married couples. The remaining ten families had adopted thirteen older white girls. These families were white and consisted of four single women and six married couples. One single woman had adopted an older boy.[1]

The eleven married older child adopters in the sample were working class or professionals. The eight single women were professionals with flexible office schedules. This profile is substantially in keeping with other researchers' findings that public agency adopters usually have less education and lower incomes than those adopting through private agencies or independently through lawyers (see Barth, Brooks, and Iyer, 1995). What the figures do not reflect, however, is the growing number of single women professionals seeking to adopt through public agencies or their subcontractors. In my sample these women seemed more like the private agency single adopters in terms of education, but generally had lower incomes than the private adopters.

PRIVATE AGENCY ADOPTERS

The adopters working through private agencies were seeking infants or toddlers: seven of the children (four boys and three girls) were from the United States and twelve (nine girls and three boys) were from other countries. The adopters were white: ten married couples and nine single women. The single women seeking to adopt were people who would have been categorically excluded from the public agency route in the state where they lived: some had been turned down already on grounds of being over age forty or being in a lesbian partnership. In one case the woman's age would not have mattered had she been willing to take an older child, but she wanted an infant.

Among the children adopted, all were infants or toddlers; of the seven U.S. children, two were considered Latina/os and two were considered to be "biracial" or "mixed race." Most of the children had been in foster care for short periods in states other than the ones where the adopters reside.

INDEPENDENT ADOPTERS

Children whose adoptions were arranged privately through the mediation of specialized attorneys included three boys and a girl from the United States and two boys from other countries. The adoptive parents were white and from professional middle-income and upper-income brackets. These adopters were college educated; the couples were dual-earners, with the exception of one of the wealthy international adopters, where the wife had no paid position.

The sole single-father adoption in the Northeast was in this group. He was a middle-income gay man who had cared for a woman with a young son while she was dying of AIDS. She had contracted the virus as an IV drug-user, but she had quit using by the time she became pregnant; her child was HIV negative. The mother had not known she was infected at the time she conceived. She specified in her will that this man be permitted to adopt her son, as he had been the only effective father the child had ever known. At the time of the adoption, the child was six but had known his adoptive father from birth. The relationship became virtually custodial as the mother's health deteriorated. In the local jurisdiction, the man's sexual orientation was considered an impediment by the family court judge, but his long-term caregiving and de facto parenting, in addition to the child's obvious attachment to him, were deemed by the judge to surmount other considerations.

It is a rarity to encounter gay single father adoption in the United States, but among the few I located, until very recently there seemed to be only two ways men located children to adopt: either through a long-term connection to the child's single mother who had died, or becoming a single father as part of an adoptive or blended family when marriage to the child's mother ended and the mother did not seek custody. The latter situation is rare; in the two families I know, the children were boys who had severe physical or cognitive disabilities. The only other single father adoptions I have found did not involve gay men: these two were adoptions of pre-adolescent black boys in state care by African American men who were social workers and had grown up in foster care themselves. In California de facto social work practices have recently begun permitting, after an exacting screening process, select gay men who are single or in partnerships to adopt children with special needs, particularly those who are HIV positive. Gay adoption remains an exception to exclusion, however, and most children are adopted privately or through a few sympathetic private and public agencies (see Mallon, 2000).

Business/professional private adopters from this same race/class strata focused on controlling prenatal conditions as much as possible. Outright purchase of children remains illegal for private domestic adoptions, but once these parents screened their potential birth mothers to rule out those who smoked, drank alcohol, used drugs, or are HIV positive, they often subsidized her medical and dietary expenses. They also provided substantial gifts to the birth mother throughout her pregnancy and upon the birth of the child. Preserving the appearance of not paying the birth mother was very important to the adopters.

Throughout the research period (1992–2004), all the independent and private agency adopters had incomes of more than twice the national median, significantly higher than the public agency adopters. In terms of education and other aspects of socioeconomic status, they would be considered upper middle class or wealthy professionals.

INTERNATIONAL ADOPTERS

Cutting across the private agency and privately arranged adoptions were the international adopters. Twelve of the fourteen children coming from other countries were infants or toddlers, that is, under the age of three at the time of adoption; the other two were under the age of five. The adoptive parents were white. Of the fourteen families, eight had gone through the adoption process as married couples and four as single women. Twelve of the families had adopted through private agencies and two went through adoption lawyers to locate their children. Four of these adopters were single mothers as far as the adoption agencies or lawyers were concerned, although two were in long-term lesbian relationships before, during, and after the adoption took place.

The families had each adopted one child: the children included four girls from China, two girls and a boy from Korea, a girl from India, two boys and a girl from Colombia, two girls from Guatemala, and a boy from Brazil. While it was not planned, the proportion of ten girls to four boys was close to the ratio (64 percent girls and 36 percent boys) in the 1992 NAIC statistics for U.S. international adoption. Despite this statistical serendipity, I was disappointed that there were no children from the former Soviet Union, Romania, or Bulgaria in the snowball sample from the Northeast: countries from Eastern Europe had joined the top-sending regions during the period of the study. I was gratified in the Southern California sample to interview two married couples who had adopted in Romania, and a married couple and a single mother who was married at the time when they adopted Russian children. To supplement this material I have used a range of secondary sources for information about these adoptions.

The international adopter group had the highest educational attainment and income levels of any of the people I interviewed for the larger study: all were college- or graduate-school educated, and salaries (of those who revealed theirs to me) were at least three times the national median. Single or married, most had supplementary income from stocks, rental property, trust funds, and corporate bonus packages. Most of the couples had second homes and all had at least part-time nanny support in child rearing.

LESBIAN ADOPTERS

Apart from Ellen Lewin's path-breaking study of lesbian motherhood, there is little information about lesbian adopters in either the analytical literature or the memoir literature (see Lewin, 1993: 72–73). In the northeastern and Southern California sites, I located women who were parenting alone or with a partner. In Massachusetts in 1993 I contacted five self-identified lesbians who were adoptive mothers who were willing to participate in the study. Two international adopters had not identified themselves as lesbians to their social workers or agencies, but told me they had stable partnerships before, during, and after the adoptions. Two of the women who had adopted domestically through private agencies also were lesbians; one was parenting alone and the other was in a long-term relationship. One of the public agency adopters was parenting alone; she had disclosed her sexual orientation to her sympathetic social worker, who decided to suppress the information. The private agency adopters all had contacted the agencies because of referrals from other lesbian adopters. Only one had to be completely closeted to her agency.

The four others were acceptable to their agencies in what one mother called a "semi-out" fashion. When I asked why, I was told jokingly, "They were more interested in two-parent families than in straight singles." As she explained further, the agencies made it clear that the adoption would be to her as a single mother and only that mother would be allowed to take the child to court for finalization, but that partners were welcome in the pre-adoptive training sessions and in the home study interview process. Like single women adopters in general, most of the lesbian adopters had been questioned about their attitudes toward sexuality during the screening process. When I asked the heterosexual couples about this point, none had been questioned.

In addition to these five women, in 1993 I made contact with a lively, close-knit network of lesbian singles and couples who had established an informal post-adoption support group. Most of these women were in long-term, stable partnerships. All had adopted through one particular agency and all of their children had come from one out-of-region locale in the United States. After considerable discussion within the group, the group decided to refuse access to me:

> No reflection on you, but some of us are real paranoid: We know you'd keep our names out of it and all that, [but] if anyone figured out who or where we were, maybe the agency would shut down to people like us and we just can't risk that. Some of us want to add to our families and it's so hard to find an agency that understands.[2]

I asked if I could relate just the information above and they agreed. Given the degree of homophobia in the United States and the well-documented legal problems even birth mothers face in custody cases if they are openly lesbian (see Lewin, 1993: 163–179), I considered their concerns well founded. By the time I interviewed the Southern California lesbian adopters, lesbian adoption was still not acceptable throughout the country, but there were pockets where it was far more possible, and a few situations in which it was not difficult. The six "out" lesbian adopters in the Southern California sample were aware of constraints many of their friends or acquaintances from other parts of the country encountered, but were confident that things "really had changed" toward acceptance in their own localities. The ballot initiatives of 2008 would seem to make this confidence premature.

With these methodological and ethical considerations in mind, we can turn to key issues explored through the adopter narratives and the participant observation.

ADOPTION AS PRACTICE: THE POLITICS
OF CLAIMING AND DISCLAIMING

I posed several questions about adoptive kinship. First, how do gender, race, and class hierarchies and ideologies influence adopter perceptions of their children? Second, how do adopters come to prefer some children over others placed for adoption? Third, how do adopters conceive of families and enact relationships with their children? Fourth, based on the results of the first three questions, what does adoption provide to theories of kinship?

The following chapters consider how public agency adopters, older child adopters, transracial adopters, and international adopters spoke of their children and their parenting experiences. They reveal tensions between ideologies and practices of kinship, between gender and racial ideologies, and how in some cases the difficulties of class mobility for the children challenge the adopters' unspoken commitment to their own class reproduction.

Chapter 2 introduces public agency adopters, where class and gender dynamics intertwine with those of race. The issues of single-mother adoption and adoption by people of color and working-class married couples cluster in public adoption. Here, too, we encounter domestic, transracial adopters for the first time in the study. The public adopters also represent the only group in the United States that consistently adopts older children.

Chapter 3 delves more deeply into the experiences of interracial adoptive families, from the viewpoint of the parents. The stress here is on white adopters of African American and black children, as the issues of race in that setting are the starkest and the highest, given racial politics and the life prospects for African American boys and girls in the United States. Some of the issues of single-mother adopters range into this chapter as well, given the demographics of transracial placement in public agency adoption.

Chapter 4 examines the experiences of parents who have adopted older girls through public channels. It gives the reader a sense of the impact of gender on adoption practices in ways much of the literature fails to appreciate. It also links issues of race with gender, both among the adopters and adoptees.

Chapter 5 considers the experiences of parents adopting internationally, across cultural and sometimes color lines. Here we can discern the role of private agencies in addressing parental desires. Here again, although we are often trained not to see it, the role of social class enters strongly, and issues of class and gender also shape parental wishes and practices.

Finally, Chapter 6 addresses the questions posed in the study in examining kinship formation among these adopter groups. These adoptive parents' experiences inform the changing ideologies of kinship in the United States, but they do not do so in isolation. The structures and policies that constrain support for them and their children point to family formation as a highly contested arena.

TWO

"KIDS NEED FAMILIES
TO TURN OUT RIGHT"

Public Agency Adopters

*Without the support groups, one or both of us would be dead.
You've heard the African proverb, "It takes a village to raise a child"?
Well, it's taken the whole damned East Coast to rear my daughter!*

—SINGLE MOTHER, PUBLIC AGENCY ADOPTER, 1999

There has long been a socioeconomic divide between those who adopt children from foster care and those who adopt privately or through private agencies. For decades, most foster parents have come from the working and lower-middle classes (see Mandell, 1973: 43). Public agencies did not actively solicit adoption applications from these caregivers until reforms of the 1970s permitted foster parents to adopt. Public agency adoptions began to permit kin adoptions in the 1970s, followed by greater acceptance of single-mother adoptions in the 1980s. Kin adoptions reflected the class and racial/ethnic backgrounds of children in foster care. Single-mother adoptions included more middle-income professionals and whites than the children's backgrounds would predict.

The ten couples I interviewed who had adopted or were seeking to adopt through public agencies—whether through the state's Department of Social Services or its designated private agency partners for adoptions labeled "special needs" or "hard to place"—shared certain characteristics. The ones who remained throughout the screening and training process were less well off than the people I interviewed who were seeking private or international adoptions. Based on the wives' and husbands' self-reported occupations, in most cases, the public agency adoptive couples' household incomes were comparable to those of the single professional women seeking to adopt through public channels. Public agencies also provide home-study services to people not planning to obtain children from public sources. These participants in the preadoptive training/home study sessions are more likely to have higher incomes. One prosperous white couple remained in the training sessions to complete their home study. They opted for international adoption after expressing a fear, based on the pre-adoptive parental training sessions they attended, that they would never get a healthy infant going through public channels. The prospective adopters in the training sessions I observed were not all white, in contrast to those in the private agencies not contracted to the state for special needs and older-child adoption. But compared with the children awaiting adoption, there were a disproportionate number of whites nonetheless. The public adopters' class composition mirrored what stable employment, freedom from addiction, or relative nonviolence would have made of the vast majority of foster children's birth families. In short, public agency adopters shared class characteristics with the parents of foster children, but proportionately more were white. The public agency adopters as a group, however, showed the greatest ethnic and racial diversity of any prospective adopters (private agency or independent).

NOT THE "HONEYMOONERS": WORKING-CLASS COUPLES AS ADOPTERS

The discussion of family in these working-class adoptive couples' narratives all stressed the desirability of a stable nuclear unit within a wider net of supportive kin, but otherwise their situations and reasons for adopting varied. The white couples in the sample tended to be younger and most had infertility issues; the one middle-class African American couple was adopting for infertility reasons. The two working-class African American couples were seeking to add to their families, as were three working-class white couples. Two of the latter were adopting because they were starting a second family as a result of remarriage; in both cases the husband had non-resident children from a former marriage and did not wish to sire any more children. The remaining middle-class white couple revealed their baby-boomer status when they identified their motivation to adopt as arising from an interest in "Zero Population Growth."

The two working-class African American couples were in their mid-forties, older than all but one of the other couples by a decade. They were starting second families: their first set of children had grown and moved out of the house. As one of the mothers, Simone, put it, "We have room in our home and hearts now that the kids are grown for another family." Her husband, Aaron, added, "Children need families and we did a fine job with our other ones." When asked what their older daughter thought of their adopting, Aaron laughed and said, "Well, at first she was jealous that they were going to eat up her inheritance, but she came around." Simone added,

> I took her to look at that notebook [a state Adoption Resources book with descriptions and pictures of children available for adoption]. When she saw all those kids just waiting, she just had to agree with us. It just is the right thing to do.

The other working-class African American wife, Velma, murmured, "Mm-Hm. You said it." Her husband, Louis, patted her hand, perhaps in affirmation, perhaps to remind her it was too white a setting for call-and-response.

A common theme was the hard work needed to win over an adopted child to the family's ways. One of the white husbands, Robert, said,

> I wouldn't have made it through that first year without Mary Pat [his wife]. She kept saying, "Don't give up on him, he just has to learn he's one of us. Don't let him win and keep being a loner." We just kept showing him our ways and expecting him to live up to them. Then, one day almost—after that horrible birthday, remember? He just sort of came around. Since then, he's done better in school, made friends, shown us more respect. We still have our ups and downs, but it's like he decided we were really going to be his family, that he was one of us.

Mary Pat added, "I thought I would melt the first time he hugged me without wanting something from me except a hug in return. That's when I knew we'd won, we'd won him over." Sandra, another white mother, described how their adoption came about:

> We set out to adopt a baby and one day [the social worker] just called us up and said, "We have three girls who've been through a lot. They've been physically and sexually abused. One doesn't talk and one sets fires. They aren't legally free yet. Can you take them?" I looked at Johnny [her husband] and said, "Are you ready for this?" He said, "Hell, no! Are you?" So, crazy fools that we are, we got in the car and went to get them. It sure was a roller coaster at first, but each of them had strengths that helped the other ones along, and we could build them up that way. My mother helped out a lot, and I practically moved my sister in with us. Now it's four years

later, and they're doing fine. It made me and [Johnny] feel real good about ourselves—we did it, we made it work. What's funny is that each of the girls is like me and Johnny but in different ways.

Velma, reared in a loving foster home herself, laughed about why she and her husband adopted a toddler whom they knew two other black couples had rejected because of her appearance: "She has bad hair and is too dark, but then, look at our family: We're all a mess!" More seriously, she added,

> The real work with that child had to be done on the *inside* and that's where we got down to business. She needed to know that she belonged *somewhere* and that 'somewhere' was *us*.

In these narratives there is a strong sense that adoption means bringing a child into an ongoing family system, and a belief that the values of the family are solid, good for the child and everyone else. The parents I interviewed do not neatly fall into gender roles typical of the working class as described in the analytical literature (see Rubin, 1976), although husbands deferred to wives for child rearing and there seemed more reliance on kin from the mother's side during critical periods. Both husband and wife expressed strong support of one another, and stressed the strength and endurance of the other in periods of difficulty. They also affirmed that parents should be authority figures, not their children's friends.

The adoptees faced risks in these families, including a propensity for at least some of the relatives—often not the parents—to use corporal punishment. Despite pre-adoptive training sessions that stress disciplining children through logical and natural consequences for inappropriate behavior, using time-outs and other alternatives to physical violence, adoption social workers I interviewed admitted that spanking, if not belting, remained a commonplace punishment in working-class adoptive homes. One experienced adoption social worker stated:

> I know some of our kids are going to homes where they will be hit. Some will be belted. I'm not defending it, but you have to realize that the kid is probably better off in a permanent family with hitting than a series of foster homes without hitting.

Another adoption social worker explained,

As long as the kid isn't being singled out for punishment, he'll figure it's just the way things are. That's not great for the next generation, but unless the kid was tortured earlier, it won't make things any worse probably.

When I probed about what she meant by "torture," she elaborated:

Listen, when you work in public adoption, you see it all: cigarette burns, scalding, welts and scars from beatings, broken bones, skull fractures. Some of these kids have been through hell and back again for years. It never ceases to amaze me how they can come back from all of that, and most of them do. The resiliency of these kids, given half a chance, takes your breath away.

Given the profiles of children awaiting placement in public agencies, the working-class adoptive couples openly discussed the risks they saw themselves taking (Barth, 1988; Cahn and Johnson, 1993). The white couples spoke of their fears that the children would not turn out right. What was absent from their discussion of risk was attributing failure to the child herself, that is, to purported innate qualities. The risk was that the couples would not have enough time with the kids to turn them around. I asked if they considered that the child's problems might be genetic. One white mother, Anita, shrugged and said, "Well, maybe so, but there's nothing you can do about that, right? You gotta do what you can." Her husband, Jim, added, "There are no guarantees that come with biological kids either, so what's the difference?" The wife of another couple said, "You know, you gotta be careful with those labels. A lot of people put a label on something they just don't understand." Her husband added,

Yeah, when our son was in first grade, they had him labeled every way but the right way. We went along with it for a while, they being the experts and all, but when he was gettin' worse, not better, we put our foot down and took him off the pills and made them try him out in a regular classroom. He still needs discipline sometimes, but basically he's OK.

Akin to the white working-class adopters, the working-class African American couples did not attribute possible problems to innate qualities of the child. They phrased risks in societal terms. Risk for adopted children was bracketed by the hazards facing all black children, and especially black boys. "It's genocide out there, and you don't know from one day to the next if the kids are going to make it," summarized Aaron. His wife, Simone, added,

"This place just eats some people up alive. We just hope we can give the children enough strength to get through it in one piece." Velma said of her daughter, who had been physically abused in her birth home and in foster care, and sexually abused in one of her four foster placements,

> I tell her that a lot of good people had a hard time coming up. Sure she's had a hard time of it, but she's not the only one. It don't mean she got to shrivel up and die.

What varied quite a bit in the interviews was the degree to which families discussed problems in front of the children: most black and white working-class couples did not do so, in contrast to middle-class adopters, who were more apt to have weekly family meetings. Among the working-class adoptive families, fathers would sometimes take aside older sons, as would mothers with older daughters, to discuss gender issues or the presence of problematic people in the neighborhood or family. Trudy, recently separated from her husband four years after they adopted a ten-year-old girl, said,

> When Tory started her period, I let her stay up sometimes and listen while me and my sisters talked late. A lot came out of those coffee klatches, let me tell you! It was a way of letting her know what was going on, the things women need to know to make it all work.

For boys in two-parent families, being included meant apprenticeship in home repairs or fixing cars, and attending or watching sports events with other men and boys. This inclusion provided the kind of nonverbal companionship or noisy excitement that was typical of men's leisure activities in these families. With video gaming now part of family culture—mostly a "guy thing," according to one mother—fathers and sons were often involved in parallel play.

These working-class public adopters viewed kinship as a process of progressive inclusion in adult activities. The goal was fitting in and being responsible and productive within an extended family context. The parents remembered and remarked upon changes over time in the adoptee's behavior, approach to life, and even personality (see Loehlin et al., 1987). One mother said,

> Greg was such a Gloomy Gus when we adopted him. No smiles at all, always negative. He tried to get us to be mean to him, too. I guess that was all he knew. But as a family we're just real hard to be negative around.

We work hard, but we play hard, too, and Bill [husband] is just, well, he's a card. You could just see Greg changing, almost from one day to the next. He came out of his shell. He still doesn't laugh as much as the rest of us, but he's coming along.

These working-class couples ascribed responsibility for outcome, however, to a combination of social conditions over which they expressed little sense of control and familial grappling with the effects of the child's history.

MATCHING UNDESIRABLES: SPECIAL-NEEDS KIDS
AND SINGLE-MOTHER ADOPTERS

Not much literature exists on single-parent adoption (see Groze and Rosenthal, 1991; Gailey, 2004b), partly because it was rare twenty-five years ago when many of the longitudinal studies began (Shireman and Johnson, 1986).[1] By the 1980s researchers were beginning to note that single adopters could be effective parents even for children with exceptionally difficult histories (Feigelman and Silverman, 1983: xii). Today, single parents — nearly all women — account for about one-third of all public agency adoptions (USDHHS, 2003). Nevertheless, public agencies do not target single adopters as a desirable category, and for decades single women have encountered more obstacles to adoption than have married women (Feigelman and Silverman, 1997; Jordan and Little, 1966; Kadushin, 1970).

As a result, many single-parent adopters go through private agencies. Indeed, some agencies are known to cater to this clientele, with a small number advertising their openness to single-parent adopters, which is also considered code for lesbian couples (Allen, 2002). In any case, private agency adoptions are hard to monitor after placement, so data on how these adoptions fare are lacking.

Another reason so little data are available may be that women who adopt through public agencies face a plethora of problems, but the vast majority of these single-parent families succeed despite them (USDHHS, 2003). Most of the problems appear to have little to do with single parenthood per se and much to do with social conditions and the paucity of support services (see Shireman and Johnson, 1985; Gailey, 2004b). The situation for single-parent adopters, therefore, parallels that of many single birth mothers, although single-parent adopters generally are maintaining stable employment at the time of the home study and are usually better educated.

Social workers tend to match single women with children unlikely to be adopted otherwise; the adopter and adoptee share the condition of being less desirable in the adoption scheme of things. The adopters, being on all levels except age and social class in the same category as young birth mothers, are not ideal parenting material to agencies because they are not married. An exception to this is where the agencies have an active program to recruit parents of color. Agencies may forgive the single status in the search for someone apt to address a child's identity needs. Nevertheless, the two-parent family, where at least one parent can stay home during the first few months of the adoption, remains the ideal, if not the practice.

In one private agency that conducts a lot of subcontracting work in adoption for a state agency, I noticed that many if not most of the caseworkers were themselves single parents. The reason for this, one veteran adoption worker told me, was simple, and sheds light on their insight into the difficulties of single-parent adoption:

> When you work in adoption, you end up adopting. You see so many kids who are hard to place; you end up taking one of them, or two of them. Your husband is OK with this for a while, but they just aren't cute and cuddly and they're *real* hard to show off to the folks, so, you end up divorced. I tell my friends that, if you want to avoid a custody battle, do a special needs adoption [laughs].

Thus, most of these social workers were not single when they adopted, and they experienced a rapid decline in their standards of living when they divorced. "Frankly, I try to warn off most single clients: It's just too hard," one worker stated. For those who are persistent enough to gain approval, however, this same social worker said, "I try to get them the biggest post-adoption subsidy they can get, because they're going to need it."

Another reason single women are not highly recruited to adopt is because being unmarried calls their sexual orientation into question. Ironically, because most agencies are reluctant to place children with lesbian couples, closeted single women may be the front for a two-parent lesbian family that is nevertheless closer to the ideal nuclear family (see Haldane, 2003). Another adoption social worker I interviewed said she tried to point out to her agency supervisor that they could recruit a lot more two-parent families if they allowed lesbian recruitment, but her idea was not implemented.

In any case, single women, unless they have the financial resources to adopt internationally from the roulette wheel of countries that from time to time permit single-parent adoptions, are presented with the children who are considered hard to place: special-needs children, older children, traumatized children. Among the dozen single women I interviewed who had adopted through public channels, transracial adoption of black and biracial children was considered only where the prospective adopter had a good many ties already to an African American or an Afro-Caribbean network, and where the children had been considered and rejected by middle-class black married couples.

In short, single adopters—theoretically more at risk for a failed adoption because of more limited finances than two-parent adopters, without the support of another parenting adult and more constrained by the need to work full-time unless they are in a disguised partnership—are given the children who demand the most specialized care and therapeutic parenting. Indeed, per capita, single women adopt more children labeled "special needs" than any other category of adopter (Feigelman and Silverman, 1997). Given the structural problems involved in single parenthood, we need to emphasize that single-mother public agency adoptions succeed at the same rate as special-needs public adoptions by married couples (see Rosenthal and Groze, 1992; Barth and Berry, 1988; Smith and Howard, 1991).

There are an unsurprising number of temporary psychiatric institutionalizations and a smattering of juvenile incarcerations among the adolescent and adult children of these "subatomic" families, as I discovered by attending a number of adoptive single-parent support group events on both coasts. But this, too, parallels the rates in dual-parent adoptive families. We know, for instance, that children who have been abused in birth homes or foster care are in general at a higher risk for incarceration, mental illness, early pregnancy, or drug problems in adolescence (see O'Brien, 1993: 6; Piantanida, 1993: 13). Notably, however, they are at no higher risk in single-mother adoptive homes than in two-parent ones, and almost always at a much lower risk than those left in foster care or in violent birth homes (Boyne et al., 1984; Groze, 1996).

KINSHIP DYNAMICS:
SINGLE-MOTHER PUBLIC ADOPTERS

I interviewed twelve women who were single adopters through public or subcontracted private agencies (four African American women, the rest white), whose children ranged in age from five to fourteen years old, all having been adopted at age four or over. How these mothers spoke of their children shows a highly conscious social construction of kinship as part of daily survival practices:

We're a team more than a family. We have to work together or we'll all go down the toilet. I grew up in a family where my parents never talked money around the kids. My son has seen me cry over unpaid bills, we've been near bankruptcy a hundred times. I've told him I just can't afford for him to fail in school: He just has to do his part. We've just got to make it work. We may not have much, but we're in it together.

I've always said Nicky will either end up on Wall Street or Sing Sing. I never realized before he came home how useful husbands might really be. Oh, not for helping with Nick—I'm not a fool—but just for unloading at the end of a rotten day, to keep you from killing him or yourself. I guess we bottomed out when I had to go bankrupt this year and we lost the condo. But when we were packing, he put his arm around me—he hates displays of affection—and said, "Wherever we go will be home, Ma."

Maria, who lost her job because of time spent taking care of her nine-year-old in his first year, explained:

I had no idea older kid adoption would be this rough or this costly. It's such a crapshoot. I live day to day now. I can see how much better he is now, but if anybody says it's because of my maternal instinct, I'll bite their face. We all have chores, we all contribute, we keep the place running somehow. I feel like a dictator sometimes, and sometimes like an older sister, but Jamie and I manage somehow. I just love her and she knows it, even when I yell at her. She's been home now for five years. I guess the first two years were horrible, but it's like labor—I guess—you forget how awful it was once things get better. She's fourteen now—it's such a hard time for girls—and I know now that she'll let me know if something's really bothering her. We've worked out so many problems over the years. Really, adolescence isn't that different, knock on wood!

The theme that runs through these mothers' narratives stresses daily struggle and expectations of helping one another out. The mothers acknowledge the risks involved, but see risk-taking by both parent and child (see Zwimpfer, 1983). Boundaries between mother and child are not always clear, but the sense of belonging and building something together is unmistakable.

Most of the women I interviewed expressed a longing for financial assistance or spiritual support from another adult: a husband, a sugar daddy, a rich aunt, fairy godmother, a boyfriend. Most qualified the wish for a husband almost immediately with comments like "Of course, only if he were a good guy" or "but only if he were as committed to James as I am." There is a nuclear family behind these narratives, but the women reject the prospect of marrying under their current circumstances as unworkable, unrealistic, or undesirable in the long run. It should be noted that the seven single-parent adopters I interviewed who went through private agencies and adopted internationally did not share these experiences, probably because they had greater financial resources and greater access to privatized support services, such as nannies.

Family formation for these single-mother public adopters was generally a conscious process of drawing in support people from natal and acquired kin networks. The four white mothers of African American adoptees did extra "kin work" (di Leonardo, 1987: 340), extending patterns of sharing, gifting, socializing, holiday celebrating, and so on to include black godparents and grandparents, acquired aunties and uncles. Clare said that her friendships with an interracial gay couple brought "two great uncles" into the family:

Trevor [the African American gay partner] was so happy—he'd been rejected by a lot of his own family—first, when he "came out" and then because of Steve [because he was white]. He and Steve always wanted to have a kid, and of course the agencies don't want to even *know from* gay couples. They've been together for going on twenty years now—the longest-lasting couple I know, gay or straight—and both of the guys are wonderful with Angela. Who wouldn't want a couple of nurturing, fun, and safe uncles for their kid? They're light-years better than my brother: I wouldn't leave her alone with *him*!

Another mother had joined a church that was predominantly black but ethnically diverse:

I'm not especially religious, but the community in that place is really very special. Most of the people have just taken us in, made us feel welcome. I've made friends, Monique has made friends, we all work together on special projects like the soup kitchen and Thanksgiving. Grace [an older woman] has become the grandmother my mother could never be.

In other words, the transracially adopting white mothers among the public agency adopters were not isolating their children in what one mother called "whiteland," although sometimes the networks they developed for their children were not through traditional community organizations. For these mothers, the arrival of their adopted children required them to consciously shift their family toward African American or other communities of color. This changing set of connections would sometimes create rifts with the mothers' birth families.

In contrast to single adopters of black children, the single-mother adopters of children from so-called buffer races—East and South Asians, Latinos—received greater support from existing kin networks. Most of these mothers adopted their children from other countries and did not go through public agencies. When asked, the public adopter mothers of black children said that the stakes were very high for their children in a racist society. They expressed a sense that they could not on their own provide the child with ways of negotiating racism, and thus they needed to seek community support on an ongoing basis. The next chapter, on transracial adoption, discusses the issues these mothers identified in more detail.

FAMILY IDEOLOGIES IN THEORY AND PRACTICE

While working-class white couples in particular embraced the ideology of "blood is thicker than water" in the abstract (Schneider, 1984), they nevertheless mentioned their estrangement from part of their family and discussed how they kept their kids away from relatives who might be alcoholic or drug abusers. In practice, familial networks excluded these people, even while acknowledging them as kin, and drew in a range of long-term friends, relatives of ex-spouses, and the like.

The people least invested in biological kinship as an ideology seemed to be the African American working-class couples. While one man expressed that "family is the only thing you can rely on, and if you can't rely on them, you're nowhere," "family" seemed to be a functional rather than an ideological unit for him: people who helped each other out, took care of kids together, counseled teenagers, and so on. The adoptive mother of a special needs infant said,

> Girl, this is *work*. It's work to make family happen. You gotta keep track of this one and that one, and don't be talking behind the other one's back, and take care of your niece who just lost her job, and take in the young ones when they need it. It's complicated, see? Otherwise don't *nothin'* work.

There were parallels between single, middle-class women adopters and working-class public adopters. Perhaps because they are seen as deviant, and perhaps because they expect their standard of living to fall after they adopt,

29

the single-mother public adopters seemed less invested in the notion of kinship as conjugally based or derived from blood or genetic ties. These women seemed aware of the need to develop a support system and did not have the financial resources to do so entirely through contractual arrangements.

Single-parent adopters, particularly those who were lesbian, who had adopted transracially, or who had daughters who had been sexually abused (see Chapter 5), had deep misgivings about any ideology of innate causation or nature outweighing nurture. One woman expressed her views this way: "If blood is thicker than water, then how do you explain the incest my daughter suffered?" Another single adopter commented,

> I came from such a blown-out family. I had to learn as an adult how to build healthy relationships. You have to make those ties; they're not "there" otherwise.

Of all the adopters in the sample, the public agency parents were the best trained and informed about children's issues in adoption. All had participated in at least twelve weeks of three-hour seminars on adoptive parenting, since all the adopters had to be qualified as foster parents: it would take at least six months, and in one case three years, before their adoptions could be finalized.

Despite pre-adoptive training that typically is far longer and more detailed than private agency programs, as well as extensive post-adoptive programs, public adopters are rarely given credit in the mass media for their greater preparation. Instead, public agencies tend to draw media attention most often when a child is injured in a foster-to-adopt setting or when bureaucratic snafus or impossibly large caseloads result in a child's injury or death. Otherwise, public adoption comes to public attention only during Adoption Month or when the media are interested in particular types of stories, such as those about the problems of drug-addicted or drug-affected babies, the singular (and by inference, peculiar) altruism of adopters of special needs children, and, the most incendiary and persistent theme in American adoption, transracial adoption.

THREE

TRANSRACIAL ADOPTION
IN PRACTICE

I can tell now when white people are treating me different from [her son] Rashad—better. I want him to be aware of that, and I don't want to use my being white to get things, because he won't be able to when he grows up. I have to be real careful about it. It's made me much more aware of racism than I ever was before.

—TRANSRACIAL ADOPTER, 2002

Institutional and attitudinal forms of race, class, and gender discrimination have shaped adoption in numerous ways: in the necessity for adoption in the first place, in the state's regulation of adoption and fosterage, in the categorization of children and parents, and in matching children with parents. Most researchers concur on these points, but few have put all these factors together into a comprehensive analysis of adoption and race. Even in a thoughtful study such as Sandra Patton's examination of race and class in transracial adoption (2000), gender is often overlooked or submerged.

In this chapter, the politics and practices of interracial adoption take center stage. I focus on white adoptions of black children rather than white-Asian or Anglo-Latino adoptions because ideologies and hierarchies of race in the United States have developed within the context of black-white relations. Other groups may be racialized in a certain region, such as Samoans and Tongans in Hawai'i, or racialized during a particular period, as Karen Brodkin argues through her examination of Jews in America (1998). Only Native Americans have experienced as consistent and continuous an oppression as blacks in the United States. Native Americans also suffered slavery and genocidal conditions, but blacks, in contrast, are unable to argue for the disposition of children on the basis of sovereignty. In recent years, sovereignty claims have made white-Native American adoption a unique case, exempting recognized tribes as sovereign in foster care and adoption matters (see Strong, 2002).

Most communities of color in the United States are contextually racialized and yet relatively privileged compared to African Americans due to their "buffer" position between white and black (Patterson and Spencer, 1994). Moreover, policy decisions regarding race in adoption have focused on white-black domestic adoptions. My focus, therefore, is on white adoptions of black children.

For the past thirty-five years, the great majority of black children available for legal adoption have been adopted by black families or interracial couples. But their struggles and successes have not fueled adoption studies to the same extent that white adoptions of black children have. The reasons for this go to the heart of a long-standing interracial adoption controversy.

WHO ADOPTS INTERRACIALLY?

In the United States, Joyce Ladner's pioneering study noted the proportionately greater numbers of black children relative to white available for adoption and the largely positive outcomes of white-black adoptions (Ladner, 1977). Later longitudinal studies of white parents adopting black children, particularly those by Rita Simon and her associates, provided the "positive outcome" data that informed the adoption reform legislation of the 1990s (see Simon and Altstein, 1977, 1987, 1992; Simon, Altstein, and Melli, 1994). To date, however, only the work of Patton has placed emphasis on the structures that render relatively more black children available for adoption (Patton, 2000).

Social science researchers in the United Kingdom profiled interracial adoption in ways that appreciate the combined effects of racism, class, and political-economic forces in state foster care and adoption long before these were analyzed in the United States. For example, John Triseliotis's work explored the role of the shrinking welfare state and postindustrial capitalism at home in shaping foster care and adoption in the United Kingdom (see Triseliotis, 1980). Christopher Bagley and Loretta Young held reduction of state subsidies for single mothers as primarily responsible for increasing the numbers of black and what they term "mixed-race" children in foster care or available for adoption (Bagley and Young, 1979: 193). Bagley and his colleagues also examined parental and extended family attitudes toward race and adoptees' identity formation and adolescent experiences (Bagley and Young, 1979; Bagley, Young, and Scully, 1993).

Both British and U.S. researchers concur that adoptive parents of black children are more "independent minded," less likely to be influenced about life choices by friends and family than other adoptive parents (see Bagley, 1993; Simon, 1987). One mother I interviewed put it bluntly: "You have to be 'hard-headed' to do this." Another said,

> You'd better be aware that a lot of white people—and some black people, too—are going to disapprove and say thoughtless and mean things in public to you and to your kid. You have to know how to turn that negativity around.

Several adoption scholars have attempted to categorize white adoptive parents according to their expressed attitudes toward their black or biracial children, coupled with their activities regarding their children's identity formation (see Ladner, 1977; Bagley and Young, 1979; Anderson, 1971). In the 1970s their motivations to adopt a black or mixed-race child ranged from the longer wait required for a white child to the sense that all children have a need for homes and the fact that social workers, who were usually white, had difficulty recruiting black families (Ladner, 1977: 2–6, 12–13, 44–47). By the 1990s, however, among the transracial adopters I interviewed in the Northeast and Southern California, no one had adopted a black, biracial, or multiracial child because of long waits for a white child. Almost all the adopters, married or single, expressed their motivations as some variation of "There are so many black kids waiting." "With the help of our [African American] friends, we felt we could do a decent job raising a black kid," noted one parent, and another remarked, "Our family is so mixed already, the kid would fit right in." One single white mother said,

> I remind myself all the time that I am just as single as my daughter's birth mother: only age, education, and color give me the edge. So I have a responsibility to *her* to do right by *our* daughter.

When asked, "Do you know your daughter's birth mother?" this parent replied, "No, but I would like to: they don't do 'open adoptions' much in this state." In general, the awareness of racism and identity formation issues, including a sense of accountability to the African American community, was keener among the interracial adopters in this study, which may be related to the urban areas surveyed and the snowball sampling.

Federal adoption reforms in the mid-1990s that put an end to race as a consideration in adoption placement had a swift impact on media representation of transracial adopters. From the 1970s on, in the few stories on the topic, the media focused on the ways white adopters had accommodated their lives to address the need for African American community involvement in child rearing. In the 1990s this shifted. An article in *Parade* magazine in 1998 mentioned adoption advocates who were clearly concerned about preparing black children for racism. It then proceeded to quote an adoptive parent who situates color as only one of many forms of "prejudice":

> Many people experience prejudice because they are overweight or disabled or because of their religion. All prejudice is hurtful, not just color. (Winik, 1998: 4–5)

The article argued that "love is all you need" as background socialization for surviving racism and used the term "biracial" to describe most of the African American children adopted by the families. The article then applauded the families' approach:

> But the Musicks still wrestle with racial questions, like what racial category to check on official forms. "I don't want my children to deny either side of their [biracial] heritage, so I just check 'other' and write 'special.'" (Winik, 1998: 7)

In order to avoid the discomfort of racial categorization, such children are left without solidarity with the people with whom they are most likely to be identified, both institutionally and interpersonally. The term "biracial" is itself highly controversial, with advocates promoting the blurring of racial boundaries as a move toward race blindness, while others argue that, far from race blindness, the term fractures unity within African American communities in part by activating a history in which light skin is preferred to dark. What is clear in the article is that the post-reform adopters were far from clear about such race politics or structural forms of racism, electing to focus instead on immediate interpersonal interaction.

Given the mandates of the federal reforms that demanded race-blind placement of children under threat of severing government funding, it has become even more unlikely that contemporary pre-adoption training will address this lack of appreciation for the complexities of race politics and racialized identity formation. This well-intentioned erasure of racism, by collapsing it into prejudice, on the one hand, and, on the other, distancing children from an African American identity by stressing hybridity, embodies larger problems with postmodern thinking about race in America (see Harrison, 1995).

RACIAL AWARENESS AMONG INTERRACIAL ADOPTERS

Thirty years ago, Bagley and Young found that British parents who already had birth children and decided to adopt a mixed-race child were more "racially aware" than those who adopted because of infertility (Bagley and Young, 1979: 211). Three-fourths of the adoptive parents in their study had no birth children, while U.S. studies from the same period stressed that about 80 percent of transracial adoptive parents had birth children at the time of adoption (Ladner, 1977). In my study only one of the transracial adopters had birth children, a white mother who had boys from her first marriage. After her divorce, she adopted two daughters who had been labeled black. She later married a man who identifies himself as black rather than African American.

The Bagley and Young study divided parental race attitudes into three categories: "racially aware," which meant that they had at least some black friends, were concerned with providing the kids with a sense of their racial heritage and culture, and were in the researchers' words "unprejudiced." These families were contrasted with a vaguely defined "intermediate" group and a third group called "racially unaware," where the parents had no black friends, were ignorant or unconcerned about heritage and culture for their kid, and held racial stereotypes (Bagley and Young, 1979: 210). Another study found that the white families they studied emphasized either "integration," where the child's differences were minimized, or "differentiation," where familial activities engaged issues of race and adoption (Costin and Wattenberg, 1979: 225–226).

Thirty years later, these categories require refinement, based on how children's senses of self and racial identity can shift later in their lives (see, e.g., Weinrich, 1979; Verma and Bagley, 1979). Sara Dorow's research on white Americans adopting Chinese girls emphasized how parents acted upon attitudes as well as how they spoke of their children. She categorizes responses from virtual silence to what she terms "immersion" (Dorow, 2001). I am elaborating on earlier studies to suggest that interracial adoptive families engage racial identity and racism in one of the following ways. I have included examples of the kinds of comments that define the categories. It should be noted that these "awareness categories" may apply to non-adoptive interracial families, too.

1. *Denial of child's social condition.* "This kid is mixed, not black"; "Our child is human, not black." Or, as the African American wife in an inter-

racial marriage explained to me regarding her son, "Hayden is biracial, not black." These comments indicate an emphasis on race as a biological rather than social category, even when the parents emphasize ethnic heritage mixtures. These parents show no awareness that a child's position in a socially constructed category that changes historically is not just a marker of oppression, but also a source of solidarity and strength in the face of structural racism. Such parents reject the identification of their child with other African Americans. In seeming to reject the racist categorization of blackness as "one drop of black blood" in the United States, they unwittingly privilege the notion of adding whiteness (see Zack, 1993).

2. *Denial of the importance of racism.* "We want integration and so we don't want to emphasize racial differences in bringing up our son." Here, parents fear that discussing racism will somehow make the child obsess about race and, in keeping with that fear, reject the adoptive parents. There is no evidence that making race a major point of discussion in family dynamics is harmful. Indeed, all the longitudinal studies show that acknowledging race as an issue and racism as a problem is extremely valuable in helping interracially adopted children value themselves.

3. *Awareness of the child's background, coupled with latent or explicit racism.* "Our daughter is black, but she's exceptional." "Leonard is light-skinned, so he won't have as many problems." "Our son/daughter has natural rhythm." The implicit assumption here is that race is biologically based and carries with it innate traits, a pseudoscientific belief dating back to the nineteenth century (Galton, 1925).

4. *Awareness and concern about racism, expressed through consumption.* "Our son is black and we provide him with African American history books." "We go to black cultural events." This is the commitment to culture as consumption. Parents in this category may not have African American friends or other peer connections that are visible to the children.

5. *Awareness of racism and social engagement:* "We want our child to have black friends, so we changed [schools, churches, and/or neighborhoods]." "We've gotten involved as a family in social justice issues more than before Tricia came to us." One father told me,

You can't be color-blind, because it won't work for your kid. No one's going to be color-blind toward him when he's a teenager. You have to make sure he gets the kinds of African American role models who are positive, who'll give him that strength to deal with the society.

6. *Awareness and reconfiguring the family within a black context.* Here, four adoptive mothers' comments are telling:

We've changed from being a white family with a black kid to being a black family with white members. People may not see us that way, but that's how I describe our family to them if they ask. [Do both white and black people ask?] Oh, yes, but more white people than black people—probably because I'm white.

I didn't want to be the "Great White Authority" figure in my child's life, so I created godparents and auntie/uncle relationships to surround my daughter with black family members. I know I can't do it all: there's so much I just don't pick up on yet.

I know my limits as a white parent. I rely on [black] friends and neighbors to counsel me and give my daughter what I can't, to prepare her for being a black woman in America.

I've tried to become more aware of the situations where people give me "white privilege"; I try not to exercise that privilege any more, and to point out to my daughter what is happening. . . . Sometimes I tell them what they're doing, too, and ask them to either extend the privilege to everyone or cut it out.

The last two categories comprised almost all the parents in this study. These parents seem to provide their children with an acceptance of diversity, if not always positively valuing diversity, alongside awareness of racism and a sense of belonging to both a family and a racialized community. The parents in the last category seemed the most aware of white entitlement and the most committed to addressing it in their own lives.

There have been numerous longitudinal studies in the United States and Britain of parents' transracial adoption strategies that have helped adoptees to develop positive attitudes toward both themselves and others of their race and healthy adjustment going into adulthood (Simon, Altstein, and Melli, 1994; Gaber and Aldridge, 1994; McRoy and Zurcher, 1983; Bagley, 1993; Patton, 2000). A key strategy involves the parents reorienting the family to include regular parent and family involvement with peers who are from the child's racial background. Another has everyone in the family encouraged to recognize, discuss, and debate issues of difference and racism. The adoptees showing the most comfortable sense of self, according to researchers, came from families that also provided everyday exposure and engagement with ethnic or racial diversity through neighborhood, schools, and social activities.

COLOR PREFERENCE IN ADOPTION

Interracial adoption, apart from the adoption of Asian children by whites, remains fairly rare. Despite the issues of color prejudice that permeate all communities in U.S. society and a decade of race-blind national adoption policies, most adopted black children join African American families. Although discrimination against blacks is readily recognized and discussed in African American communities, color prejudice within many African American families receives less attention. Media messages about appearance and racist values, argues bell hooks, imbue problematic attitudes within African American and other black communities (see hooks, 1995). But airing these issues in a society willing to attribute all the problems to the community itself is risky business, and hooks and others are keenly aware of the stakes. Yet the issues arise in some of the reasons parents give for interracial adoption.

Psychotherapist Marlene Faye Watson has addressed a difficult subject relevant to our discussion: that many African American families privilege or disfavor children on the basis of lighter or darker skin tone. She writes, "Internal family racism affects all African American people, yet it has long been denied, repressed and suppressed" (Watson, 1999: 54). She points out that children in an African American family that has not addressed color prejudice may insult each other based on skin tone or hair texture, or familial perceptions of who is lighter or darker—regardless of actual variations in these features. She emphasizes the consequences of such color prejudice within families: favoritism obviously affects the children who are not privileged, but it also encourages lighter-tone kids to wonder if they are special only because of their skin or hair.

Adoption researchers generally do not venture into the minefield of color preference. With some misgivings, I asked adopters questions about their own preferences and whether they knew about their child's previous history of foster or adoptive placement. I also asked six adoption social workers—two African American, three white, one Puerto Rican—about the placement histories of children classified as African American that they personally had placed with a white mother or couple. It was an uncomfortable set of questions. For African American social workers and adopters, it meant having to confront persistent patterns of color preference and racial stereotyping within black communities in front of a white person who was going to be writing a book. It meant deciding to speak or not to speak to an audience that would include whites. For some of the white adopters, it meant finding the words to talk about their children having been rejected by potential adopters who were black, without condemning a racialized community or appearing self-righteous or entitled. I could sense their struggles, and some expressed their discomfort to me. One of the African American social workers explained,

> Look, this [color prejudice] goes on, but I really don't want people to think that it's the biggest problem, right? The biggest problem is racism. Period. I'm dark. I have kinky hair. My family was not great on these issues, so my brother got privileges I never did because he was a male and because he was lighter-skinned. It's a problem, but it's not much compared to what happened to me because I was a black woman in this society. Just get that down: I want that in the book.
>
> Now, about the kids. Yes, I've placed a few kids with white folks. Those kids are usually the ones who *have* been turned down or returned, or have big problems. One was a little baby, a preemie and two different black couples turned her down because she had bad hair or would probably darken up too much for their liking. She also had developmental delays. I placed her with a white couple, but one that had black people in their extended family already. The other was an older girl, seven, who had been through hell: sexual abuse, beatings, everything. She was dark, too. I would've taken her if I had the energy, 'cause it broke my heart to see how no one [of the prospective black adopters] would even *consider* her. I put her with a single white woman who had good ties with people I know in the community—a feminist, good on abuse issues. She'd have a chance with her.

The other African American social worker said,

> It's a hard issue, that one. We really don't want to talk about it, it's too painful. . . . We do get kids that are considered but rejected because they're too dark or have "bad hair" or look "too African"—all that kind of ignorant behavior. I think it's best not to push them toward kids they're not going

to accept and love as they are. I don't *like* to place kids with white folks, but sometimes it's a choice between them or no one. I grew up in foster care and I do believe any decent family is better than no family at all. I just try my best to make sure the child will have the kind of contact and relationships with other African Americans that will give him the kind of help he'll need coming up.

Three of the other social workers were similarly thoughtful, but one gave a rather curt response:

They're not kidding when they say these kids are "hard to place." We're lucky to get anyone to adopt them. I should, but I don't even bother about whether it's transracial or not any more. The ones [social workers] I know who handle the crack kids would tell you the same. If [the prospective adopters are] alive and not child molesters, we'll place 'em.

Among the African American and white families that had adopted black children in this study, only one interracial couple expressed color preference. The African American husband explained, "We wanted a kid who would be believable—some color that you could get between Tracey and me." All transracial adopters had children who were considered dark. One of the white social workers commented,

There's no problem at all placing healthy infants or little kids who are lighter with black families. Couples are real eager to get them. It's the kids with health problems, and even the toddlers who are dark that are hard to place. I know it's the result of racism and how it creeps into every-one's heads—even African Americans'—but it's the kids that pay the price, always.

Transracial placements have been done carelessly in the past, strongly favoring white clients seeking healthy infants (see Ladner, 1977; Gaber and Aldridge, 1994). As a result of earlier adoption reforms sought by the National Association of Black Social Workers in the early 1970s, until the mid-1990s public agencies placed far fewer children transracially than did private agencies. In my public agency sample, I found that social workers placed black children with white parents only in lieu of moving from foster home to foster home or being institutionalized. After the 1996–1997 federal adoption reforms, however, public agency social workers have been constrained in their legal ability to place children preferentially in same-race families.

WHO GETS PLACED TRANSRACIALLY?

Social workers know that some children who enter care relatively unscathed suffer abuse in the foster care system. In my study, I found that eight of the ten black girls who were adopted over the age of four had been physically or sexually abused while in foster care; all of their multiple foster placements included both white and black families (see Chapter 4).

Angela is an African American girl who was relinquished for adoption at three weeks of age. She was not the child of a love relationship, but her young mother had rejected abortion due to her religious upbringing; she also had not used drugs or alcohol during her pregnancy. Angela was born prematurely and showed normal developmental delays for healthy preemies. Despite the steadfast efforts of at least two social workers (one white, one Latina) to place her, Angela was rejected at least three times in the first year by potential adopters because she was considered too dark and because she cried often; potential adopters also considered her developmental delays problematic.

The primary social worker, a white woman, sought families both in and outside the state. One interracial couple took Angela for a weekend to see if the arrangement might work; when they brought her back, the (African American) husband explained that she was "too difficult" for them. The social worker felt "excited and relieved" when a two-parent African American couple with older sons expressed interest in a foster-to-adopt placement. There were irregularities with the family's home study, but since Angela was by then twenty months old, the social worker overlooked them. Three months into the placement, Angela was hospitalized as a result of life-threatening physical abuse; the admitting doctor also found unambiguous evidence of repeated sexual abuse. She was immediately removed from the home. It was subsequently discovered that the family had had "suspicion of abuse or neglect" cases pending on their three birth children at the time Angela was placed.

After her release from the hospital, Angela lived in two more foster homes. When she was evaluated at the age of thirty months, she showed a range of symptoms of unattachment and typical responses of very young girls to untreated sexual abuse. In the subsequent two and a half years, despite loving care by an African American foster mother and significant media outreach, the agency could not locate another black family willing to adopt the child. She was rejected twice more in the process; the foster mother was asked but explained that she could not take on another child because of her own deteriorating health. Eventually, Angela's social worker allowed Clare, a single white woman who had been closely screened to document her long-term ties to black communities as well as her experience with survivors of incest and abuse, to adopt the girl. By most accounts, this was an unusually careful transracial placement.

Among the black children in this study, seven of the ten girls and three of the four boys, all of whom had been adopted after spending at least three years in foster care, had been placed in African American families. The boys were adopted by couples; most of girls' adoptive parents were single mothers, generally in their late thirties or forties, and, like the mothers and fathers among the couples, were employed full-time or nearly full-time. Only three of the ten girls in my sample and one of the boys had been adopted interracially: the girls by single mothers, the boy by a married couple. All the transracial families lived in multiracial communities (see Shireman and Johnson, 1986) and had peer relationships with African American or Afro-Caribbean neighbors and friends. All but one of those adopted transracially were older, traumatized children who had already been in an average of three foster homes at the time of adoptive placement. Moreover, all but one of the children at one time or another, generally as infants or toddlers, had been considered and rejected by prospective black couples. One girl had been rejected by four couples in her first eleven months of her life, and it is not uncommon for skin tone to be a factor in rejections of black children at such a young age. Indeed, judgment on the basis on skin tone begins at birth, notes Watson:

> When a child is born into an African American family, parents look at his or her skin tone—how light is this child? A child who is lighter skinned than his or her parents starts life with an advantage. A child whose hair is less African (blacker, kinkier, shorter) and more Caucasian (finer, straighter, lighter, longer) is seen as more beautiful. (Watson, 1999: 53)

Certainly a great many African American families are keenly aware of color prejudice and address it routinely (see, e.g., Hopson and Hopson, 1990: 82–85). Nevertheless, the interracially adopted children in the sample had been targets of this kind of informal assessment during placement, as had the children adopted by the unmarried African American women in the sample. Indeed, in their attitudes toward their children's color and placement histories, the transracial adopters in my sample expressed similar views as the in-race African American adopters. One of the African American adopters, a single mother, spoke for the transracial adopters as well when she said, "My girl was 'too dark' and had 'bad hair' so they didn't want her. Well, I did and I do."

COMING HOME: FRIENDS AND RELATIVES RESPOND

In a dominant culture where kinship is intensely biologized—"blood is thicker than water," genetic similarity as the strongest ground for attachment, and similar beliefs—we should not be surprised that extended family reactions to the adoption of a black child are strong. The adopters' parents have especially varied reactions, as revealed in both my study and the adoption literature. One cannot generalize about whether the adoptees' new grandmothers or grandfathers are more or less supportive; it seems to depend more on the relationship of the adopters to their parents, on political attitudes, and on the adults' religious or secular worldviews. Some grandparents (although not those in my study) express outright rejection through disowning the adult children or cutting off all contact. Others show initial rejection, followed by acceptance when it becomes clear that the adopters have claimed the child as their own. Some of the grandparents express pleasure at having a grandchild, but see the adopted child as second-best to the prospect of a birth grand-child or as an exception to their prejudiced view of blacks. A few show what I call "defensive favoritism," showering the adopted grandchild with gifts and attention to the extent of neglecting the other grandchildren, a kind of overcompensation that singles out the child in a divisive way. Most seem understanding and accepting on an interpersonal level, but few show active support by becoming involved in community activities around racial issues. In one case, however, an older woman friend and the father of one of her male friends volunteered to become grandparents to the adopted daughter when the mother's parents were not forthcoming.

Other relatives of the adopters in the sample responded in a range of ways to the interracial adoption. Some were supportive if not comprehending of the motives. One adoptive mother explained,

> My lifestyle and politics made me an oddball in my family anyway, so as far as adopting Lee Ann was concerned, it was yet another thing I was doing that they couldn't fathom, but they are basically warm people, open and accepting of both of us.

Other parents encountered rejection by key people. The wife of the white couple described the reaction of her husband's sister:

> My sister-in-law really freaked. I think she was sure something would hap-pen to us [the two parents] and she'd be stuck with a hyperactive black boy.

She didn't chill until I told her we'd decided that if anything were to happen to us, that Jason would be welcomed into my best friend's family. But things have cooled between us. We still see them on the family occasions, but I take her rejection personally. I've never told her, but I wouldn't trust my son to someone like her. I love him too much to give him to her.

Her husband added,

Yeah, my sister was a real jerk when we adopted Jason. So was her husband, but I've never been very close to my family, anyway. It's pretty messed up. Mary [wife] and I are a lot closer to her family, and they've been fine. Her family's real mixed and we fit in just as much as everyone else.

Another mother explained,

Monique coming home was the litmus test for our families. Most of them were cool about it, but Rob's father was horrible. The family name, that kind of thing. What a creep! Fortunately for us, his mom isn't like that. She comes over and visits and plays with Monique and takes her shopping. No one says anything to the old man about it. She wasn't going to let him stand in the way of her enjoying her granddaughter.

Two other mothers commented,

I could count on my sister to share childcare and be around, but that's about it for my family. Doug's mom was thrilled to have a grandchild, so she's been fine. I've made friends with other mothers in the park—some of them are black—so we've kind of redone our family circle to make it comfortable for all of us.

Maybe I shouldn't have been, but I was surprised at my brothers' and sisters' reactions. They were all OK around the adoption, but the one who reacted best was my oldest brother, who's the conservative one. Looking back, I think it's because in his military training, the idea is you can shape anyone into anything and he has this image of our family as a great thing. So, of course she will be "a real [family name]," of course she'll turn out fine. It's weird, but it works. Tamica feels his acceptance and likes him the best of every one of the uncles and aunts.

Friendships, too, sometimes changed or dissolved after the adoption:

My so-called best friend asked me why I was ruining my life. She thought I was doing it for political reasons. What a joke! I told her I wasn't out to prove anything: I just loved this little girl and thought her [personal] history and mine made us a good match.

I had a friend who just couldn't deal with it. He thought [my wife] and I were crazy. "Isn't life complicated enough?" he said to me. I said we wanted this kid so much, why couldn't he just accept it? He said something like, "Integration is one thing, but this is 'out there.'" . . . I mean, he rejected my family, my own kid. How could I be friends with someone like that?

In the literature and among my families, a few parents were engaged in African American or Afro-Caribbean community activities prior to adoption:

In the neighborhood there are kids who've been adopted by grandmothers, kids from mixed [interracial] families, kids whose father is African and mother is English, so when we decided to adopt, we knew our family wouldn't really stand out. Outside the neighborhood it's a different matter, but we're comfortable where we live.

Everyone thinks my husband and I adopted the girls, but actually I adopted them before I met him. We kind of adopted him!

Most of the parents had some relationships with their kin sour due to the adoption, but overall they proceeded to emphasize relationships that were more positive. Several invented new relatives or forged new friendships to replace the lost ones. Some of the parents had staked out an area of personal autonomy within their families of origin long before the adopted child was on the scene, which seemed to normalize the adoption more than for those who tended to conform to familial scripts.

WALKING THE WALK: CREATING KIN SYSTEMS

The four white unmarried mothers, who had worked through public agencies or subcontracted private agencies to adopt their black children, did more kin work than did the wives in transracial adopter couples. These single mothers extended patterns of sharing, exchanged labor, pooled rides to school and to grocery stores, expanded their gift-giving networks, and in general stepped up their socializing, holiday festivities, and the like to include black godparents, grandparents, aunts, and uncles. They created or inserted their family into a kin system that included what Patricia Hill Collins has termed "other mothers": experienced women who advise parents on child rearing, counsel children, and act as role models and mentors (Collins, 1990a). One mother remarked:

> Some of the African Americans in [this urban neighborhood] don't approve of our family; some of the whites don't either. They stay away from us and we stay away from them. But I've learned so much from the women who have taken a positive interest in Kenya. Ms. Wells has taught me how to grease and braid her hair, my neighbor Danita showed me the best lotions for her skin, Mrs. Hicks told me which schools were better for "our children," and on and on. I really feel supported, and believe me, I listen when they tell me something. They know what it's like to be black in America: I don't.

Other mothers explained,

> Whenever there's an incident at school or in the park, I call up my friend Barbara [an African American woman]—I work with her and like her kids—and ask her what she would do. I make up my own mind, but I weigh her words a lot.

> Hey, if I don't give Monique examples of all different kinds of black people, she'll take the stuff on TV as reality. What's out there on TV for black women? Hookers, addicts, or rich housewives, plus the talk shows and a few athletes. Well, where we live there are all kinds of black women— secretaries, teachers, day care people, even an apprentice electrician. There are jerks, too. But I want her to grow up knowing the good people, so she has some real choices.

The fourth mother said,

> You give up some control to do transracial adoption right. You need people from the community involved with your kid, and that means you have to be involved in your community. You also have to be willing to admit your limitations, to learn and be taught, and that's not always easy. But sometimes you have to draw the line, like when one mother said a little physical discipline would teach Lee Ann a lesson. I thanked her for her advice. No way will I do it, but I'm not going to tell her that either. And I do feel great

when Lee Ann gets compliments on her hair or skin, because it means I've learned a thing or two.

One of the mothers summed up this way:

> When you're the white mother of a black child, there are many eyes watching you and your kid. If the kid makes a mistake, some white folks will think, "See, even in a good environment 'they' mess up," while some of the black folks will think, "Look at that poor kid with a white mother: no wonder he's a mess." I figure he'll be fine, and it'll be everyone's "fault": mine, his, our crazy mixed-up family, the people who helped—everyone's.

Two of these adoptive mothers had sought the support of Big Brother/ Big Sister programs to provide their sons and daughters with mentors from African American or West Indian communities; others used recreational programs known to have diverse staff and participants for sports, after-school activities, and summer day camps. In other words, the mothers in this snowball sample were not isolating their children in all-white surroundings. For all these mothers, the arrival of the children and the concomitant, consciously undertaken shifts in family orientation toward African American or other communities of color created rifts in their birth families. As one mother put it, "Taisha coming home sure brought out my sister's true colors!" Interestingly, the structure of single-parent adoption, coupled with the awareness most of the women had about the controversies surrounding transracial adoption, led to a situation where the women had constructed networks of support and strategies of survival reminiscent of Carol Stack's account of life in an urban black community (Stack, 1974).

According to these parents, school officials, teachers, neighbors, and shopkeepers tended to show attitudes reflecting the range of the wider society. Parents told me and a number of other researchers about outsiders treating the parents in a patronizing way (e.g., "You've done a noble deed"), showing undue attention or favoritism that marked the child as different, or offering concern about biological or heritage problems ("Aren't you worried about 'bad blood'?"). These comments might seem unbelievable for their blatant insensitivity, but parents from a range of studies tell similar stories (see, e.g., Bates, 1993). Unfortunately, the quarter-century that separates the earlier longitudinal studies from the current ones have not revealed great differences in the attitudes of outsiders toward interracial adopted families, even though the number of interracial families in the United States has increased significantly.

Considerable realignment and invention of kinship seem to accompany single adopters of black children, far less so for those adopting children from so-called buffer races, such as East and South Asians and Latinos. When asked, these mothers of black children explain that the stakes are very high for their children in a racist society. They express a sense that they cannot on their own provide the child with ways of negotiating the racism: they need community support and seek it out. Acknowledging this, they proceed to adopt many of the strategies taken by African American parents (see Hopson and Hopson, 1990). Some international adopter mothers of Asian and Latino children discussed in Chapter 5 claim to be race-blind, not to notice their child's color, a situation that most researchers argue is not healthy for identity formation. Here, it is enough to point out that a few of the international adopters express concern that their children might be hurt by prejudicial comments or have difficulties with dating in adolescence. Issues of survival, however, are not present as they were for the white couples or single-mother adopters of black children.

"BIRACIAL? YOU *BLACK!*"
CHILDREN'S ADJUSTMENTS AND RACIAL IDENTITY

Even the early research on transracially adoptive families shows that the children of parents who are racially aware, not out to be heroes or missionaries, and socially engaged with the issues of racial identity and community develop a healthy personal identity, a sense of belonging within a black community, and the ability to negotiate complex racial issues (Anderson, 1971; Jaffe and Fanshel, 1970; Grow and Shapiro, 1975). These results are echoed in the later studies (Silverman and Feigelman, 1981; Simon and Altstein, 1987; Simon and Altstein, 1992; Simon, Altstein, and Melli, 1994). And in both earlier and later research, non-black children in these families, whether by adoption or birth, develop an appreciative sense of diversity (Pohl and Harris, 1993).

If such outcomes were the only issue, there would be no controversy surrounding the neoliberal adoption reforms of the 1990s. But saying that placing black children with racially aware and engaged white parents works is not the same thing as saying race should have no part in placement. Indeed, the British studies stress that placement with racially unaware parents is detrimental to adoptees' identity formation. Yet the U.S. reforms limit the ability of public agencies to probe potential adopters' racial awareness and strategies for inclusion.

The federal reforms of the mid-1990s hearken back to positions that fore-grounded adoption issues and deemphasized racial identification issues. For example, researcher David Anderson asserted, "The fact that an interracial adoption is an adoption is more important than the fact that it is interracial" (Anderson, 1971: 104). The adopters of black children in my sample, however, whether interracial or in-race, would disagree with this position: all stress the structural and interpersonal forms of racism in the larger society that pose abiding challenges for their children, and all refer in one way or another to the prejudice their children face as blacks or adoptees, depending on the context. At first blush, having a child that does not resemble one or both parents would seemingly make it necessary to make adoption a topic of family discussion from the outset, and all researchers concur that open discussion of adoption is beneficial. A white mother, however, can bear a black child, so even outside the context of transracial adoption, the presence of a white mother and black child raises questions about miscegenation. Indeed, in my sample more than half the mothers told stories of strangers in public places asking if the child's father was black.

A surprising silence in the social science literature, however, concerns the negotiation of racial identity between transracial adoptees and children born to interracial couples, although Heather Dalmage discusses the complexi-ties of identity formation among African American and mixed-race children adopted by interracial couples (Dalmage, 2006). One incident related by a white adoptive mother in this study suggests that the comparison warrants research:

> My daughter was six when she was invited to a birthday party. At first there were no other African American kids there, and when one boy came in, my daughter ran over to him and said excitedly, "Now there are two black kids here!" He came in with his [birth] mom, who was African American. Well, when my kid said that, he started punching her, shouting, "I'm *biracial,* not black!" I leapt over to separate him from my girl, which pissed off his mother, who was watching but doing *nothing* about the punching. My daughter, who was standing her ground and fending off the blows, but *not* punching, was snaking her neck and saying, "Biracial? You *black!*"
>
> Looking back on it, I'm still proud of how Angela handled the situation. . . . I can understand people's desire to bring up their kids [to] emphasize both parts of their heritage, but I don't think it was going to help that kid—he was so *angry*—to feel so separate from other African American kids.

According to transracial adoption researchers, in cases where identity confusion arises for adoptees, it is usually during adolescence, surrounding issues of dating, friendships, and relations with teachers and school staff (Simon, 1992; Grotevant, 1999). Longitudinal studies of transracial adoptees similarly show that racial identity issues are prominent in adolescence (McRoy and Zurcher, 1983), but, overall, adoptions are deemed successful according to a range of measures, not limited to those related to identity. It is thus worth noting that adult adoptees, despite identity issues during adolescence, have fared well, including on various measures of racial identity (Shireman and Johnson, 1986; Simon and Altstein, 1992; Gaber and Aldridge, 1994).

Most of the adopters of black children in this study spoke of their adolescent adoptees' animosity toward them for being inadequate or embarrassing because of their whiteness. Most of the interracial adopters I interviewed who had adult children said their sons and daughters had gone through a "cultural nationalist" or "ghetto" phase. As one mother put it:

> I was so worried that Nina was going to hate me forever. I asked one of my [African American] friends how her daughter dealt with race issues in high school. I had told her that Nina never wanted to be seen with me because I was white, when before it had been at least OK. My friend laughed and said, "Honey, you could never be black enough for her at that age! Kendall [her daughter] said I was too 'white-acting' to be seen around her and her friends when she was sixteen, too!" My friend is pretty dark—it kind of put things in perspective for me.

Another mother told of how she became the focus for her daughter's anger toward some of the "skinheads" and "rednecks" in a highly diverse urban middle school:

> She called me all kinds of names: "racist white bitch" was probably the worst. When I asked her how I was being racist, she said, "Because you always want me to know about African American history and racism and stuff like that." I said that wasn't what people usually meant by racist. After we both cooled down, I asked her what it was really about, and she said one of the white boys had called her a "jungle bunny." We talked about how it made her feel, what she did about it—she walked away—and what she wanted to do about it. The next day I went with her to the principal's office to lodge a complaint. The assistant principal was good about it: The kid was suspended. . . . We were lucky: He stayed away from her after that.

Adolescents whose parents are inattentive to racism tend to fare ill in these identity-sorting years, having been reared to think of themselves as white and suddenly having to negotiate a world in which they are judged immediately on the basis of skin color (Thompson, 1974; Costin and Wattenberg, 1979). During the first transracial adoption controversy, while most researchers found the children were well adjusted in their placements, Ladner noted there were some failures (Ladner, 1977: 30). One family did not hold or touch their black child as much as their white ones; consequently, the infant became a "failure to thrive" child. Another family included their adopted child on family outings when she was little, but stopped doing so later because the child made the adoptive parents' family and friends uncomfortable. In London, Bagley and Young found that mixed-race kids of "racially unaware" parents tended to identify themselves as white, to prefer white role models, and to harbor some negative stereotypes about blacks (Bagley and Young, 1979: 210–211); children of "racially aware" parents had no such confusions.

Rita Simon's early research was an uncontrolled study of 120 black and 37 Asian and Native American kids in white homes in five midwestern cities, along with the 167 white children in the same families (Simon, 1975). She used a version of the Clark and Clark doll play study, where children are asked to talk about dolls of different colors and ages, to group them in various ways, and so on. When the kids were asked to construct a family, two-thirds made one that was racially mixed. While all young children showed some negative feelings toward the black dolls, the older the children were and the longer they had been in the adoptive homes, the more they associated the black dolls with positive qualities. It should be noted that at the time, the few black dolls available used the same molds as white dolls but with unearthly shades of gray-brown plastic. Simon did not explore this as a possible reason for children's responses to the dolls. When I showed one of these 1970s-era black dolls to an adult transracial adoptee, it evoked this comment:

> Shows how little [manufacturers] cared about us then! No little girl wants to play with something that looks like chocolate been left in the fridge—all ashy! Those dolls didn't even look human.

The early studies were done at a time when Great Society policies provided better support for struggling birth families and thus made it more likely that the children being adopted were healthier and younger at the time of placement than would be the case today. Later longitudinal studies of transracial adoption, conducted before the adoption reforms and used to bolster arguments for their passage, have shown the absence of harm in transracial placements where the family does not avoid racism as a concern, and where the family connections and communication patterns support the child's identity formation process. With few exceptions, however, the widespread success of most black adoptions in providing positive identity formation, and the benefits to minority race children of growing up in a community where they resemble many people in some way, are given little attention (but see Willis, 1996; McRoy, Zurcher, et al., 1982).

INTERRACIAL ADOPTION TODAY: ELIMINATING CATEGORIES WON'T ERASE PROBLEMS

Most of the authors writing when the transracial adoption controversy first emerged called for improving the parental evaluation process where interracial placement was a possibility. This seems crucial, considering the reports that exist about identity confusion and the damaging and sometimes catastrophic experiences black and Native American children had in some families (Costin and Wattenberg, 1979; Jaffee and Fanshel, 1970; Weinrich, 1979). A large number of studies underscore that there is sustained interest in adopting in-race among African Americans, especially regarding healthy babies. A recent national survey, however, has showed a disturbing shift in attitudes toward adoption along racial divides:

> About one in three of the blacks said adoptive parents got less satisfaction out of raising an adopted child than a biological one, compared with one in seven of the whites. . . . Overall, women, whites, and those with a college education had more positive views of adoption than men, blacks, and those with less education. (Lewin, 1997: 16)

Why this might be the case is not at all clear in the report. It may reflect the greater likelihood that children adopted within black communities have experienced greater trauma and therefore are more difficult to rear; it may reflect a pro-natalist desire within a community facing life-threatening violence. It may act as reinforcement for the pressure within African American communities placed on young mothers to keep their children. Indeed, 69 percent of black respondents said teenage mothers should rear their children themselves, which is twice as many as among whites (Lewin, 1997: 16). Particularly since this survey was conducted after federal welfare and adoption reforms were implemented, the discrepancy between black and white respondents regarding teenage mothers and adoption may well reflect a keen awareness among blacks of the problems black children encounter in the foster and adoption scene (see Bachrach, Stolley, and London, 1992).

Such results should spur community activists, adoption advocates, and public agencies to increase educational and recruitment campaigns in African American and Afro-Caribbean communities. There has been excellent, nationally conducted research that identifies barriers to in-race placement that could be addressed with a modicum of commitment by the state and adoption agencies (see Kroll, 1991: 1–3). But there are no federal monies to step up such recruitment and, indeed, the 1990s federal adoption reforms make it unclear if such targeted outreach campaigns would be legal. The burden of attracting community homes for children in foster care falls disproportionately on the shoulders of African Americans themselves.

In reference to interracial and single-parent adoption, some researchers urge that the screening procedures be altered—no less stringent, but on a different basis, asking different questions. They argue convincingly that identity formation and belonging to a community that includes people like the child need to be more central to the screening process. Carole Klein's argument over thirty years ago for single-parent adoption holds ever more true today:

> Many people now feel that an adoption caseworker should . . . concentrate on educating . . . a person who wants to adopt. Show them what is really involved in adoption, and then trust they will be able to make the decision of whether they should in fact become adoptive parents. (Klein, 1973: 95)

By saying race should not be a factor in foster or adoption placement, federal reforms leave ambiguous whether or not public agencies are forbidden to conduct screening that places ethnic or racial identity formation on the table. Even given the numbers of black children awaiting adoption, refusing to acknowledge the role of racism in their placement augurs ill for their healthy development (see Kroll, 1993).

Over the past thirty years, the picture for transracial adoption has changed in a number of ways, even as many of the issues persist. According to the adoption social workers I interviewed, there is no difficulty in placing healthy black infants who are legally freed for adoption in black homes. The children who wait, and who are therefore shunted in and out of foster homes, are those who are called "legal risk" children, or those who have a "positive toxic screen" (indications of illegal drugs in the body) at birth, developmental delays, or other special needs. For these children, a few public agencies negotiate what is called "open adoption"—where the birth mother or relatives retain contact with the adoptive parent(s). But open adoption is not an option for children born to alcoholic or drug-addicted mothers, a situation that cuts across ethnic and racial categories, especially since the methamphetamine epidemic of the current decade.

Most public agencies created foster-to-adopt programs following the first transracial adoption debates. Here, children are placed in foster homes where the parent(s) have indicated a desire to adopt the child. There is always a risk (up to 10 percent in one estimate) in these cases that the child will not be freed for adoption (see Lee and Hull, 1993). Alternatively, the child may eventually be freed, but the case can take up to seven years in the courts. The federal adoption reforms targeted the legal relinquishment process for special attention, and the impact thus far has been to speed up the relinquishment of birth-parent rights. Until these mid-1990s reforms, white adoptive foster parents might be asked to provide a rationale for how they could give the child a sense of African American identity, community, and so on. Many court proceedings urged reunification with the birth mother as the goal if at all possible, a policy emphasis of the 1980s referred to as "family preservation." This policy was criticized by many reformers as enabling drug-addicted parents to enter rehab in order to regain custody, lapse, and repeat the process for years on end, while the child experienced numerous placements. The 1990s reforms limit the time and circumstances in which birth mothers and fathers can regain custody: a "permanency plan" must be in place within eighteen months of foster placement.

What appears to be in "the best interests of the child" (see Simon, Altstein, and Melli, 1994) is taking place in a context that targets the poor. The flow of drugs into inner-city neighborhoods has been increasing since the 1970s, with wave after wave of highly addictive substances eroding many family ties, even generational ones: crack cocaine followed by methamphetamine and designer drugs. HIV infections are rising among heterosexual women, especially women of color and the poor. Drug treatment and medical care are nearly impossible to tap for those most exposed to damaging conditions on a daily basis. As a result, the children entering the public foster/adoption system are less healthy than thirty years ago.

Adoption reforms came into being at the same time that qualifying for welfare benefits became far more difficult, and strict time limits were imposed. The welfare reform laws have led to harsher conditions for poor mothers, especially as the economy slows. Because race overlaps class hierarchies significantly in this country (Oliver and Shapiro, 1995), a disproportionate number of black mothers face losing their children to foster care and adoption for reasons of neglect, including holding mothers responsible for conditions such as unheated rental units over which they have no control.[1]

Acting in "the best interests of the child" might be seen as supporting struggling birth mothers and their families, but this has been discredited as the failure of "family preservation" efforts of the 1980s—a time period when severe cutbacks in the social safety net were put in place. Yet the funding needed to support poor mothers was never there. The federal response is to speed up relinquishment of parental rights and make it easier to place children into adopting families.

As a result of these factors, interracial adoption centers on those kids who are considered difficult to place. These days, this means compounded or conjugated special needs: older children, those who have suffered abuse, those who are legal risks, drug- or alcohol-affected infants, and so on. But because race cannot be considered as a factor in placement, there are no increased federal monies for recruiting families of color. The shortened relinquishment period sometimes makes no distinction between whether the child was placed in foster care because of abuse or because of neglect that can be traced to poverty and/or 1990s welfare reform programs that cut off benefits. This combination means that, while more black children are likely to become available for adoption and the younger children among them have a greater likelihood of finding permanent families, African American and other children of color will be more likely than ever to be placed transracially or not at all.

Timely and decisive permanent placement is in "the best interests of the child." But the context in which placement into foster care and relinquishment of parental rights occurs privileges white claims in domestic adoption. The situation, according to many African American scholar-activists and their supporters, provides federal legal and financial support for what they consider to be white entitlement (see Howe, 1995, 1997).

Under the reforms, African American children are treated as if they just happen to be black, as if race in America is an option. Anticipating that race-blind policies will corrode structural racism as a force in these children's lives is funding policymakers' hopes in the face of life-threatening conditions for the children. The children and the group with which they will be identified throughout their lives are disserved if their adoptive parents are not prepared to address the very real dangers they face. The families need to rear children to value themselves as black in a society that structurally devalues them, and to develop strategies for confronting racism in its myriad of institutional as well as interpersonal practices.

FOUR

MAKING KINSHIP IN
THE WAKE OF HISTORY

Older Child Adoption

I was an egg dropped on the sand; a pauper by nature, hunted from
family to family, who belonged to nobody—and nobody cared for me.

— MARY WOLLSTONECRAFT, *MARIA, OR THE*
WRONGS OF WOMAN, 1798 (1975: 56)

Older child adoption[1] in the United States today is a story of forming kinship bonds in the aftermath of personal and community-based trauma,[2] specifically, violence that has simultaneous gender, race, and class dimensions.
Adoptive parents and children struggle daily with a set of intersecting ideologies of child development, personality, and kinship that make change, tran-
scendence, and healing appear impossible. It is a story that often revictimizes
children by making them appear helpless and ignoring their strengths. Parents
who subscribe to society's dominant narrative of kinship as an expression of
genetic replication, inheritance, and possession, and who reinforce society's
gender hierarchies and sexual double standards, may further traumatize their
adopted older children by silencing them and remaining silent themselves
on these issues. Since adoption of older children is one of the few arenas in
which these issues are confronted on a daily basis (see Carney, 1976), we can
learn from the experiences of parents about the dimensions of recovery from
gendered violence.[3]

I consider "gendered violence" as bureaucratic or personal action or in-
action that systematically truncates chances for mental and physical health or
survival, with differential focus and intensity depending on how the perpetrator perceives the target's gender. The utility of this concept as an analytical
category owes to the ways gendered violence attacks what is in many societies
a central facet of social personhood, namely, one's gender identity and often
one's sense of bodily integrity as a gendered person.

Situations in which violence is gendered help us understand the coercion inherent in reproducing gender hierarchies (see Gailey, 1988). Foster care and adoption provide vivid situations where we can see how gender ideologies articulate with kinship ideologies in exposing children to forms of sexual and physical violence. Having a notion of gendered violence, in turn, helps us see how perceived kinlessness opens girls and boys to specific forms of violation and, when children are removed from the violent context, the different ways gender expectations inhibit or facilitate their recovery.

Violence directed at children is gendered when coercive enforcement of culturally defined, stereotypical gender behaviors is involved. If we do not analytically distinguish gendered from other forms of violence, we hamper efforts of the victims to recover from histories of trauma (Briere, 1989). Moreover, ignoring the gendering of violence reproduces the very circumstances that create more victims.

Gendered violence involves a set of practices that vary culturally and help replicate gender hierarchies. In societies riven by racial, ethnic, and class hierarchies as well, gendered violence is itself affected by the simultaneous operation of these other structures that entail violent practices. Saying that the cross-cutting or intersection matters in our analysis does not mean that we are justified in submerging gendered violence or that it is secondary (hooks, 1990: 75–76).

In U.S. older child adoption, gendered violence operates at several levels: first, at the level of risks within birth or foster homes; second, at the level of adoptive parent preferences; and third, after adoption, even where adopters themselves are not violent. Let us consider how children come into care and what their risks are within birth families and in foster care.

CLASS AND DEFINITIONS OF ABUSE

I interviewed parents from twenty families who had adopted twenty-three girls over the age of four from foster care. Violence was endemic in most of the birth or foster homes where the older adoptees in my sample had spent significant periods of their lives. To understand the impact of this violence on children's later lives, we need to see the gendering of child socialization in working-class families, including both underemployed and unemployed sectors. Most foster and birth families are working class and, with exceptions having to do with individual family cultures, education, and some ethnic practices, there is an overarching class dimension to kinship ideologies and child-rearing beliefs (Rubin, 1995). Foster parents, most of whom are recruited from the working class, must attend parent-effectiveness training workshops prior to being certified; the amount of training varies from state to state. As a rule, such foster parent training stresses nonviolent approaches to child discipline, focusing on natural or logical consequences and time-outs or temporary ostracism as effective responses to unacceptable behavior. Physical punishment was discussed in the three state-contracted agency training programs I attended; in each, several of the foster parent trainees objected to being told not to use corporal punishment.

Notwithstanding variation in family and ethnic cultures, what are general parenting expectations and child rearing practices among the U.S. working class? For many decades researchers have noted that parents expect girls more than boys to obey and assist their mothers in home maintenance and child care (see, e.g., Henry, 1963: 133–134); girls also are held more accountable for rebelliousness or resistance, especially in adolescence, than boys (Rubin, 1976; see Gillies, 2007; Trudge, 2008). Boys tend to have more freedom of movement outside the home and less supervision in it.

Most of the working-class parents in my study viewed corporal punishment as a necessary or at least as an inevitable or unavoidable part of child rearing. There certainly are working-class families who do not espouse corporal punishment, including several parents in my sample. Still, it is rare to find this as a long-term, transgenerational pattern (see Rubin, 1976). All the children adopted over the age of four discussed in this chapter had lived in working-class foster homes and all had been hit, slapped, belted, or beaten by parents in those homes.

There is no consensus among American parents about what constitutes physical abuse, although leaving marks seems to be a dividing line of sorts. Indeed, the working-class parents in my sample did not agree on appropriate physical punishment that falls short of child abuse. Some parents focused on the intensity of the punishment: mild slaps are not abusive, but hard slaps or slaps on the face are. Most thought that leaving a mark that lasts more than a few minutes is abusive. For others, spanking with the hand is acceptable if the infractions are well understood, but punching or kicking is not. Still others said it depends where the parent strikes the child: spanking through clothing or on the thigh is acceptable, but not on the naked bottom. A few remembered occasional beatings in their own childhoods, with a hairbrush, leather belt, rod, cane, or stick as "deserved"; these parents considered such punishments abusive only if they left marks, were in response to small infractions, or erupted in the heat of anger (see Henry, 1963: 345–348). Yet the working-class adopters I interviewed said they only used spanking as part of disciplinary practices that also included time-outs.

Physical abuse of children by parents certainly is not limited to the working class. Middle-class parents in my study, however, were more likely to express general condemnation of corporal punishment. Nevertheless, they evaded discussing their personal practices or "mistakes" in that regard. Perhaps they were less violent than working-class parents. Perhaps they were more likely to resort to emotional or verbal punishment, or perhaps they were more cautious about how they might appear in an interview.

A small number of mothers said that when they spanked their child, they used the sole of a shoe or the flat side of a hairbrush. In other cases the parents said they avoided physical punishment, but that one or another of their relatives hit their own children. One father elaborated:

> We try not to have my mother babysit for us, but sometimes that's impossible. She hits first and asks questions later, which drives me and my wife nuts. But the kid is on to her by now and knows when to lay low. When she does hit him, he tells us and we talk about it. I tell him what she did to me and my sisters when I was a kid. He knows we don't approve of it.

None of the middle-class couples in my study, whether adopting through public or private agencies, admitted to hitting their children. Almost all the single-mother adopters—most of them through public agencies and most middle-income professionals—admitted they had "lost it" sporadically and slapped their children. All these women, however, said they had not hit their children repeatedly; they denied using corporal punishment on a routine basis; and all claimed they had only used their hand to hit. Most said they "felt awful" or "felt I had failed" after hitting the child.

Another dimension of U.S. kinship ideology is that mothers associate fathers or father figures (uncles, mother's boyfriends) with disciplinary action more than themselves, although national child abuse statistics indicate that mothers are as likely as fathers to strike children. Almost all the parents I interviewed who approved of occasional physical discipline considered father figures to have the right or even the responsibility to conduct more severe punishment and to punish older boys, while mothers should inflict lighter physical punishment and punish adolescent girls.

Because of the gender division of labor in the family, mothers tend to be more in charge of child monitoring, which also means that girls face more supervision. The effect is that both girls and boys risk physical punishment by adult men, but girls also face a greater risk of routine physical punishment from their mothers. In adolescence, gender segregation for physical punishment is typical: fathers or father figures discipline boys, and mothers or their surrogates discipline girls. Older boys, however, have more opportunity to evade physical punishment than older girls because they are freer to roam outside the home. Thus, while physical punishment appears to be a generic risk for both girls and boys in the homes from which most older children are adopted, the gender of the perpetrators influenced the degree of severity, the age at which physical punishment might begin or end, and the type of physical punishment.

Beyond physical punishment, girls run an additional risk of sexual abuse in both birth homes and foster homes at the hands of fathers, brothers, male relatives, neighbors, or mothers' boyfriends. One controlled study conducted in Illinois found that children in foster care who had been sexually abused in their birth homes were significantly *more* likely to be reunited with these birth families than were children who had been placed in foster care because of neglect (Schuerman, Rzepnicki, and Littell, 1994). Why this can occur requires us to explore the intersection of gender with kinship ideologies in greater detail.

GENDER AND KINSHIP IDEOLOGIES: "DAMAGED GOODS" OR DOOMED TO KINLESSNESS

A discussion of the violent traumas that older child adoptees have often experienced requires a better understanding of how ideologies of kinship shape the categories of vulnerable and protected children. These ideologies are reflected in the patterns of violence experienced by children in foster care, often resulting from the widespread assumption that the only real kinship is based on genetics. Because mothers are often more closely associated with their daughters and fathers with their sons, and men are commonly believed to have weaker ties to their nonbiological children, this gendered ideology denies to men any strong, nonsexualized role in creating kinship with their adopted or foster daughters. At the same time, patriarchal ideology delegates familial protection to fathers as an outgrowth of what is purported to be a natural aspect of masculinity, namely sexual possessiveness.

In the patriarchally defined domain of family ideology, being without an effective father is a dire circumstance. But being fatherless has different consequences for boys than for girls. Single parenthood among white professionals or in stably employed, white working-class sectors carries with it a certain stigma, but more sadness than anger. These days the media present it more as an economic and social hardship than as a moral taint. The same courtesy, however, is not extended to single mothers of color, or to impoverished white single mothers: the media invariably portray their children as living without parental control. Regardless of plentiful data to the contrary (see Rubin, 1995; Collins, 1990b: 115–137), the media depict single mothers as promiscuous teenage girls predisposed to bearing drug-addicted babies, staffing the sex trade, or living lives of welfare dependency. Young men from single-mother families have long been represented as street gang members, violent drug runners, sexual predators, or parasites on ordinary taxpayers (Fredrickson, 1971). In the politics of cultural representation, having "only" a mother means de facto having a dysfunctional family or virtually no family. The condemnation carries with it a justification for and a heightened risk of abuse.

Kinlessness is a dangerous liminal state in a society that devalues anything other than blood connections. Without patriarchal possession, women and children appear unclaimed and thus vulnerable. This notion of the patriarchal aegis providing protection continues despite long-standing evidence that patriarchal fathers are implicated in much of father-daughter incest in America (Herman, 1981).

Removed from birth families, and often from single-mother families that already face ideological devaluation, children relinquished for adoption and living in foster care become categorically kinless. Girls in these circumstances have a somewhat better chance of escaping chronic kinlessness in fosterage because of the slight preference for girls in older child adoption. This slight advantage, however, is outweighed by girls' far greater risk of sexual abuse.

The patriarchal kinship script outlined above, with its emphasis on genetic connection as primal and its differentially gendered implications, means that adults in general tend to identify girls with their birth mothers and boys with their birth fathers. Birth mothers who relinquish or are forced under new federal guidelines to relinquish children to foster care are presumed, in many cases erroneously, to be unwed, underage, incompetent, promiscuous, and/or drug-addicted (see Ninivaggi, 1996). Such a demeaning imagery of their birth mothers renders the girls particularly vulnerable to sexual abuse by men around the birth, foster, or adoptive mother, be they uncles, boyfriends, fathers, or stepfathers. And black girls in foster care have the additional burden of racial discrimination.

One of the gendered dimensions of this script paints white women as instinctual, natural mothers, an essentialized view of motherhood denied to black women. Black women are figured instead as hypersexual and hyperfertile (Collins, 1990: 77), in a cultural setting where women's sexual agency has been opposed to concepts of good mothering since at least the eighteenth century. Thus, the mass media depicts black birth mothers as irresponsible breeders rather than as caring mothers in difficult circumstances, and the population at large consumes these images without questioning (Collins, 1991: 78). Consequently, the daughters of black women are seen as inherently promiscuous, oversexed, and/or seductive regardless of their behavior or age. Such raced and gendered patriarchal scripts permit, indeed promote, sexual violence.

In most states, foster and adoptive parents receive very little information about their children's birth parents, increasing the likelihood that negative stereotypes in the media will prevail. Among the sparse information that social workers disclose to adopters is: if the birth mother and, when known, the birth father were of "normal intelligence"; their ages and educational attainment; their height and general family circumstances; whether the birth mother took illegal drugs or drank alcohol heavily during pregnancy; and if the child was removed from the home for reasons of neglect or abuse. Only three of the parents in my study were told who the suspected perpetrator was in cases of sexual abuse.

Social workers may not know about sexual abuse at the time of foster placement: physical evidence may be ambiguous, and not all children reveal molestation to a psychiatrist they may only see once or twice. If the social workers do know, they generally provide the relevant information to foster or adoptive parents. Given the highly uneven funding for medical and mental health care between states, however, there is no guarantee of therapeutic treatment in foster care or adoption.

Indeed, if a fostered or adopted girl is known to have been violated, she risks additional consequences of a gendered double standard for sexuality in the United States: a common assumption is that the daughter of a violated woman is tainted by the association. Once violated, acquaintances of the family or sometimes members of the foster family (again, there is no research on incest in adoptive families) may view the girl as openly available to others or as being inherently seductive. One young black woman explained that she was raped in foster care because she was seen as "belonging to no one" and "damaged goods anyway," even as a young teenager.

The older the child and the more traumas the child has survived, the less concerned state or private subcontracting agency social workers are with racial matching. Irrespective of color, few families are willing to add a member who has survived a litany of traumas if less injured children are available. Given the difficulties social workers encounter finding any family prepared to address the effects of multiple traumas in the past, we would expect to find more transracial placements in this type of adoption than in others. Unfortunately, states do not track placements with such detailed attention to children's histories of sexual abuse.

GENDER AND RECOVERY FROM TRAUMA

According to the adoptive mothers and fathers I interviewed, histories of gendered violence heavily influenced the ways their daughters related to their bodies, their expectations of relationships and the future, and their self-esteem (see also Beitchman et al., 1992). Parenting practices either facilitated or obstructed the processes of family formation in adoption and recovery from unattachment or sexual abuse. Some parents were willing to address the gendered violence experienced by their children, while others were re-luctant. Some parents actively addressed strategies devised by the children to explain or adapt to conditions of bodily threat: a few left the children to their own devices, or attributed difficult or destructive behaviors to other causes. For example, when one single mother's five-year-old adopted daughter suddenly attacked an older boy in plain view and without provocation, she separated them, had her daughter apologize to the boy, and took her aside to discuss it:

> She said she wanted to kill big boys. When I asked her why, she said, "Be-cause they just want to hurt you down there," pointing to her pubic area. I asked if that boy had ever done anything to her and she said, "No." I asked her if she was afraid he would hurt her and she said no, that "Kyle was nice." "Then why hit him?" I asked. Then she got real quiet. She hardly ever cried back then, but I could see tears in her eyes. "You can tell me. I won't think you're bad," I said. That did it. She burst into tears and said, "Because Paul [a former foster brother about the same age] used to hurt me there all the time!" She must have cried in my arms for at least a half an hour. Well, I knew there had been sexual abuse from the agency report, but that was the first I heard her talk about who did it. I felt it was a real breakthrough in her trusting me. From what I've read about sexual abuse, her naming her perp[etrator] was important.

Parents in another of the families clearly did not want to probe into their six-year-old daughter's motivations:

One night around bedtime she took this red marker and just scribbled all over her favorite baby doll's bottom: and I mean *all* over it, underneath. I asked her why she did it and she said, "Because she was bad." Well, my husband overheard this and said, "Bad or not, it doesn't give you the right to make a mess." I told her she had to help me scrub it all off and not to do it again.

Such silencing can occur analytically as well. One adoption advocate, for instance, outlines six characteristics of adopted adolescents at high risk for delinquency, substance abuse, teen pregnancy, and school failure, outcomes that most researchers concur have a detrimental effect on overall life chances: early acting out, lack of parental support, lack of basic skills (that is, being one or two years older than other children in their grade at school), lack of resistance to peer pressure, living in a disadvantaged neighborhood, and depression and stress (Dryfoos, 1993: 13). That this author did not sort these into structural causes and psychological effects, or relate the data to overall rates of depression and stress by gender and age, unintentionally encourages blaming victims. Feminist therapists in particular have stressed that helping everyone involved see a survivor's agency is crucial to recovery, since it can help a range of caregivers devise effective interventions (see Brown and Ballou, 1992).

Being supported in remembering the trauma (if possible), speaking out about trauma, uncovering shared experiences in settings viewed by all participants as safe, and getting involved in social action regarding issues of violence are related avenues of healing, according to a range of researchers (Root, 1992). Given support, some survivors can come to situate their experiences politically and socially, which can help to further both personal and political change (Hoff, 1990). For example, a call for submissions to an anthology edited by a former foster child stresses the sociopolitical dimensions of long-term foster care:

Attention Foster Care Survivors! Are you an adult who survived foster care? Would you like to help teens in foster care by sharing how you survived/recovered from your foster care experience? . . . The publication will be geared toward teenagers in care and emancipated youth who are looking for life models, and who want to know that they *can* make a good life for themselves after being raised as state wards. (*Adoptalk*, 1995: 17)

The call implies that state care is a kind of incarceration demanding creative action to survive and escape. Children entering and spending time in

U.S. foster care, even if they are adopted later, are placed sometimes from birth in circumstances that increase their risk of trauma. That their trauma is not a focus for social action further victimizes these children and youth.

As we turn to the narratives of parents adopting older girls, black and white, who have been in state care, we need to link the ways in which birth or foster care homes entail gendered violence with policies that could help to prevent the forms of trauma that girls and boys experience differently and also facilitate their recovery.

ADOPTING OLDER GIRLS: PARENTING NARRATIVES
OF TRAUMA AND RECOVERY

The claims of some adoption advocacy groups aside, adoption alone cannot be a panacea for children's problems, particularly in a country like the United States where post-adoption services are scanty and monitoring all but non-existent. Studies by anthropologists, sociologists, psychologists, and social workers have shown repeatedly that adoption can facilitate recovery from even the most profound abuse—saving children's spirits and lives—but loving a child is not enough (see, among others, Jewett, 1978; Katz, 1986). Kin formation in the anthropological sense works in a wide variety of settings, but it requires a fairly consistent access to material and community resources (Gailey, 2004).

Attachment can and does occur in foster families. Sometimes foster parents ignore many states' training guidelines that stress limiting kinship outreach to the child and thereby increase the risk of grief and loss for all involved if the child must be moved. But such foster attachment is viewed in other state manuals as beneficial. A range of child psychologists have stressed that an attached child can reattach, while an unattached child will continue to have difficulty trusting anyone (see, for example, Cline, 1979; Jewett, 1982).

All five adoption social workers I interviewed considered grief and loss preferable to unattachment. If the child is not buffeted about in foster care, but has a stable and loving foster family, the loss she experiences being moved to an adoptive home is not permanently scarring. Unclaimed in foster care, one social worker explains, can cause a child to "shut down," to become unwilling to risk another abandonment. It is ironic that in most states it is legally easier for an older adoptive child to stay in touch with former foster family members than with birth family members.

The crisis for adoption social workers dealing with burgeoning caseloads of children over the age of six is finding homes with any promise of continuity and safety. There is consensus that continuity and safety are paramount in ensuring children's mental health as well as physical well-being and that a spiral of foster care placements is detrimental to children. Long-term foster families are increasingly difficult to recruit,[4] particularly for children who may have been born with drug addictions, HIV infection, or profound physical or mental disabilities. Adoptive families are even more difficult to find.

In my sample of older child adopters, twenty families (thirty-one adults) had adopted twenty-three girls between the ages of four and twelve at the time of adoption, which was within the past decade. Ten families had adopted ten black girls; these families consisted of two single African American women, three single white women, three African American married couples, and two white married couples. The remaining ten families had adopted thirteen older white girls. These families were white and consisted of four single women and six married couples. All eleven of the married couples in the group were working class or professionals; all were in dual earner households.

Of the twenty families, eight had first identified the girls who would be-come their daughters in adoption resource catalogues, from which they gave information about those children to their social workers. In eleven other cases, social workers had identified a child for the parent(s). The remaining family had identified a child in their community whose foster family encour-aged them to adopt her. Although it did not occur in my sample, it is com-mon for long-term foster mothers or parents to adopt older black children unrelated to them, particularly if the foster parents also are black or were in foster care in their youth (Shireman and Johnson, 1986; Meezan and Shire-man, 1985).

The racial dimension of gendered violence can be seen in the differential exposure of black girls to violence and particularly sexual violence in and out of foster care. This is largely an unspoken phenomenon. I could find no reli-able statistics on the rates of sexual abuse reported against black girls before or in foster care anywhere in the United States. Thus, I have no way of knowing if the alarming incidence of sexual abuse (eight of the ten) in my snowball sample is representative. If it is, sexual abuse of black girls in or before foster care is normative. Moreover, all these girls had been physically abused, most habitually so; four bore scars from beatings, cigarette burns, scalding, knifing, or razor cuts. The literature on transracial adoption does not deal with the aftermath of trauma in addition to the issues of racial identity formation (see Simon and Altstein, 1992), but neither does the literature on in-race adoption. These issues continue to be dealt with as if they were separable in children's lives. Particularly where the perpetrators also were black, which should never be assumed and was not the case in two of the black girls' cases, the issues are deeply entwined with racial and gender identity formation.

Before adoption, the ten black girls had experienced from two to seven foster placements: half had had three placements in four to seven years. The thirteen older white girls in state care had experienced one to four foster placements at the time of their adoptive placement. Almost all these girls had encountered physical abuse in birth relatives' and foster homes, most on a routine basis. Sexual abuse was reported in three cases. These three were sisters and the violation had occurred in the birth home by the birth father. Their foster placement was precipitated by starvation and beatings; the sexual abuse was discovered only later in the medical screening for the physical abuse.

Five of the nine parents whose girls had been sexually abused before or during foster care were willing to talk to me about it. The parents of the three sisters above and the white mother of a black girl said health workers diagnosed the sexual abuse after the children had been removed for reasons of physical abuse or profound neglect in birth or foster homes. Of the remaining twelve girls in the sample, sexual abuse was suspected but not proven in four other cases, based on a configuration of behavioral and cognitive symptoms, including flashbacks associated with being sexually violated (see Brown and Ballou, 1992). Only two of the diagnosed girls had explicit and detailed memories regarding incidents of sexual abuse, but all eleven had experienced flashbacks.

All but two of the eleven girls known to have been sexually abused were currently or had been in counseling or psychotherapy since coming home to their adoptive families. Of the twelve girls who had not been diagnosed as sexually abused, four were currently in counseling or therapy and two others had been in therapy earlier. Given that psychotherapy is not covered under most workers' medical plans in the United States, the expense for treatment averaged about five or six percent of the parents' annual income. Some of the parents used the entire post-adoption subsidy payment to cover their daughters' therapy expenses.

The short version of this story is that all the children had had histories of being violated, witnessing violence, being verbally lambasted, and being moved from one foster home to another, or back and forth to a birth home where they were not safe. With these histories, recovery from post-traumatic stress (Figley, 1985), rape trauma, or incest is paramount in the family formation process (see Herman, 1981). But they are not always perceived that way by the parents or social workers involved. Most adoptive parents are not given in-depth training in therapeutic techniques directed at redressing unattachment (Cline, 1979), or the kinds of post-trauma or rape-trauma behaviors their daughters may exhibit (McNamara and McNamara, 1990). Moreover, such therapeutic techniques are counter-intuitive to typical middle-class or working-class parenting styles.

Many towns and cities do not have ongoing support groups or programs, such as respite care, that might give the stressed parents a break, or help them devise or gain access to appropriate activities or groups that might help their children. Schools and day-care centers are ill-equipped to understand or respond to the child's needs, and parents are often inappropriately pressured into overmedicating or placing a child who is in no danger to himself or others into separate educational settings focused on behavior modification, particularly if the child is also African American (see Goldberg et al., 1992: 440). The stage is thus set for parents who do not have the personal or financial resources to arrange support, therapies, workshops, educational advocacy, and the like, to eventually give up on the child or be forced into institutionalization.

Often, newly adoptive parents wish to focus on those issues common in most adoptions, namely, adoption transition: resolving grief and loss the child feels, forming loving bonds to the child, and explaining to the child how she or he came to be adopted (Burlingham-Brown, 1994). The parents I interviewed all began the process with the assumption that nurturing and love would be sufficient to "turn the child around," as one father put it. For the children, issues of transition and kin formation are intertwined, conflated, and confused with those of the multiple traumas and losses they have experienced. According to one mother, when her daughter arrived at the age of six, even after having visited the family over a period of two months, she "was sure we would kill her once we got to know her, because that's what happened to her when she was little." Another mother told me that her twelve-year-old daughter had recently showed her a passage in her diary that she had written during a time-out period, a year after coming home at the age of eight. In the journal, according to the mother,

> She writes about how we talk too much, how we scream at her but don't hit, and how she can't trust us, because she doesn't know what we're going to do to her. She must have been so frightened!

Anthropologist Judith Modell has argued that the kinship of adoption is more akin to marriage than to the formation of family ties through birthing, although she also argues that adoption is a model for all kin formation (Modell, 1994). While Modell's concept of "kinship with strangers" describes aspects of some adoptions, it cannot capture the terror and resistance trau-matized children experience in their adoptive settings.

A more suitable analogy for these children might be the family formation of Holocaust survivors in the wake of the death camps. In approaching the complex task facing these rape and abuse survivors and their families, the im-portance of the parents and other relatives' stances toward the girls' histories cannot be overemphasized (Jewett, 1978). As psychologist Maria Root states:

> Current theories [on post-traumatic stress disorder] do not account for the interaction between the environment and an individual (mind, body, and spirit) as it shapes the development of post trauma responding and heal-ing. . . . Factors such as isolation, blame, loss of social status, and effect on ability to care for one's self and/or family add to the trauma of the original event. (Root, 1992: 235, 237)

Most of the girls in the sample had blamed themselves for their physical abuse. One mother viewed her daughter's self-blame as at least in part an effort to retain a sense of control in a powerless situation. Most of the adop-tive mothers' narratives give an optimistic past tense to these feelings of self-blame, and most parents had encouraged the children to see themselves as unaccountable for the violence:

> She thought that she had caused her scalding by bothering her mother.

> Molly believed her father wouldn't have hit her so much if she'd been a better kid.

While none of the families blamed the girls for their trauma, several of them expressed reluctance to discuss the child's history of violence with her "un-less absolutely necessary." One seven-year-old survivor of physical violence, who was described by her parents as "on the shy side," had parents who, four years into the adoption, were satisfied with her silence about the past: "A lot of people have had terrible things happen to them in childhood. In our family we encourage people to get on with their lives," said her father. Her mother added, "That was then, this is now. If she really needs to talk about it, of course we'll listen." Another mother said of her sexual abuse survivor, who had memories of the events, "I don't want her to obsess about the pain in her past. I try to listen for a while, then get her to talk about more cheerful things." In terms of recovery, these strategies, which cut across both middle-class and working-class parents, act as vehicles of silencing.

One common symptom of survivors in safer surroundings is the onset of flashbacks. Flashbacks are unplanned, uncontrolled bursts of memory that flood the survivor's sensations; flashbacks place the survivor back in time and without reference to the current space she inhabits, to the scene of trauma. Some flashbacks may be triggered by sound, smell, the position of light, a word, or a facial expression, but others seem to the person experiencing them to have come from nowhere. These "teleportations of pain," as one of the mothers described her daughter's flashbacks, are terrifying, unbidden re-visitations of a horrific experience. For the girls who had flashbacks, ignoring the past was not an option. Most parents were able to recognize flashbacks as such, particularly if they had had some experience of abuse themselves or training in abuse recovery and if the girl was over the age of eight. In one case, however, the mother viewed the daughter's actions as tantrums, because "she was too young to remember." Other mothers, particularly the single parents, disagreed strongly with this response. "My kid was only two when she was raped, but you can't tell me she doesn't remember it," said one. The others had similar reactions:

I really get freaked by [five-year-old] Makenzie's flashbacks. It's like she isn't even in this world. . . . I just hold her and talk calmly to her till she comes round again.

No one [at the agency] prepared me for the flashbacks. One day it just happened—like a seizure or a thrashing tantrum—Lee Ann [then four] was so terrified! She was right back there in that scary place with those horrible people. She was reliving it! [voice breaks] I was a wreck afterward. I had to tell the day-care staff about [the flashbacks]. It just wasn't fair to spring them on them. I mean, what would they do? I wanted them to know that they shouldn't be afraid of her: she was the one who was terrified. I told the staff to pull her onto their laps or into a rocking chair and rock, soothing her with touch and soft words, to call her little spirit back to our time and place. It only happened once, but all of us were glad I did the training with them, and Lee Ann got the help she needed.

Monique [now twelve] doesn't want me to tell anyone at school about them [the flashbacks]. I got her a beeper [cell phone] because of them. So, the deal is that when she has them at school, she puts her head in her arms on the desk, and then calls me as soon as she can. I just want her to know I'm always there for her.

These mothers articulated their own stress and upset in trying to support and cope with their child's difficulties (see also Katz, 1986). A number of psychotherapists have called the transfer of trauma from the victim to the caregiver "secondary post traumatic stress disorder" or "compassion fatigue" (see Yassen, 1995). Others consider symptoms like the ones these mothers express to be different from stress. Root, for example, offers the concept of "indirect trauma" to describe when one is "traumatized by the trauma sustained by another with whom one identifies in some significant way" (Root, 1992: 240). The mothers' comments would support the latter contention:

When she suffers, I suffer. I didn't go through what she went through, but jeez, how can you hear a six-year-old kid saying, "I want to kill myself I'm so bad" and not feel that pain?

Her flashbacks sometimes trigger mine. So in a real intimate way, we're in this thing together, right?

The latter quote points to an arena virtually unexplored in the current adoption literature, namely, how unremembered sexual abuse in the adoptive parent's history can be discovered through parenting a sexually abused child (see, for example, McNamara and McNamara, 1990). This particular mother had sought therapy for herself as well as her daughter, but she also was among the most active parents in developing and sustaining support networks (see Briere, 1989; Beitchman et al., 1992). Again and again, when parents spoke of having support, probing revealed that they had to assemble the resources and networks on their own (see Piantanida, 1993: 13); further probing found that mothers did the vast majority of this resource identification and access work.

Given such levels of anxiety and constant strategizing (Katz, 1986), in the more forthcoming of the narratives mothers and fathers risked revealing their defeats: the foresworn swatting in anger, the harsh words, their fear of breakdown (theirs or the child's), the humiliation when other relatives boasted about their children's achievements, periodic feelings of being swallowed by another's madness, the fear that if the family struggles were revealed, the child would be taken away, lost forever in the maw of foster care:

I have to tell you, one of my nightmares is someone hearing me yell at Molly or find me trying to hold her during her rages and calling the cops. I'd be devastated if she were taken away [into foster care] and God only knows what would happen to her. It scares me to death. It scares me even to talk about it.

Other themes that run through the interviews are children constantly testing boundaries, "pushing my buttons," needing to know the threshold for violence in their parents, what made the parents feel crazy, "in a way, balancing the powerlessness [that the children] feel" (see McNamara and McNamara, 1990; Mansfield and Waldmann, 1994). Several parents noted their child's fear of establishing anything other than violence as a basis for trust:

It blew me away when I first saw her actually trying to get me to hit her, like it was a kind of reality check. She couldn't trust love.

I lost it once and slapped her when she kicked me. She smiled, and I knew right then that she'd won some kind of contest, and lost at the same time. I promised myself I wouldn't repeat that mistake.

My daughter was a master of subverting her own good times. I used to think of it, when she'd begin shrieking and writhing in the Science Museum and have to be carried home, as "I can't trust pleasure. Pain may suck ducks, but it's at least predictable." It was pretty sad, but now she can do Christmas, Halloween, birthdays, traveling, whatever without a crisis. Pissy behavior, yes, but nothing horrible.

Placation and manipulation are often responses by the powerless to those who have the potential to harm. For girls who have been victims of severe physical or sexual trauma, there is a repertoire of behaviors aimed at disarming potential abusers. These behaviors may have saved the child's life in the past, but they stand in the way of her attachment and trust in those adoptive settings that are safe. Parents seem acutely aware of the manipulative behaviors: some described them as merely quantitatively different from other children's wheedling ways, while other parents considered them as distancing and power games. Most discerned a difference between "real" or "genuine" affectionate behavior and what one mother described as "play-acting like she loved me." One father said,

When I saw the movie *The Bad Seed* and the girl says, "I have the most wonderful mother!" in this really fakey, singsong voice, I wanted to throw up. That was our daughter: 100 percent. She could do that and then turn right around and kick the dog if she didn't get her way.

Other parents described what they felt were indications of growing trust and bonding:

> I'll always remember the first time Monique hugged me without wanting anything from me.

> Can you imagine? I jumped for joy the first day she felt safe enough around me to shout, "I hate you, Mom!" instead of always being on her guard.

Only two parents linked the placating behavior to the girls having lacked control over their physical safety earlier. One father even called this "seductive" behavior, suggesting that he holds his daughter at least partly accountable for her own earlier abuse. All but two simply responded to such behavior with negative attention, comments such as "Stop that right now!" or "Be real." One of these two remaining mothers, who worked in an agency addressing the needs of battered women, drew an analogy between her daughter's actions and battered wives' behaviors toward their husbands: "It's so hard to learn to trust anyone once a loved one injures you."

Parenting narratives, particularly those of mothers, tell of small victories in everyday life and a growing awareness of their daughters' strengths and cues:

> One day, it seemed like Carly finally understood that if you behaved good, you got to do more things. I guess there wasn't much of a tie between what you did and what you got where she come [sic] from.

> It sounds weird, but there was one day when Lee Ann was five when she spent a whole day in her body, here with me, on earth. I can't explain the feeling, but she was really there, 100 percent there, a real kid doing real kid things—all day.

> I knew she was on the right road the morning she hugged the dog and said, "I wish we got you before they cut your tail: Mom and I would have stopped them!"

> Her second grade teacher told me she comforted a kid at recess, who said her mom's boyfriend had beaten her, by saying, "You should think about getting adopted."

The timing and location for these breakthroughs are not always optimal. One mother laughed when I asked her and explained:

Are you ready for this? One night we were in this restaurant and Monique ordered a hot dog. She *never* ate hot dogs. Never! I asked her if she was sure and she said, loud enough for the next table to hear, of course, "Yeah, now I know it's not really a penis going to choke me."

These "first times" are not the usual stuff of parental nostalgia (see also Wadia-Ells, 1995). "I never knew I had such a range of emotions," one exhausted mother commented about her experiences with a recent preadolescent adoptee. "I ride this roller coaster every day. I see my friends' [birth] kids and, like, mine is theirs times ten! Lord, have mercy, some days I just don't know if she'll ever turn out right!" Several mothers, but particularly the single mothers, echoed her emotional weariness:

I've given up the five-year plans and college plans. Now I make thirty-minute plans, hour plans.

All my life people pushed and pushed me to make long-term plans. I learned how to do it. Now, because of my daughter, I've had to unlearn it and learn how to live in the present. Where she's at demands it.

I feel like I've rewritten the Twelve Steps [a recovery program for alcoholics], but instead of "one day at a time," it's more like one minute at a time [laughs].

When Desirée [age fourteen] ran away for the third time in two weeks, I called up my friend whose kid [adopted daughter] had had a kid at sixteen. "Does it ever end?" I asked. "Yeah," she says, "in a way, but not in the way you have planned. Emily just finished her associate's degree and has a full-time job at a bank. I am so proud of her, and I love being a grandmother. She's still seeing that stupid schmuck [a marginally employed man—not her child's father] but at least he's not a batterer." We had a laugh at that one.

What is apparent in the narratives as well is that older child adopters benefit as much from support groups of family, friends, or other adopters as their children do (Groze, 1996; Smith and Howard, 1991). Indeed, therapists working with traumatized patients have written eloquently of the need for various behavioral stances, forms of social supports, and social activism as strategies for preventing "secondary traumatic stress disorder" among therapists treating trauma survivors (Yassen, 1995).

But the crisis among adults attempting to do therapeutic parenting is acute. Few of the people in my larger sample, including those who had not adopted older children, received help or advice in developing support networks, finding relief when the tensions were too great, or locating or organizing workshops through state or private agencies. In the two-parent families adopting older children, the wife was the one who sought out and kept the support group ties functioning. For the single mothers, it was "not really a choice: I'd either do it [find support] or collapse." Typical were these responses:

> The only thing that kept me going that first year was the telephone. I think one of us would be dead today if it wasn't for that phone. I'd call and just bawl my eyes out once she was in bed, or when I wanted to strangle her. Thank God for my friends and this group of other adopters I found.

> I remember calling up a friend of mine—also an adoptive mom, but whose kids are grown—and saying, "I don't know who I want to kill more, her or me." And she laughed and heard me out. She was a lifesaver.

What of the failures? Social work literature sanitizes adoptive parents' voluntary return of their adopted child to state care as "disruption" rather than what is sometimes parental rejection or abandonment of the child (Barth, 1988). Parents returning children to foster care is acknowledged by social workers to be far higher for older child adoption than infant adoption, higher for special needs adoption than ordinary adoption (Boyne et al., 1984). If, like the children in the public adopter part of this study, a child is adopted at age four or older, the chances of having the adoption fail are ten to twelve times as great as that of a child placed in infancy (Barth and Berry, 1988). If the child is of any age but has special needs, the disruption rate is over fourteen times as great (Groze, 1986).

What remains unclear, however, are the gender and abuse dimensions of this kind of abandonment or parental rejection (Sack and Dale, 1982). Adoption advocacy groups appear reticent about collecting such data, but the North American Council on Adoptable Children (NACAC) research on the disruption literature pointed out services that could reduce it:

> A complete history of the child and a realistic appraisal of disruption risk should be mandatory. . . . Parents need education, skill training, develop-

ment of support and referral networks, and intervention strategies prior to placement and any crises it may bring. . . . Special needs adoption . . . requires post placement services of adequate duration and intensity. . . . Experienced adoptive families . . . suggest streamlining of services, creating consistency in services, reducing adoption costs, and providing appropriate and timely respite care, case management, and counseling. (*Adoptalk*, 1993: 4)

The narratives in my study stressed again and again the need for training and support groups, including advice from experienced adopters (see Katz, 1986; Groze, 1996): "After exactly one month, I knew I had to find some help. I asked around and joined a group for adoptive parents in the area." No one in the sample felt their adoption agency had lied to them about the child's condition, but many felt that there was minimal or reluctant information sharing. For others, much was unknown at the time of placement. Most of the parents were under the impression that "love and stability were enough."

The parents of four of the adoptees who were placed as older children did not want to talk extensively about the trauma of the child's past. Their narratives indicated some formality or reticence about adoption in general as less than real kinship. For instance, "We love her like our own" and "I didn't used to think much was inherited in people before we adopted Amanda, but now I really think there are a lot of things like personality that are nature, not nurture." Do these stances indicate any predisposition to give up on a child? Several studies strongly imply that distancing of any kind predicts what used to be called "failure" (Barth, 1988; Smith and Howard, 1991; Zwimpfer, 1983). It is recognized that abuse often accompanies failing adoptions (Sack and Dale, 1982), although this is a decidedly under-researched area. Labeling situations where parents relinquish an adopted child as a "disrupted" adoption exonerates the parents and constitutes another part of the hidden violence in older child adoption. Adults are rarely considered "disruptive," while "disruptive behavior" is often used to describe children's socially unacceptable actions.

Gendered violence is exacerbated when adoption, already cast in the dominant ideology as inferior and as a more fragile kin connection than genetic linkage or birthing, intersects the brutal circumstances that have made the girls or boys "hard to place." The causes of their trauma lie less in neglect, the consequence of poverty, than in the evaporation of state aid for birth mothers and their children in the contemporary United States. Other causal agents are patriarchal gender ideologies and racism that promote physical and sexual abuse in birth homes, foster care, and (in all likelihood, to an extent) in adoptive homes. What is important for people engaged in facilitating survivorship rather than further victimization of children is understanding the gendered dimensions of the violence, particularly the sexual abuse or gender-targeted torture that children have endured and how that affects their subsequent sense of personhood, bodily integrity, and relationships.

The 1990s adoption reforms provide increased federal expenditure for post-adoption support services. These are certainly needed, but they come at a time when more children are likely to come into state care, given the welfare reform laws that cut off federal aid after five years and local jurisdictions that seek to remove children for reasons of neglect alone. Programs for birthmother support and foster care training and support are sorely needed and unlikely to occur under the present neoliberal political climate.

Moreover, pre- and post-adoption training and support programs need to address parenting approaches specifically geared toward recovery from rape or incest trauma, as well as physical injury and the more commonly acknowledged issues of abandonment, grief, and loss. To presume that the gendered trauma that poor girls, especially poor black girls, encounter in or before state wardship is generically akin to other forms of trauma creates a situation where recovery is thwarted, because the causes are submerged and the voice of the survivor silenced. Inept or ill-informed parenting can re-silence or re-victimize the child survivor and can make it likely that the girls will become involved in self-destructive or abusive relationships in their adoptive homes, in young adulthood, or as mothers themselves.

There are marked analogies between these older adopted children's histories and the gendered violence experienced by other state wards in situations with minimal state intervention, such as refugees, war or famine orphans, and institutionalized abandoned children. As more of these children, too, are created and sometimes enter into the international adoption market, parallels become even clearer. Children can and do transcend horrendous traumas given committed familial intervention, structured guidance, and love (Groze, 1996; McNamara and McNamara, 1990). As one mother told me,

> My [fourteen-year-old] daughter's been home now for seven years. We all know each other's crap and we fight like dogs sometimes. Not physical, arguing. But we're real tight, her and me. The other day she said, "I want to do something about child abuse. I don't want no other kid to hurt the way I did—and still do, sometimes." I hugged her. She's going to be a fine woman. *She is on her way.*

Still, we must remember that "those transcendent survivors should be used for hope but not as standards for comparison" (Root, 1992: 236). Community intervention and support are also crucial for both kin formation and for recovery from trauma. Global economic restructuring and conservative demands for dismantling existing welfare states are formulas for digging additional pitfalls for recovering children and their families.

Recognizing ways that gendered violence operates through U.S. adoption practices means demanding that social services be increased and redesigned to more effectively address and prevent violence against girls and boys. Social scientists, social workers, and caregivers need to understand better how girls and boys recover from traumas that they experience in common and distinctively. The need is pressing for services at all levels involved in adoption. For birth families, multifaceted services are needed to curtail the need for removing children and to help provide the material and social resources needed for supportive kin formation. For foster families, services should ensure the safety and mental well-being of children entrusted to temporary state care. For adoptive families, training and support of parents are needed to ensure that the child can develop a healthy sense of self and agency and can sustain relationships in the wake of trauma.

FIVE

THE GLOBAL SEARCH FOR
"BLUE-RIBBON BABIES"

International Adoption

*We chose China because we heard there were healthy infants there.
My husband was persuaded because he thought a girl
would be easier to raise than a boy.*

—ADOPTIVE MOTHER, 1997

In 1992, international adoption[1] represented only 5 percent of all adoptions in the United States, far less than domestic adoptions through public or private agencies. By 2001, that percentage had tripled, a level it continues to maintain until today. As with domestic transracial adoption, the dramatic increase can be traced in part to the adoption reforms of the 1990s. The number of international adoptions to the United States keeps growing steadily, from about 6,472 in 1992 to 20,679 in 2006. As such, the United States is the largest importer of adopted children in the world, a trend that shows no signs of changing.

Why would U.S. citizens pursue international adoption rather than seek a child domestically? Gaining an appreciation of the racial, gender, class, and colonial dynamics in the history of U.S. adoption moves us toward an answer.

CONQUEST, COLOR, AND ASSIMILATION DREAMS:
A BRIEF HISTORY OF U.S. INTERNATIONAL ADOPTION

The history of international adoption in the United States cannot be disassociated from the history of U.S. military occupation. Technically, the first international adoptions took place early in the history of the British colonies that later became the United States. Missionary groups and white settlers sometimes sought to adopt Native American children; often, indigenous groups accepted these offers, as within their cultures adoption meant extending kinship links across differences, ensuring peaceable relations and creating other kinds of ties, such as trade and marriage. Later, they shunned offers when they learned that adoption among Europeans was qualitatively different from adoption they practiced: it was nonreciprocal, irrevocable, and entailed a transfer of all rights to the adopting group (Leacock, 1980: 37; see Ouelette, 1999). From the outset, then, any notion of "gift children" was a myth (see Triseliotis, 1999). White adoptions of Native American children continued, often following the massacre of the children's parents, but they were rare prior to the professionalization of adoption social work in the twentieth century. Twentieth-century adoptions of Native American children tended to be highly irregular in terms of frequency, with termination of parental rights frequently due to coercive or uninformed consent. The rise of the Red Power movement in the 1970s, however, along with similar efforts to assert Native American sovereignty, helped to reverse this trend and give Native Americans greater control over the adoption of their own children.

The history of international adoption beyond the borders of the United States, its territories, or its founding colonies is far more recent. After World War II, occupation officials relocated German and other European war orphans to the United States, primarily to military families, but also to some civilians. This spate of adoptions from the late 1940s through the mid-1950s was part of both the U.S. de-Nazification program and its public relations efforts to paint U.S. military occupation as a beneficent and healing force. Within the United States in that period, public adoption agencies routinely practiced religious as well as racial matching—even matching hair and eye color—with a clientele that was almost uniformly white, married, and middle income. Under such conditions, placement of "Aryan" children was not difficult, even those who were older. There were also placements of Japanese war orphans, but in far smaller numbers.

The international adoptions from postwar Europe, many of which involved children who had survived soul-searing conditions during the war and in its aftermath, occurred in an era when post-traumatic stress went unrecognized and psychiatric treatment was viewed as an admission of moral weakness or madness. Those seeking treatment were viewed with suspicion and often shunned by their neighbors. The results of these adoptions, as we might expect, were highly uneven—some of the children suffered severe, lifelong emotional and social problems (see Dodds, 1997). Few of the adoptive families were prepared to address their new children's multiple emotional needs.

The first continuous flow of adoptees in U.S. international adoption began in the 1950s, in the wake of the Korean War (see Berquist et al., 2007). These adoptions, confined primarily to the recruitment of adoptive families within the U.S. military, presented the available children as war orphans, many of whom were children of U.S. soldiers and Korean women. The children from these unions were rarely welcomed into Korean families, who viewed (and still view) racially mixed children as a taint on family honor. Mothers often had to abandon the children under extreme pressure from their families; in other cases, the reassignment and relocation of soldiers contributed to mothers and children continuing alone. All abandoned children in Korea were permitted adoptive placement in the United States, and, as Kristi Brian has found, one American religious adopter and entrepreneur established a virtual monopoly on Korean adoption in the United States in that era (Brian, 2004). Eventually other private agencies in the United States and, in recent years, European state agencies became involved in relocating Korean children. From the 1950s to the 1990s, approximately 100,000 children were adopted by U.S. parents (Sperry, 2008).

The racial stratification that still marks international adoption today can be seen in the complexities of what constituted permissible and prohibited transracial placement. The color hierarchy between black and Asian was marked. Children of black soldiers were not slated for U.S. placement and remained in orphanages until they reached adulthood, facing a lifetime of discrimination in Korea. At the time, fathers of these children were neither permitted to marry Korean women nor to adopt their progeny. White soldiers were discouraged by the military brass from marrying Korean women but generally were not prohibited from doing so. Many who requested permission to marry, however, were transferred to other locations in short order. Racial miscegenation was not encouraged by the U.S. military in that era.

Today, military personnel still enjoy expedited legal processing and a far shorter wait for Korean adoptees compared with U.S. civilian families. Among the couples I interviewed who had adopted from Korea within the past decade, the average wait for the non-military families was a year after the home study was completed. For two military couples with whom I corresponded, the wait was six weeks in one case and six months in the other. Both of these fathers told me independently that other military couples they knew who had adopted from Korea also waited six months or less.

Even today, black Korean children have little likelihood of being adopted by Americans, although some African American servicemen have been successful in adopting children born to Korean women with whom they had been involved or whom they had married subsequently. More of these outcast children could be placed if South Korea permitted single-mother adoption, either domestically or internationally. The country's policy is consistent with the view that women having children outside of marriage is dishonorable; a recent compendium of letters Korean mothers wrote to be given to their relinquished children makes it clear that this is still the case (Dorow, 1999). Single women, Korean or foreign, cannot adopt even those children who would otherwise grow up in orphanages and who face certain poverty and intense discrimination in adulthood. After growing up in orphanages, there are few options: boys generally end up in the drug trade or other criminal activities; the sex trade claims many of the girls.

Although almost none of the 1950s Korean adoptions involved children who could be construed as black, they nevertheless posed a challenge to a country still marked by miscegenation laws and segregated schools and public institutions.[2] What made them even more distinct from the earlier German and smattering of Japanese adoptions in the United States was the prevalence for the first time of infants and toddlers rather than older children. An experiential history of the first wave of Korean adoptions has yet to appear, although narratives by later generations of Korean adoptees exist (Cox, 1998).

In addition to the explicit racial hierarchy marking the Korean American children for both Koreans and white Americans, World War II and the subsequent Cold War produced a submerged racial discourse that still percolates today. During World War II, Japanese Americans were forced into internment camps, and the media reinforced the dominant notion that these citizens could not be true Americans (see Suzuki, 1980: 36–39). This compounded an already widespread conflation of disparate Asian peoples in the mass media as a "yellow horde," although there was a temporary effort during the war to portray the Chinese, or at least Chiang Kai-shek's faction and the Nanking population, as victims of Japanese aggression (see Chang, 1997). With the shift in the late 1940s and early 1950s from anti-Japanese portrayals to those painting the Chinese as communist aggressors, the adoption of Korean infants seemed at least in some way a laboratory for assimilationist beliefs in the redemptive qualities of capitalist culture and Christianity. These children were going to become "real" Asian Americans, because they would be reared by white, middle-class, conservative, patriotic Americans.

For the next twenty years, international adoptions continued to draw upon postwar U.S. military occupations, increasing U.S. presence in various locales. Korean adoptions remained dominant, followed by adoptions of Filipino children—again, at first mostly by U.S. military families and, again, in keeping with a significant U.S. military presence in the islands. Similar to the Korean case, the perceived specter of communism spreading to the

Philippines targeted these children, too, for "model minority" adoption. The expansion of U.S. interests in Latin America through the 1960s Alliance for Progress spurred adoptions from countries that the United States deemed strategically important, either for investment or for stemming the spread of communism.

The number of international adoptions to the United States remained very low until the 1970s, when demographic changes—delayed childbearing among whites, greater acceptability for keeping children born outside of marriage, the legalization of abortion, and the rise of privately arranged adoptions—led to extended waiting periods for healthy white infants through domestic public agency channels. Private adoption agencies expanded services to include adoptions from other countries, initially through church-related networks and later through legal networks and local agencies in other countries. The major increase in international adoptions, however, followed two major transformations in geopolitics: the collapse of the Soviet Union and the opening of the People's Republic of China to international adoption, after two decades of its one-child policy.

WHO ARE THE INTERNATIONAL ADOPTERS?

Judging from the literature and interviews with adoption lawyers, most international adopters are white married couples or single women who do not have sustained links with their child's country of origin. The parents generally visit the country only long enough to arrange and finalize the adoption; some revisit years later if their child wants to undertake what are termed "cultural tours" for international adoptive families. A less well recognized but important group of international adopters remains military families whose children often come from countries where U.S. servicemen have been stationed. These parents, as well as those who work overseas as international agency workers or academics, may be able to establish contacts with local orphanages.

International adoption requires a substantial outlay of cash, akin to the down payment on a house, although this may be eased if the adopting parents have ties, through friendship or work, to people from the child's native country who can assist in navigating intricate legal bureaucracies. The overall costs of international adoption are as much or more than domestic independent infant adoption (contracting with a pregnant woman through a lawyer) and considerably more than domestic private agency adoption. Thus, given the added expenses of travel, missed work, possible residency requirements in the child's natal country until the adoption is finalized (often as long as six weeks), and unpredictable cash outlays due to bureaucratic delays and snafus, it is not surprising that international adopters tend to be more prosperous than most Americans (see U.S. Federal Reserve, 2004; Child Welfare Information Gateway, 2009).

For this phase of the study I developed two separate snowball samples, one of international adopters who were from wealthier strata, typical of U.S. international adopters as a whole, and a smaller snowball sample of academic and non-governmental organization (NGO) workers and academics, middle-income professionals with sustained links to the countries from which their adopted children came.

The first snowball sample consisted of twenty adoptive parents: eight married couples and four single women that I refer to as the business/professional parents. In all but three cases, adopters had never visited their children's countries of origin prior to staying there for the required period that some countries require while the adoption is legalized. Judging from their homes, automobiles, and furnishings, these adopters appeared to have significantly higher incomes and wealth than the second snowball sample of eleven adoptive parents: five single mothers and three married couples, which I shall call the NGO/academic group. I interviewed the latter sample after the business/professional parents; I was acquainted with three of these adopters before beginning the study.[3]

The business/professional international adopters viewed adoption as an inferior substitute for childbirth, but once they decided to adopt, they entered the process with careful planning regarding the child or infant they were seeking. Six of the eight married couples, none of whom had birth children, told me in one way or another that they had come to believe (if they hadn't always believed) that they were incomplete without children. As one stated,

> We wanted a child of our very own. My parents were getting older and it was time, you know, and then we had trouble getting pregnant.

One of the husbands described what I call a "nursery ceiling" for male executives in the Fortune 500 corporation that employed him—the inverse of the "glass ceiling" for female executives:

> If you're in your mid-thirties and on your way up, people expect you to be a "family man." If you don't have kids, you're left out of a lot of the talk at company picnics. I mean, what do you say when they're all talking about day care and you and your wife are undergoing fertility treatments?

Being a father, it would seem, is a distinct asset in such a corporate environment. For their working wives, however, the expectations are quite different: as professionals they are judged by productivity, and many U.S. corporate managers continue to assume, despite ample evidence to the contrary, that being a mother is a workplace liability. For these professional women, the "glass ceiling" that may hinder promotion because of motherhood was not as worrisome as the impaired fertility that accompanied their delayed efforts to conceive until their mid-thirties. Through adoption, these women sought to redress infertility, as did many of the other infertile women in the larger sample. Unlike the working-class adopters, however, these women spoke of their infertility as a kind of betrayal by their bodies or, in some cases, gender failure:

> I'd always been so successful, first in school, then in my career. I put off having kids because of my career — it's really held against you [as a woman] in my firm — and then, after we got married and decided we wanted a kid, it was . . . well, like staring failure in the face. Devastating. I became so obsessed with the fertility treatments and, well, I guess adoption was about not admitting defeat. I was going to have a kid one way or another. I was *not* going to be held back by my body.

Her husband added,

> She brought the same kind of drive and single-mindedness that makes her so successful at work to the adoption process. I knew she'd pick out a great kid, 'cause she never settles for second-best.

Domestic independent adopters I interviewed shared many of the demographic characteristics with the international adopters: mid- to late thirties, higher income brackets, dual incomes except at the highest income levels, corporate careers, college and postgraduate professional training. My snowball sample of independent adopters was very small, not surprising given that the entire process operates under attorney-client privilege: four married couples and three single women. (Nevertheless, independent has been the most rapidly growing form of adoption for the past decade.)

For almost all the business/professional international and domestic private adopter groups, unambiguous rights to the child mattered a great deal (see Berry, 1992). They set out to avoid the possibility that birth parents might seek to reclaim control of their children. Such a situation not infrequently arises with foster-to-adopt programs, where legal ambiguity over parental rights may last for months or even years (see Lee and Hull, 1983). It was also clear that these international adopters had no desire for anything like the open adoption arrangements that are common among public adopters (Baron and Pannor, 1993). One couple, both professionals, had lost a child in a court battle over a private domestic adoption. The birth mother claimed duress in her decision to relinquish, and the courts rescinded the relinquishment and granted her custody. This couple stressed to me their desire to establish secure legal rights to their adopted infant. "Going international," in the husband's words, was at least in part to avoid any subsequent claims by birth parents.

The NGO/academic international adopters saw their adoption efforts as part of an ongoing commitment to the people of the country where they worked. These adopters contracted for a home study either through public or private agencies in the United States, but finalized the adoptions by working through lawyers they already knew or had contacted through their own networks in child's country. Almost all had adopted a particular child that they had identified or come to know, usually through women in communities where they lived or worked. All spoke a local language and had either tried to locate their children's relatives or knew them already. One single-mother adopter and her daughter spent every summer in Mexico near the birth mother. Over the years, the initial boundaries between the families became blurred. The adoptive mother became like an elder, college-educated sister who lived in the United States but sent money and brought needed items whenever she visited:

> It's funny: I used to see so many Chicano families in Chicago who would send money back home and go back to visit with these gigantic suitcases filled with stuff for everyone back in the village. I'd worked in Mexico before, doing research, but until I adopted Rosa, I never dreamed I would become one of them!

Full-disclosure open adoptions, where all parties know each other and have periodic contact (see Grotevant and McRoy, 1998; Grotevant, 1999), were typical of the NGO/academic international adopters. Indeed, a few merged their kin networks in practice. At least one adoptive mother's memoir describes such openness (see Sutphen, 1995). In contrast, among my sample of business/professional adopters, no one had sought full disclosure or any other kind of open adoption. Indeed, the majority expressed deep suspicion of having any direct or indirect contact with the child's birth family (Berry, 1992; Jardine, 2000).

Adopters in the NGO/academic sample told me of colleagues who had adopted children that had survived civil wars after the loss or execution of their families, like the more than 150,000 orphans left in the 1990s after the civil war in El Salvador or the unknown thousands following the genocidal campaign in Rwanda. One of these adopters, then a worker with a secular relief agency, had adopted a nine-year-old girl who had witnessed the massacre of her entire family and, like her mother and sisters, had been raped and left to die among a pile of corpses. This single mother explained:

> I had worked in the area for two years when the "ethnic cleansing" began. I didn't know her family personally and I hadn't really planned to adopt, but I really did feel it was my responsibility to do what I could for the survivors, especially the girls. We [international relief workers] had already seen what had happened to some of the girls afterward: they had suffered so much, and had no one left, so they ended up on the roadsides, in the streets, peddling sex for food.

This mother had strong opinions about most of the U.S. international adoption she had seen operating:

> I don't really approve of much international adoption: it seems to me that most of the time, it's just poverty that makes people give children up for adoption. I think in a lot of cases the kids would be better off if the Americans or Europeans would just donate the $30,000 or whatever to the kids' mothers and leave the kid there. But war is different, genocide is different: there really are no families for these kids. But then, these aren't cuddly little infants—they're scared and angry and humiliated; they've been through hell. They need counseling big time. You have to know about PTSD [post-traumatic stress disorder] to get anywhere near where they're coming from. I've met some of these people [international adopters] through support groups and adoption get-togethers in my town, and frankly, I can't see most of these people doing the kind of work with the children that you need to, to help them recover.

The NGO/academic adopters, in large part through their work in the home country and their contacts there, are often able to delve deeply into their adopted children's sometimes traumatic family history, in contrast with most international adopters, although in many cases, as with children abandoned as newborns, there is little to no information available.

SEEKING "THE BABY YOU WANT" ON A GLOBAL SCALE

The majority of international and independent domestic adopters in my sample were reluctant to take what they consider unacceptable risks in adopting an older or public agency child. The married couples that adopted independently in the United States or internationally through a private agency wanted a child that white Americans would consider white or at least light-skinned. One father stated his preferences succinctly: east or southeast Asian, Latin American (but not Mexican), or from the Indian subcontinent. None of the international adopters in my sample desired a child, even an infant, who would appear black in the United States.

Indeed, a number of the couples actively sought physiological matching beyond simple in-race adoption, a practice that stopped in most U.S. public agencies in the 1960s. That most were looking for children with particular traits—even if these implicitly reflected ethnic or racial stereotyping—was unmistakable: "My wife and I stand to give some child tremendous opportunities they could not dream of in their own country," one father explained, before he outlined the traits they sought in an infant. Web sites, brochures, and other advertising materials from a range of private agencies and independent adoption intermediaries reveal how much these agencies and brokers stress that such prospective parents have the "right" to "adopt the baby you want" (see Christy, 1990: A30). The neoliberal emphasis on choice, for those who can afford it, is unvarnished in these promotional materials, although the language used is often that of altruism. Implicitly, the language of choice presumes that the goal is a child as much like the adopters as possible.

Most of the couples I interviewed, including domestic adopters, stated that race should not matter in adoption and condemned anything but race-blind placement in domestic public adoption. The comments of international adopters about the kind of child and countries of origin that would be acceptable, however, indicated that race or color mattered a great deal to them. In this regard they resembled domestic independent and private adopters, who also sought same-race children or those with lighter skin tone.

The reasons international adopters gave for not considering infants from Afro-Caribbean or African countries were related to health concerns—above all, HIV infection—or governmental bureaucracies, what one father called the "unknown quantity." With the exception of adopters who did business or research in the region, these parents seemed unaware that many countries of Latin America include sizeable populations of African descent. A few noted that Brazil was a place where "some people were black"; these respondents showed more interest in Colombia but seemed unaware of Afro-Colombian populations. In general, Indian descent was deemed more acceptable than African. Regardless of where they eventually obtained an infant, the majority varied in their perceptions of children from Latin America: some said the agency had told them that their infant would be white, of German extraction, or mixed white and Indian.

International adopters expended a major effort to locate a very young child from an institution or through a lawyer who had a reputation for providing adopters with healthy infants, describing their developmental condition honestly, and skillfully navigating both foreign and domestic family courts and other bureaucracies. In Latin America the orphanage systems and adoption facilitators sometimes contracted with individual families to foster infants destined for foreign adoption and to monitor their diets and relative health. In Guatemala, for example, these private foster homes are popularly known as "fattening houses" because they often tend to low-birth-weight babies.

In the face of global capitalist expansion and neoliberal ideologies, adoption policies and practices are affected in predictable ways. With recurrent crises in local economies following austerity programs or denationalization of industries, international adoption is a ready source of income for the poor in countries where the government is either indifferent to their welfare or unable to address their problems (Tousignant, 1994: B1). These conditions are rarely appreciated by the adoptive families, however, who nevertheless are able to provide their adopted children with a standard of living far higher than they would have experienced in the countries of their birth.

VULNERABILITY, MARKETS, AND ENTITLEMENT: INTERNATIONAL ADOPTION IN AN AGE OF GLOBAL CAPITALIST EXPANSION

In a world dominated by rapid shifts of capital investment and migrations or displacements of people, where regions have differential power as a legacy of colonization and investment priorities, the search for "Baby Right" depends on the rapidly shifting vagaries of national and international politics and the operation of markets (see Gailey, 1999; Gailey, 2000a). Nowhere is an outright market in children legal, but mediated payments are commonplace in many countries (Zelizer, 1985; Anagnost, 2000). In this country and others, vectors for obtaining healthy infants also depend on a number of coexisting forms of gender hierarchy that variously pressure poor, unmarried, working, or raped women into relinquishment (see Anagnost, 2000; Ninivaggi, 1996; Gailey, 1988).

Children are in an increasingly vulnerable position in this new world order (Gailey, 1998b: 249–251). There are a burgeoning number of street children worldwide, children who in countries like Brazil become targets for death-squad activities or who must engage in life-threatening activities to eat. In some particularly poverty-stricken countries in the wake of civil war, some of these street children may offer themselves to foreign tourists, claiming orphan status. Other street children are kidnapped, sold, or otherwise forcibly re-cruited into dangerous occupations. The international sex trade preys on girls especially, as in Western European pedophile rings or the recent arrest and prosecution in Italy of a group of "adoptive fathers" transporting adolescent Chinese girls via Rome, destined for the brothels of Miami. In countries ex-periencing genocidal or other high-casualty wars, as in war-torn Rwanda in the early 1990s or the Sudan today, local boys have been kidnapped to work in militias and girls stolen to serve as sex slaves for military groups. Through-out Eastern Europe and the People's Republic of China, infants and young children are institutionalized in unprecedented numbers.

In the context of this global vulnerability, the media in the United States have depicted international adoption as providing a necessary sanctuary or as an altruistic gesture. A rescue theme ran across the business/professional and NGO/academic international adopter narratives in my samples. The dif-ferences between the groups lay in how aware adopters were, or tried to become, of their children's origins and circumstances. Alongside these nar-ratives the same theme appeared in interviews with three private adoption lawyers. One of these men worked with a network of private facilitators in the United States; two maintained relations with adoption lawyers in several countries. One of the latter—with a thriving practice arranging adoptions in Peru, Ecuador, Colombia, Guatemala, Paraguay, and Uruguay—told me,

> I think we're doing our part to give these kids a break. No one asks to be poor. No one wants their kids to be poor. We get approached all the time by parents wanting to give us kids, because they know we'll do right by them.

Without American international adoption, such depictions imply, the maw of illegal markets gapes to consume young lives. Absent from this sal-vation imagery, however, is any accompanying discussion of the roles played by the legacy of Euro-American colonialism, Cold War policies, international lending agencies, structural adjustment policies and austerity programs, and virtually unregulated international investment and transfers of capital. Col-lectively, these processes intensify local poverty and the political instability or totalitarian rule that are the foundation of burgeoning markets in illegal drugs, the sex industry, and, on a far smaller scale, the availability of children for adoption.

The outright sale of babies to foreign adopters is a horror that the news media present as both regrettable and exceptional (Sharp and Punnett, 1982). Such sales are typically disguised as donations to facilitators to help their "charity work," as major donations to public or private orphanages, or as gifts to the birth family to help with other children. This international market is conditioned by patriarchal structures that chastise single mothers or women who do not bear sons, national policies that restrict categories of potential adopters by age or marital status, and policies that discourage domestic adoption. Beyond these constraints, there are a range of countries where religious and inheritance law have the effect of discouraging formal adoption; these generally recognize only patrilineal bloodlines. In addition to endemic and increasing poverty, the proliferation of children made available to foreign adopters often reflects bureaucratic indifference or an inability to address widespread kidnapping and disappearances of young children. In such cases underpaid professionals in the legal-judicial arena become susceptible to bribery in order to support their own families: the bribery would be handled by the local lawyer, so the potential foreign adopters need never know that a bribe has been paid.

In the face of recurrent scandals (see Trimborn, 1983), the last decade of the twentieth century saw important international efforts to regulate inter-country adoption (Houston, 1992). These regulation efforts, orchestrated through what is now known as the Hague Convention, centered on the ways children come to be available for intercountry adoption, the treatment of relinquished or abandoned children within sending countries, protection of birth-parent rights, emphasis on plenary adoption that severs any subsequent claims by birth parents or other biological relatives, screening procedures for assessing the home studies of proposed adopters, and standardizing legal processes, thereby reducing graft and preventing what the U.S. State Department calls "illegal child trafficking." The Hague Convention on the Protection of Children and Cooperation in Respect of Intercountry Adoption took effect in May 1993; thirty countries had signed the treaty by March 1994. The United States is currently implementing the provisions of the Convention. While many of the major sending countries[4] have ratified the provisions, a number of francophone nations consider its call for plenary adoption a form of cultural imperialism, since it is in opposition to kinship as ordained by the Napoleonic Code, upon which many postcolonial states have based their constitutions (see Collard, 2000; Jaffe, 1995). Plenary adoption involves the permanent transfer of all kinship-related rights and obligations, including inheritance, to the adoptive family. Napoleonic Code adoption permits transfer of some rights, but cannot sever inheritance claims and includes the obligation to care for elderly birth parents. The two systems are clearly at odds. Beyond this debacle, uneven implementation creates a number of irregularities in many sending countries.

Despite the relatively small number of children adopted into the United States each year, international adoption attracts disproportionate media coverage and thereby helps to shape adoption discourse far beyond the actual numbers of children involved. Although the increase in the number of international adoptions over the past decade has made it a newsworthy topic, the numbers of children involved trail other types of adoption. A more reasonable explanation for news coverage that eclipses step-parent and public agency adoptions has to do with the class and race composition of the readership of major newspapers. International adoption stories attract reader interest because prosperous, educated, white professionals are the vast majority of both newspaper readers and international adopters.

In some dimensions much more is known about international adoptions than any other kind. The U.S. State Department issues visas for all foreign-born adoptees, so statistics on the numbers and countries involved are reliable. We can therefore track the top sending countries through time. We also know that the vast majority of these children are under two years of age upon entry into the country. Publicly available information on the adopters, however, does not include marital status, whether the adoption was independently arranged or through a U.S.-based adoption agency, or whether the adoptions were by military personnel. And, as with domestic private agency or independent adoption, little information can be gleaned about the outcomes of these adoptions. There are a few states that provide information about outcomes of public agency adoptions. But for independent or private agency adoption, whether domestic or international, we do not know the rates of child institutionalization within five years, the number of attempts to return the child to an adoption agency or country of origin, or children's physical and mental health after five years. Indeed, my interviews suggest that the privacy of such adoptions following the legally mandated home study by an accredited agency is one of the main reasons adopters seek independent or international adoption in the first place.

Sending countries vary widely in when and how official termination of birth-parent claims occurs and is documented; in some places, relinquishment by the birth mother alone is necessary. Also variable are the length of time a child has to be in state or private care prior to international adoptive placement, how long prospective adopters must stay in the country prior to finalizing the adoption, and the restrictions on who may adopt with regard to age, marital status, and financial condition. Some countries are rigorous in delineating the role of courts and lawyers in the adoption process. Others, as in many of the former Soviet bloc states during the 1990s, have such poorly functioning infrastructures that none of the parties may be certain when or if the adoption can be legally finalized (see Nash, 1991). Because international adoptions can be a lucrative source of hard currency, states generally are quite interested in regulating it, although the infrastructure costs for running orphanages or foster systems, or expanding family courts, may not allow this. Moreover, scandals concerning child trafficking have led some countries to place a moratorium on international adoptions (see Granelli and Reyes, 1984; Perlez, 1994; and Stanley, 1997). Particularly in Latin America, several countries have restricted foreign adoptions because of demands from middle-class nationals for greater access to adoptable infants (see Nash, 1991).

Until 1991, the South Korea provided the most adopted children to U.S. families, followed distantly by Colombia, India, the Philippines, and Guatemala. Children from these countries were all considered more acceptable in the American racial hierarchy than those labeled as black, whether foreign or domestic, due to various forms of racism, both in society at large and, more subtly, within adopting families. But when the Soviet bloc collapsed and China opened its state orphanages to foreign adopters in the 1990s, the racial and national configuration of international adoptees changed almost overnight (see Brodkin, 2000).

When the Soviet bloc began to crumble in the late 1980s, the prospect of obtaining unambiguously white children from abroad arose for the first time. Prospective U.S. adopters flocked to Romania, opting for race matching over all other considerations. As a result of the pronatalist ban on abortion for ethnic Romanian women during the Ceauşescu regime (Beck, 1992), many unwanted babies ended up in ill-funded and understaffed orphanages. The availability of thousands of blond, blue-eyed children of all ages for adoption was presented in the U.S. media as both a condemnation of the evil communist regime that had fallen and a golden opportunity for childless white couples to obtain the children they desired.

Some couples who traveled to Romania to adopt an infant came back not only with a baby but sometimes with an older child or two as well; the older children were often presented as the baby's siblings. Other couples were quoted in the media as being ecstatic when their new child ran up to them with hugs and kisses, calling them "mama and papa" (see Hunt, 1991). Beyond the likelihood that orphanage personnel coached some children ahead of time, such parents were almost certainly unaware that children spontaneously greeting strangers with the kind of affection generally reserved for kin signals a history of emotional trauma.

Attachment disorder, not well known at the time, is common in children who have experienced severe trauma, disruptions of care, or emotional deprivation. As a result, these children exhibit outward friendliness to anyone who might give them attention, but in fact harbor a profound mistrust of others. Another adoptive mother and I watched a television interview with a couple who had adopted from Romania. They had been moved to tears when their little girl ran up to them "right away—no fear at all, like she knew we were her mother and father." My companion, whose daughter had been helped a great deal through therapy for attachment disorder, exclaimed,

> They [the adopters] think they're moved to tears now, just wait till she greets the grocery store clerk the same way, and the mailman, and the mangiest bum on the subway! They don't realize the kid is terrified and trying to protect themselves by being charming. She doesn't trust them at all and they just don't see it! They'll find out soon enough: no kid can sustain an act for very long. The flip side of the charm is some serious lashing out—at her parents or herself or younger kids, or the family dog.

While not all children who have experienced disruption and trauma fail to become attached to their adoptive parents, it is a frequent outcome for those who come from institutionalized settings. By leaving children untreated or misinterpreting their emotional withdrawal as early (and desirable) independence, parents unwittingly overlook the fact that such children can become self-destructive, violent to others, and insensitive to feelings of compassion.

American adoptions of Romanian children reared in institutions mushroomed from only 121 in 1990 to 2,594 in 1991, about a third more than Korean adoptions the same year (1,818). After the number of children in the state orphanages declined and the children began to manifest not only attachment disorder but also HIV infection resulting from the reuse of needles for transfusions and injections in the orphanages, the number of such adoptions fell precipitously. Americans then turned to non-state sources in Romania's urban areas, and what can only be described as a baby market sprang up. One major American newspaper described Romanian women being pressured by their husbands to give over their infants for sale to foreigners, with some women having been impregnated by their husbands with this goal in mind (Hunt, 1991). Ironically, the infants in question were predominantly Tsigani, the despised and racialized Gypsy minority within Romania who nevertheless were considered white by their American adopters.

When such infant trafficking became too great an international scandal, the Romanian government moved to restrict foreign adoptions (*New York Times,* 1990: A8; Houston, 1992: A5). The number of Romanian adoptees to the United States plummeted in 1992 to 121; the number slowly rose again to 895 in 1999. But scandals persisted. Since it has not complied with Hague Convention provisions, Romania has now closed its doors to foreign adoption.

But even as the Romanian market was stemmed, the floodgates opened in Russia and Ukraine soon after: from 324 Russian and Ukrainian adoptions in 1992 to 1,530 in 1993 and 4,348 in 1999. In 1999, 29 percent of all children adopted into the United States from abroad were from Russia. Again, the prevailing explanation for the desirability of Russian infants is that they are white. Unsurprisingly, the heavy interest in Russian babies led to new infant trafficking scandals (*New York Times,* 1995: A8), in part due to the rather ineffective efforts of the local governments to regulate adoption (Stanley, 1997). The revolving door of states that alternately open and close to foreign adopters has come to characterize countries in the former Soviet sphere as well as in Latin America. The difference is the deeper experience in Latin American countries with U.S. adopters and, in most cases, better governmental regulation.

If race explains the attraction to Eastern European children, it does not explain why China has outstripped South Korea so dramatically in the past few years. It now runs a close second to Russia as the largest sending country, although very recently they have increased restrictions and wait times. The number of Chinese children adopted into the United States has jumped from only 61 in 1991 to 4,101 in 1999, or 28 percent of U.S. adoptions from abroad. A leading reason for this exponential increase is the fact that China set fewer restrictions on prospective foreign adopters; unlike several other sending countries, China did not disallow parents over forty from adopting, and only in 2005 did it change its rules regarding single parents.

Moreover, the conditions in most of China's state-run orphanages were superior to those in Eastern Europe. Nevertheless, there are substantiated reports of Chinese orphanages rationing their limited resources, resulting in neglect and early death for some children, especially those with disabilities (Johnson, Banghan, and Liyao, 1998). Chinese and Eastern European orphanages also differ substantially in terms of personnel. Many of the Chinese orphanage workers are single or older women, often sterile, who treat the children as if they were their own. In Eastern Europe, the women who work at orphanages are typically mothers who are expected to carry out the full range of domestic duties at home as well as in their profession. Many of these women, who are also woefully underpaid, are unable or unwilling to give the same personal attention or emotional commitment typically found in Chinese orphanages, and the result is that these children are neglected, almost as if they lived in a warehouse (see Ames, 1995: 1–2; Talbot, 1998: 24). Thus the emotional stimulation that is essential to normal development is more prevalent in China than in Eastern Europe, notwithstanding shortages in staffing and state funding in China. As such, Chinese adoptees are more like those from church-run orphanages of South Korea or Latin America than those from Eastern Europe, and China quickly developed a global reputation for having reliably healthy infants available (see Dorow, 2002).

Chinese adoption is unique in that the children made available are almost all girls, in many cases abandoned as newborns. This is a direct consequence of the state's one-child birth control policy in a society where parents have a distinct preference for boys. China differs from all other countries that provide children for adoption in another way, too: domestic adoptions are virtually banned. Ann Anagnost has pointed out that Chinese citizens, seeking to adopt baby girls, usually to balance their families with a child of each sex, fall afoul of officials enforcing the one-child family policy, whether the second child is born to that family or not (Anagnost, 2000). Recent reforms in China make adoption impossible for Chinese couples who are under the age of thirty-five or who already have a birth child; moreover, the bureaucratic obstacles even for those who would qualify are daunting (Johnson, Banghan, and Liyao, 1998). We cannot know, therefore, the degree to which the many thousands of Chinese girls awaiting adoption are truly unwanted, as so many foreigners presume.

Until China permitted foreign adoptions, most U.S. international adoptions, like most domestic ones, involved almost equal numbers of boys and girls. Because of China's relatively permissive adoption policies, the sex ratio of U.S. international adoptions now favors girls. And to look at how some adoptive parents speak of their Chinese daughters, it is impossible to separate racial issues of acceptable exoticism—the role of East Asians as a buffer race in the United States—from the stereotyping of Asian women as sweet and docile. Three of the couples and one of the single women in my sample had adopted Chinese infant girls. One father remembered, "There she was in the airport—our little China doll!" A married mother noted,

There are just swarms of people over there. They don't like girls much, either. So there are just all these unwanted little girls. So we had our pick, really. We chose Karen because she was so sweet and delicate and fair—like a porcelain doll.

The single mother drew on another widespread stereotype about Asians:

It's so tempting to look for mathematical ability in her. I know it's stereo-typing, but wouldn't it be great if it were true? My daughter, the math genius!

The intersection of gender and racial stereotyping among the business/profes-sional adopters of Chinese girls in my study contrasted with the views of the academic adopters, many of whom were knowledgeable about the dilemmas faced by the birth mothers. One told me,

I know there are young wives who are under enormous pressure from their in-laws to bear a son. In some regions it's almost as bad now for women as it was before the Revolution. . . . I want Mei-mei to grow up knowing how strong her mother had to be to bring her into the world. When she's older I want her to learn the history of women's struggles in China so she can resist the kind of "Asian doll" crap that she's likely to encounter here. We'll be traveling back and forth [to China] because of my research, so there'll be a network for her if she wants to use it later on.

Although this particular adopter knew the circumstances of her daughter's mother (a married woman who had had amniocentesis and opted not to have an abortion, even though the child was a girl), such knowledge is highly un-usual. Far more typical in adopting from China is knowing little or nothing about the child's background. And while in some orphanages in some coun-tries, adopters are able to select a baby, most are presented with the child that has been selected for them.

This brief survey of the relationship of international adoption to gendered racial discourses provides a ground for appreciating why international adopt-ers from the United States prefer some countries over others, even when infra-structure issues and selection criteria may be similar. Beyond the question of racial discourses, the policies related to gender hierarchies lead governments to institute a revolving door that at times may be open to single international adopters (mostly women) and at other times may be closed to them. These policy shifts produce tremendous uncertainty for single women as prospective adopters: a country may suddenly restrict single mothers from adopting between the time they are matched to and notified about a particular child and the time the adoption is finalized, as has happened repeatedly in Latin America and more recently in China. For single women seeking international adoption, these openings and closures have increased the expense beyond that for married couples.

With regard to adoption from Latin America, there is the additional issue of U.S. imperialism in the region and the heightened local awareness of the subject. Latin American countries have been sending children to the United States longer than the Chinese or Eastern Europeans, and in that time there has been sporadic popular resentment, sometimes stoked in the media, to the virtually unimpeded access of white Americans (particularly married couples) to local children (see Hoelgaard, 1998). Occasionally this animosity at what many see as another example of U.S. imperialism has taken the form of violence. In the late 1990s, for example, an American woman understood by her family and friends to be seeking to adopt in Guatemala was murdered in a rural area of the country; investigation uncovered that local people suspected her of child theft. More often, opposition to foreign adoption has come from middle-class, married couples within the sending countries demanding their own access to children for adoption.

The agglomeration of gender, nationality, and marital status makes single foreign women far more likely to be targeted with either bureaucratic impediments to adoption or outright violence than couples. Because of national gender hierarchies, however, it is usually easier for a foreign single woman to adopt than a local single woman. It remains virtually impossible for openly lesbian women to adopt in most countries, although closeted American lesbians often can, playing class, race, and education off against marital status.

ADOPTER MYTHOLOGIES

International adopters, particularly those seeking children in Latin America, are often unaware of the social, political, and economic realities that underpin the foreign adoption network. A slew of neoliberal policies imposed by states and international lending agencies have made the struggle of daily subsistence more difficult rather than easier for millions of people. Many have moved to squatter settlements on the fringes of urban Latin America in an effort to eke out a living no longer possible in the countryside. The majority of the children adopted by foreigners come from these poor communities, as do legions of street children (Brooke, 1994), most of whom have living relatives and periodically reside with their mothers or other family members. In Brazilian slums, impoverished mothers routinely send a child to live with neighbors or at a state orphanage as a short-term solution to an endemic crisis (Fonseca, 1986). Chronic malnutrition and child death from preventable illnesses rendered lethal by malnutrition are characteristic of the *favelas* of Brazil (see Scheper-Hughes, 1993) and their counterparts in other countries of the global South. State- or church-affiliated orphanages are ill equipped to handle the number of children placed in their care. Claudia Fonseca has written of the tragedy many mothers encounter when they come to a state orphanage after their economic circumstances have improved a modicum to reclaim their sons or daughters, only to find out that their parental rights have been terminated and the children are gone (Fonseca, 2001). There is no recourse.

What must this look like to the mothers in these desperate neighborhoods? Faceless enemies are stealing the children. The angel of death stalks the malnourished, but poor neighborhoods also are hunting grounds for kidnappers and paramilitary death squads. These forces have no faces. Orphanage personnel and foreign adopters are less dangerous, more safely identifiable, than the police or kidnapping gangs, and so frequently are easier to blame.

The scale of kidnapping and of selling children is hard to gauge. Clearly it occurs: relinquishment papers can be forged, bribes paid, and the paperwork can go forth legitimately. There also is in some cases a dynamic at work that accusations of kidnapping disguise. To give away a child or to leave one at an orphanage is acutely distressing for a poor mother. Besides her own grief, she risks community condemnation and possible beating by the child's father. What if a lawyer offers the child's father money for the baby? In some cases it is easier for everyone involved to say that the child has been kidnapped. This does not mean either that parents are uncaring or that kidnappings do not occur. But face-saving belief that one's child has been kidnapped receives little media attention because it challenges patriarchal control over relinquishment and ideologies of motherhood that constrain the lives of so many poor women.

The illegal or gray market for children, including children who will be adopted by prosperous nationals or foreigners, continues unabated (Perlez, 1994). Kidnappers may sell infants or young children to unscrupulous adoption lawyers (Williams, 1994). Foreign adopters working through private lawyers remain shielded from direct knowledge of these dynamics, if they do not probe beyond the courteous and bureaucratic surface. Most foreign adoptions, therefore, are technically legal.

But the "disappearance" of children to satisfy American or European desires—whether through ill-understood conditions of relinquishment of parental rights or through shady trafficking—should stimulate people of the global North to reassess two dangerous myths: the naïve and perilous belief that so-called free trade benefits everyone eventually, and the notion that international adoption "saves" unwanted children. Even if the children are voluntarily relinquished, the fact of relinquishment does not automatically mean the children were not wanted, only that the mother or parents were unable to care for them.

While most of the international adopters I interviewed seemed aware that markets for infants existed in many countries, adopters in the business/professional group stood out in that they insisted their own adoptions were above board and involved no illegal actions beyond the graft typical of countries with underpaid civil servants. They chose lawyers for their track records, which usually boiled down to their efficiency, and these parents did not apparently consider that efficiency might involve underhanded activities.

The business/professional narratives revealed that these adoptive parents sought children overseas rather than domestically as a result of their fear of open adoption and their assumption that the children from other countries come from "better stock," in the words of one father, or, as a mother put it, from people with "greater moral fiber" than the birth parents of those available for adoption in the United States. The way the moral discourse was elaborated reflected racialized representations of the regions from which the children came, largely from mass media rather than information from adoption agents or agencies.

The couples adopting from Eastern Europe believed their child was born to a middle-class unmarried woman from a "good" family who had become pregnant by mistake. Since the adoption agencies had not discussed the social origins of the children with these couples, the rather 1950s imagery of a "nice girl in trouble" was unchallenged by any knowledge of conditions in post-Soviet countries. Interestingly, the nice-but-unmarried-girl imagery paralleled the adopters' understanding that their child was white (regardless of local racial classification schemes).

Those adopting from Latin America thought their children came from married women who already had several children and could not provide for yet another. The "poor but responsible" moral imagery did not leave room for imagining unmarried mothers. The adopters from China based their assumptions about the birth mothers on media representations of a young married woman caught between her in-laws wanting a grandson and the government's one-child policy. This is clearly the case for many girls left at orphanages, but again, no conceptual room remains for unmarried women. In all cases, the adopters thought their children's birth mothers were morally superior to those relinquishing children for adoption in this country.

In the pre-adoptive training sessions I observed, couples who planned international adoptions characterized the birth mothers as irresponsible for giving birth to children they couldn't care for, but responsible enough to give them to people who could. I sensed that a lingering grief over their own infertility might have explained the reluctance most of the couples showed when asked to talk about their child's birth parents. One couple stated that the parents were "too poor" to care for the child adequately, and so had turned the child over to an orphanage. "They had so many children to feed; they wanted this one to have a chance in life," the wife said. Indeed, birth mothers' perceptions of the adoption scene in the sending countries is a story waiting to be written: Claudia Fonseca in Brazil and Chantal Collard in Haiti have led the way in examining the impact of international adoption on local communities and adoptees' birth relatives (Fonseca, 1986; Collard, 1991).

Significantly, the business/professional adopters did not extend the poor, ignorant, but well-meaning birth mother stereotypes to birth mothers in this country who relinquish their children. These women were characterized as less moral, less enterprising, and less deserving of compassion than poor mothers in other countries. The discrepancy seems to be based on the assumption that the children of the poor in the other countries were healthier, or at least less damaged, than those born into poverty in the United States, usually an unfounded assumption given the incidence of malnutrition and disease in many sending countries.

We enter here into the nineteenth-century notions of the deserving and undeserving poor, with the direct correlate that the children of the poor in the United States are less appealing and more apt to be problematic than the children of the deserving poor, that is, the poor from somewhere else. In other words, the poor you think you know (from the media) are worse than the abstract poor who are considered simply unfortunate victims of circumstances beyond their control. Here are comments from a wife and husband:

We looked into [public] adoption, but it was such a sad situation—so many permanently damaged children. No fault of their own, of course, and maybe we're selfish, but it's so much to take on. Parenting a healthy infant is hard enough, without all those inherited problems.

Even the private agencies couldn't guarantee us a healthy infant without a very long wait.

Despite the understanding of most of the business/professional adopters that their children had been born into poverty, they nevertheless assumed that being placed for adoption somehow immunized or rescued the children from the effects of malnutrition and disease. Several of the parents made these assumptions explicit:

I don't think there is the drug problem in Brazil that we have here in the U.S.

They [the poor] may have less to eat, but they don't seem to have the kind of moral decay that is such a problem here.

The agency there told us our son's mother was a good, hard-working woman, so I'm sure she took as good care of herself when she was pregnant as she could.

There are a lot of risks you take in adopting a kid from [Latin America], but one thing you don't have to worry about is fetal alcohol syndrome or crack babies.

The adopters that asserted these "facts" had very little knowledge of local conditions. There are countries, such as China, where the drug trade and HIV infection are not acknowledged as pervasive problems. There are few if any sending countries where HIV infection, alcoholism, and drug abuse do not accompany the sex trade. And chronic malnutrition is generally a problem in the communities where the children are born or in the institutions where they are placed.

The international and independent domestic adopters I surveyed focused their thoughts about their child's birth parents solely on the mother. In keeping with gender ideologies in the United States and elsewhere, the health of the birth father was not seriously considered. The domestic independent adopters had even outlined for themselves, in writing or in conversation, the characteristics they most wanted the birth mother to have. With regard to the infant, several of the international adopters had drawn up lists of characteristics they were looking for as well. One of these trait lists had been kept by a couple adopting from Latin America, who showed it to me:

Top priority:
infant
healthy (get examined by our doctor)

alert/intelligent (find out the reaction tests and do them)
normal development (ask doctor)
good background
Important:
European heritage
Not as important:
Brown hair
Blue eyes

When I asked why they had kept the list, the mother explained,

> I guess we're just "list" people. Before we got married, we drew up a list
> of things we needed to do. When we bought our house, we made a list
> of features we agreed about. It just seemed like a good way of organizing
> ourselves around it . . . and he's everything we asked for!

The concern to acquire a child as healthy, intelligent, and as near to newborn
as possible was pervasive among the international adopters. The expectation
of a high-performance child was clear from their expected trait lists and insistence that their agency was "top-flight," a sharp difference from the NGO
and public agency adopters in my sample. The NGO and public adopters
assumed that even very young children can suffer loss, may still be attached to
birth relatives, and may have developmental problems that might not reveal
themselves at time of placement.

One couple had planned to go to Romania and use some of the husband's
business contacts to obtain a child. When reports started coming out on the
psychological problems of post-institutionalized children there (see Johnson
and Groze, 1993; Johnson et al., 1992; Talbot, 1998), they decided instead to
adopt in Colombia, where (up to the 1990s) 37 percent of the U.S. children
adopted from South America were born (U.S. Bureau of the Census, 2000;
see Kreider, 2003: 13). "They've been at it longer and the procedures are more
straightforward," the father explained. "And the orphanages are clean and
well run; they do so much with so little," the mother went on. "Our little girl
was well taken care of, you could just tell from her alertness." She went on
to say that alertness is an indication of intelligence, paralleling a widespread
folk belief in the United States.

But race remained a motive for most of the international adopter couples.
One woman said international adoption was a way of "making sure you get
a blue-ribbon baby." When I asked her what a "blue-ribbon baby" was, she
laughed a bit self-consciously and explained,

Oh, you know, smart, blond, blue-eyed. . . . [A pause as she looked at me; I am dark-haired.] Well, I mean looking like us as much as possible.

According to Betty Mandell, "blue-ribbon baby" was a term used in the 1970s as an adoption "trade euphemism for a white, healthy infant" (Mandell, 1983: 43).

In an era when less and less emphasis is being placed on children's physical resemblance to their adoptive parents, the concerns of the international business/professional adopter group were actually closer to those seeking assisted conception and surrogacy than other adopter groups (see Ragoné, 1996). This was not the case, however, among the single women adopters of this group: the single women international adopters shared an awareness that their lifestyles would have to accommodate the children's need for role models and community. A few of the couples said they didn't care about color, so long as it was not black, which one woman said she was "not prepared to handle." Yet these parents' knowledge about racial and ethnic diversity in other parts of the world was scanty at best, which could indicate inadequate preparation for dealing with a child who isn't lily-white and with the various issues that face mixed-race families in the United States.

At a major adoption conference, for example, I met one prospective adopter who told me that she and her husband were going to adopt in Brazil, because of the shortage of white infants here and the legal intricacies and uncertainties of contracting with a birth mother in this country. "It turns out to be less expensive, even when you include the bribes for the local officials," she added. I asked if the color of the child made a difference to them. "Well, we want a white child, of course, because we're white, and we've been assured by our agency that Brazil is the right place to go." I probed to see if she had any sense of the racial diversity of Brazilians, particularly in the classes where adoptable children are apt to be born. She looked visibly upset and snapped, "Well I don't know about that," and turned abruptly away.

At the same conference, a headline in the newsletter of one major private adoption agency in New England announced, "Caucasian children from India now available." Since children darken in skin tone in the months after their birth, one wonders how race-conscious adopters would respond as their baby darkens, whether or not they are aware of the ways South Asians were included in the nineteenth-century racial category "Caucasian." Physiological and race matching have been abandoned in U.S. public adoption since the 1970s, excepting efforts to recruit black families for black children, but these remain among the many options in international and independent adoption today.

In addition to color, if not outright racial matching, almost all the independent domestic and business/professional international adopters in my survey had deep concerns that their new children show signs of intelligence and physical health. Fears about unanticipated genetic disorders or organic problems were pronounced in these groups. Many insisted that the infants they were considering for adopting be assessed by up to three different specialists for developmental delays and screened for HIV infection beforehand.

The effectiveness of these precautions is questionable. One particularly forthcoming international adopter, herself a social worker, was interviewed for a public television documentary on transracial adoption. She had adopted a child from Latin America as a newborn who had normal physiological development, but as time went on he displayed severe learning disabilities. At the time of the interview he was a healthy, socially adept adolescent who attended a special needs high school. With an anguished voice this mother admitted, "Would I have taken him if I knew all that ahead of time? Much as I love him, heart and soul, in all honesty I can't say definitively yes" (WGBH, 1994a).

At one adoption conference, a session about AIDS testing in international adoption was packed with women and a few men whom I presumed to be professionals. Many were taking notes. Most showed signs of distress when the speaker, a pediatrician who treated many internationally adopted children, said HIV testing has a high false positive and false negative rate in children below eight years of age and is therefore considered unreliable.

All the business/professional adopters in the international sample had accepted as provisional the representation of the infant's health and developmental status they had received from an adoption agency or lawyer, subject to their encounters with the infant in the sending country and their arrangement for independent medical examinations both there and afterward in the United States. Most accepted the agency's representation of the age of the child, although there have been cases where a particularly small child has been portrayed as younger to disguise the effects of malnutrition. None of these adopters considered that there may be cultural and financial factors involved in assessing cognitive potential in infants. None were aware that an absence of developmental delays in infancy does not mean that cognitive problems may not surface in time.

With the increased availability of genetic testing and counseling, the opportunity arises to screen young people for a range of genetic potentialities or risk factors. The accuracy if these tests is debatable, especially given the methodological vagaries of the human genome project (see Marks, 1995). But at a recent biotechnology conference on patients' rights, a genetic counselor at a major East Coast medical center said, "We've had a number of calls asking for just this kind of thing" by prospective adopters about kids available for adoption (Saltus, 2000: A1). Given the costs involved, more of the independent and international adopters in my sample expressed keen interest in these developments "as a safety thing" than did other categories of adopters. Indeed, only one of the international adopters expressed mistrust or dismay at the thought of genetic testing of children for potential parents.

It is hard to imagine the business/professional adopters accepting the kinds of children the NGO workers or public agency parents had adopted. When asked, none of them said they would have considered adopting an older child or one considered to have special needs. Their search for a healthy and acceptable infant paralleled their reluctance to take risks where there might be profound disruptions to work or ongoing life plans. One husband explained,

> I admire people who do that [special needs adoption], I really do, I'm glad someone's doing it, but it just wouldn't work for us. We just couldn't devote the time. Given our schedules, we need to have things as much like normal around here as possible.

These adopters talked more than other couples or single parents about risks and all had painstakingly questioned the agencies or lawyers through whom they worked about potential problems, including "no return" policies. One wife commented, "Life is so unpredictable. . . . We just want to start out with as healthy a baby as possible." She added, "You know, as close to the real thing as possible."

The goal these parents expressed, albeit implicitly, was to minimize the effects of early environment on the child. The adoptee was to be as young a child as feasible and from as stable a background as possible. Most of the private agencies or adoption lawyers understood their clients' anxieties well and provided prospective adopters with assurances that the children for whom they contracted were being cared for in well-run and sanitary orphanages or in affectionate foster families.

EASING ENTITLEMENT TO CHILDREN: THE ORPHAN MYTH AS POLICY

In the international adoption literature, anyone legally relinquished for adoption is labeled an orphan; foster care facilities are called orphanages. Anthropologist Chantal Collard was the first to bring this terminology problem to the attention of adoption researchers (Collard, 1991). As she points out, defining children as orphans when one or both parents are alive is clearly misleading. Persistent use of the term by international adoption agencies and lawyers creates a scenario where even children embedded in extended family networks may appear kinless and, therefore, unwanted.

In international adoption agency and legal parlance, including the Hague Convention, the term orphan includes children whose birth mothers and birth fathers have severed parental rights, either by having relinquished the children to the state or by the state having taken them. In either case, the legal fiction of orphan status contributes to an important set of images about international adoptees that has consequences for their later questions regarding origins (Smith, 2006).

Outside of war-torn areas, few of the children made available to foreign adopters have dead parents. Most have been relinquished for reasons of poverty, because social conditions do not permit the mother to rear the child, or because birth parents were ignorant of the meaning of legal termination of parental rights. To declare these children orphans disguises the conditions through which they came to be in state care.

This legal fiction has a certain appeal to adopters in search of clear-cut, exclusive rights to a child, even though general practice in pre-adoptive training urges prospective adopters to tell the child about adoption, to make it a common item for discussion at every developmental stage. On the basis of a number of longitudinal studies on adoption outcomes, over the past twenty-five years U.S. adoption agencies have shifted from practices that urged parents to tell the child about adoption on a need-to-know basis only, with secrecy as the goal, to urging parents to tell children from the outset, in language appropriate to their age level, about their adoptive status and about their origins.[5] The parents in my sample were all versed in this new approach, but some seemed content to present to the child the myth of orphan status as truth:

> We don't really know if he really was an orphan or whether he was simply left on the doorstep of the orphanage. We don't want him to worry about his mother or father, so we're just keeping it simple. [What do you tell him?] I just say, "They told us you were an orphan."

While waiting in the country for the adoptions to become legal, few of the parents apparently sought to explore their children's social histories beyond establishing the health of the birth mothers and/or fathers. Few had visited the neighborhoods or sectors where many of the children's mothers had lived.

There were, however, two exceptions to this among the business/professional adopters, both single mothers. One of these mothers elaborated:

I wanted to find out everything I could about his mother, so I could answer his questions later on—maybe even help him with a search if he wanted to. I couldn't find out her name, but I did find out she was living—married, very poor, very religious. She'd discussed giving up the baby with the sisters [it was a Catholic orphanage] before she did it. The sister told me she was a good woman. I guess she just couldn't face one more kid to feed. [Has he ever asked you about his birth mother?] From time to time. I'm really glad I found out as much as I did—it helps me, too, to feel a kind of connection with her—you know, a kind of responsibility to do right by him, for her sake as well as mine.

For an international adopter to remain in a foreign country longer than necessary to finalize the adoption is so unusual that it can attract U.S. news coverage, as in the case of an adoptive mother who spent considerable time in Romania trying to find out her infant's history (Cunningham, 1997: A29). But while few of the business/professional parents were so committed to answering their children's potential questions about origins, only one of the couples I interviewed seemed completely evasive once the children began asking. The husband said,

When she asks about her mother, I tell her about [my wife] until she catches on who I'm talking about. It's a kind of teasing game with us.

His wife later added, "I don't like him playing that game with her." When I asked her what she told her daughter, she said,

Your mother must have been so pretty, because look at you . . . that sort of thing. You know, so she feels positive about her. . . . [Is her birth mother alive?] Oh, probably, somewhere, but I don't want to confuse her with all the unknowns. I just focus on the positive.

I was particularly concerned with how parents adopting Chinese girls would deal with the widely recognized pressure young married women in China today face to give up daughters if their in-laws want a son, or the pressure unmarried students who do not opt for abortion encounter if they desire to keep their daughters. Few of the parents I interviewed had considered this before I asked, preferring to think of the girls as unwanted. A married mother said:

I suppose I'll tell her that in China, people prefer boys, but that I really wanted a girl.

One couple clearly was thinking out loud:

Wife: I, uh, I guess we'll tell her that her mother didn't want her—no, that would be awful. Honey, what do you think we should say?

Husband: Uh, maybe, that the government made it hard for . . . no that doesn't work. I guess we'll have to give that one more thought.

Another couple responded:

Husband: The best thing would be to say that her mother loved her and wanted her to get a loving family.

Wife: Well, that'll do when she's little, but at some point she's going to have to sort it out for herself.

None of them were aware, as indeed few scholars are, that domestic adoption in China is extremely difficult, as noted above (see Anagnost, 2000). It seems from their responses that the parents had not considered how to help their daughters value the cultural dimensions of their country of origin, given their birth mothers' difficult situation, trapped between government policy and patriarchal practice.

Whatever the country of origin, most international adopters also express a fear of a custody battle. Accepting the minimal story regarding their child's origins—the word of the orphanage director or the adoption lawyer—without much probing helps to assuage this concern. Several of these parents mentioned the fear they felt when they read of domestic adoptions that had ended in the courts when a birth father or mother claimed that their legal rights were not terminated (see Maloney, 1994: 430–431; Haberman, 1990: A4). One mother said, "We discussed the possibility of surrogate parenthood, but the Baby M case scared us."[6] Another explained what she thought was a major virtue of international adoption: "Once the child is out of the country, you can relax—no custody fights years later."

The concern for exclusive possession and the adopters' often charged feelings surrounding infertility make it difficult for these parents to discuss their children's histories beyond a very general outline. The curiosity or serious concern so many adoptive children have about their origins and especially about why their birth mothers gave them up (see Burlingham-Brown, 1994), usually beginning around age eight, represents a communications time bomb for parents uncomfortable with their children's origins.

The language of international adoption policy, thus, creates conditions where the adoptee's birth parents become socially dead (see Collard, 1991). Beyond calming the fears of reclaiming the child, the social death of the birth parents also stems many of the parents' insecurity around the potential that, as an adult, their child might wish to find lost relatives. This insecurity reveals that, despite expressions to the contrary, on some level the parents realize their child was not an orphan. One of the business/professional single mothers who openly acknowledged that her daughter had a birth mother said:

> What would I feel if she wanted to find her birth mother? Oh, God . . . like I failed her somehow, like she didn't really feel like I was her mother. It would scare me. [Would you help her search?] I don't know, I really don't.

One of the fathers responded:

> I guess I'd see it as a kind of test of our commitment to her. Yeah, I'd help and so would my wife. We'd probably take a trip to Colombia with her, hire a lawyer. I doubt anything would come of it: things are pretty messed up around that area. [How would you feel if she did find her birth mother?] Whew. That would be tough. I don't know. Threatened, I guess. I know I'm her father, her real father, but . . . well, I just hope she knew that deep down.

None of the business/professional adopters adapted their lifestyles to immerse themselves in or to engage on any sustained basis the culture or cultures from the country where their child was born, in contrast to some of the families that had adopted Chinese girls in Dorow's study (Dorow, 2001). Some had children's books of stories from that country; some had decorative objects in the child's room. One family had hired a housekeeper-nanny from that country. Dorow explores the ways that race and culture become conflated in some parenting narratives, while in others culture becomes homogenized—as, for instance, a single Chinese culture—or reduced to food, song, and dance (Dorow, 2006). I found this to be the case with the business/professional adopter couples, although two of the single mothers and all the NGO/academic adopters had more complex views of culture, on the one hand, and more engagement with people from the child's natal country, on the other.

About a third of the business/professional international adopter couples and all the single mothers, however, seemed open to going on what have been called adoption tours. In Western Europe and the United States, some travel agencies arrange guided tours for adoptees from a particular country; adolescents or young adults and their parents usually compose the tour groups. In addition to lectures on music, dance, and the dominant traditions of the local society, tour companies often arrange visits to major orphanages. This permits some sort of search for birth parents or at least reunion with early caregivers or people who knew the caregiver (see Yorkshire Public Television, 1998). More typical for the couples, however, was the kind of insecurity in their status as parents revealed in the quotes above. Although adoption as a social fact would seem to challenge notions of genetic kinship as the basis of attachment, and although these parents felt attached to their children, often the fear (and therefore the commitment to genetics as a stronger basis for families) remains.

One of the mothers in the sample expressed a concern that some kind of connection between mother and child, stronger than nurturing, might exist (Gediman and Brown, 1989). International adoption acts to reduce the potential for successful searches, just as it reduces the possibility that birth parents might find or reclaim children. The myth of the orphan, made real through the legal erasure of the birth parents, makes it easier for adopters to commit to their children. The consequences of the myth for the children, presumably, are secondary.

THE PRESUMPTION OF FUNCTION: CLASS AND HOME STUDIES

An incident occurred during the early part of this study that, in its implications for policy, attained the status of what the French call a *crise révélatrice:* an event that reveals a crucial set of dynamics. Following up on a lead by a private adoption lawyer, I telephoned one of the many private agencies specializing in international adoptions. I was on the verge of telling the person that I was conducting research when she asked me if I was a prospective adopter. Since at the time (1990) I was in the midst of a home study myself, I said I was. She then launched into a spiel about the services they offer their clients, who are, as in all private agencies, the adopters rather than the adoptees.

She informed me that they did home studies. When I asked how long these took, she told me that it was usually six weeks, half the average public agency time, but that it also depended on the clients' needs. I thought of a colleague of mine who had an approved home study already and who had just found out about the child she was adopting from Peru, so I asked, "What if I knew of a child in Peru who was available for adoption now?" She answered, "Then I suppose you want a home study done as soon as possible. An expedited home study would be possible, but it would require an additional fee." "Of course," I replied. "How long would it take and how much extra?" "Our usual fees are $5,000 for the home study." This was about twice as much as the public agency fee in that state at the time. "The expedited study would be $10,000, but we could have it done in two weeks." "How can you do it so fast?" I probed. "Well, we can start the paperwork right away—today if you want." "I heard you have to attend those training programs and that would be very difficult to fit into any professional's work schedule." "We could send you the materials to read and go over them with you on the phone if you can't make it to our seminar." "What about the home visits? I'm really busy at work these days and don't get home until late." "Well, that is a bit of a problem, but we could arrange to get the information we need over the phone." I told her I would think about it.

Even in 1990, pre-adoptive home studies in Massachusetts public agencies required two on-site home inspections by a licensed social worker. State agencies never relied solely on self-reporting by the prospective adopter. Then as now, public agencies in many states expect prospective adopters to participate in a twelve- or thirteen-week, three-hour-per-week training seminar. This seminar acts as a screen in and of itself, entailing a major commitment of time and effort. The seminar typically informs prospective parents about nonviolent child-rearing techniques, bonding and attachment issues, grief and loss issues, questions adopted children may harbor about their origins, fetal alcohol syndrome and the supposed effects of maternal cocaine or other drug addiction on children, emotional and behavioral disturbances that are seen in adopted children who have been institutionalized or suffered multiple foster settings, and the kinds of support groups and therapeutic services available in the area and through the agency. The seminars are conducted by one or more adoption social workers and generally at some point involve guest speakers who have adopted through the agency. Some agencies include adult adoptees as informants.

The idea that this kind of intense training could be replaced by telephone interviews is absurd. Moreover, in the conversation I gave the woman every indication of being a workaholic and therefore hardly a good candidate for parenthood, especially single parenthood. The warning flags were out, but the focus on her part was accommodating the client's needs.

That a person whose face-to-face contact with the agency was minimal could adopt a child teetered on the brink of illegality. A well-heeled client could hand over $10,000 plus the additional $20,000 or so for the out-of-country adoption and have an infant or toddler placed with her. When I told a public agency adoption social worker about the incident, she snapped,

> That "client" of theirs could be a child-beater and no one would be the wiser! . . . I can't believe we [the public agencies] are the ones everyone thinks are the problem, with our "red tape" and accusations that "no one examines birth parents, why adoptive parents?" and all the rest!

Private agencies thrive on the mistrust people with substantial means tend to have about bureaucracies, on the one hand, and, on the other, the long wait for or unavailability of healthy white or "acceptably colored" infants. Those with means can indulge the pervasive American insistence on privacy, because money allows one to minimize the amount of scrutiny into one's personal history. Certainly many private agencies are highly ethical and conscientious about their home studies, including the one that allowed me to observe its pre-adoptive training sessions, but the relative laxity of state and federal regulation permits practices that verge on child endangerment.

None of the international adopters I interviewed had had such an expedited home study. Most of the private agencies through which they worked had similar fee structures, and most had attended a once-a-week, two-hour seminar on child rearing, but for six weeks rather than the longer period demanded by public agencies. With only two exceptions, the private agencies did not inform prospective parents about sustained emotional, cognitive, or behavioral issues in some adopted children, particularly those who had early experience in institutional settings. Two of the agencies did bring up problems encountered with many post-institutionalized children, but in keeping with most media coverage, localized the problem as "Romanian" and emphasized that they did not arrange Romanian adoptions. They did, however, arrange Ukrainian and Russian adoptions, where orphanages are run in a similar manner and where maternal and paternal alcoholism are as frequently encountered (see Nakashima, 1996: A1).

The reason for what appears to be a lack of candor is obvious: the agencies are, first and foremost, businesses, not social services. Although legally private adoption agencies must be incorporated as non-profit organizations, the proceeds from the adoption services underwrite salaries of the owners and workers, and there are many time-honored ways for accounting to disguise profit as operating expenses or overhead. In practice, then, most operate as businesses, albeit technically non-profit ones, and frightening the clients is not a wise business practice.

Most of the agencies strongly imply in their advertisements that they provide their clients with healthy and intelligent children. Indeed, most of the business/professional adopters I surveyed were not aware that many long-term effects of severe maternal malnutrition or emotional deprivation, for instance, may not show up in the first few months of life (Rutter et al., 2000). Furthermore, those international adopters whose children later showed cognitive or emotional problems reported that they had not been informed by the agencies or their lawyers about the potential for these kinds of difficulties, a common refrain in U.S. international adoption (Hart, 1997: B3).

Two social workers I interviewed in one private agency believed that, because they had long-term connections with orphanages and adoption lawyers in particular countries, they were able to provide the "best" children for their clients. Since most agencies do not have exclusive arrangements with local orphanages or most of the lawyers, the notion that they would have access to "the best" is questionable. Both agency workers believed that a very young child is a virtual blank slate who will not have any problems with bonding or attachment. Similarly, one mother who had adopted internationally because fifteen years ago it was virtually impossible for even a well-educated, middle-class, white woman to adopt domestically if she had never married, said in an interview for a public television documentary,

> My kid was a bright-eyed, alert little baby. I got him at eleven days old, an empty slate, I thought. Only later did the learning disabilities emerge, probably due to prenatal malnutrition. (WGBH, 1994a)

Despite a growing number of testimonies about the effects of early institutionalization on child development or emergent developmental delays among severely malnourished infants, it seemed unnecessary to these private agency workers to add to the prospective adopters' anxiety by telling them "a bunch of horror stories," as one of the women put it. When I asked if any of the agency's clients had tried to return a child, one said, somewhat evasively, "None of *my* clients . . ." and the other said, "Rarely." Even if parents attempt to do so, however, this agency, like most that specialize in international adoptions, cannot comply unless under court order.

What happens to "returned" children? In some cases they are turned over to state care; in others, the agency uses its clout with the local orphanages to return the child, but this involves monumental legal intricacies. According to a social worker in the agency involved, one couple received an infant from India whom they returned after a week, because—contrary to the way the agency had represented the child—he seemed to have marked developmental delays. The agency not only returned him to the orphanage, but subsequently no longer worked with that institution. According to one of the international adoption lawyers, returns are known but infrequent in his practice as well, but returning children to the agency or legal practice is permitted only in extraordinary situations, such as outright fraud:

> Occasionally an orphanage or local agency tries to switch children from the ones we've identified, but that doesn't happen twice. Every once in a while, a couple, having adopted, discovers that the wife is pregnant, but we've never had a problem with anyone deciding not to keep the adopted baby as well. I always tell my clients that there are no return policies for birth kids, but you know, these people are usually so traumatized by their own infertility issues that they just want everything to be predictable.

In their successful attempts to protect their privacy and reduce agency demands placed on their time, the international and independent adopters received far less preparation for their first-time parenting than public adopters did. They received little information on physiological and psychological repercussions that many children who suffer from early physical or emotional deprivation exhibit (see, for example, Verhulst, Althaus, and Bierman, 1990). In contrast to the public agency adopters and the NGO/academic international adopters, the business/professional private agency and independent adopters were ill prepared to address whatever physiological or psychological problems their children might have.

For the additional expense of an independent or private agency domestic and international adoption, clients receive a home study that takes half the time of those conducted by public agencies, and with far less scrutiny of familial histories and current lifestyles. In some cases, this permits otherwise well-qualified people who are categorically excluded because of sexual orientation or age to adopt. In other cases, however, such an expedited process helps to approve people whose motivations to adopt or whose willingness to devote the time and effort needed for effective child rearing might be questionable.

The business/professional adopters, both independent domestic and international, referred more than other adopters to continued feelings of failure regarding their impaired fertility; they also were the ones most likely to see adoption as a series of daunting risks they needed to minimize. These adopters' intense desire for successful, high-performing progeny was an explicit agenda they brought to the adoption process. Having screened agencies or lawyers to the best of their considerable ability regarding the average wait, cost of services, ease of home study screenings, and reliability of children's health screenings, the adopters seemed willing to believe what their agents told them. While public adopters similarly expressed a willingness to believe the information provided by their social workers, they explained that somewhere in the screening process they had been told that, in contrast to the "bad old days" of secrecy, the state mandated public agencies to disclose as much about the children as legally permissible.

In contrast, agencies or lawyers for the business/professional adopters were structurally predisposed to present infants or toddlers as the kind of children the adopters were seeking because the adopters were their clients. Furthermore, in responding to express client wishes for an expedited approval process, agencies often limited parental training to general issues in adoption, including the need for children to be told that they are adopted and the need for parents to understand that there is a period of adjustment after placement that demands patience and understanding.

Such inadequate preparation for child rearing following early disruption and sometimes malnutrition or maltreatment often ill serves both parents and children, especially if the children begin to show signs of developmental delays or emotional distress. Perhaps as a result of the less rigorous adoptive parent training they received, the business/professional group also entertained romanticized ideas of adoption. They accepted models of child rearing that stressed negotiating discipline with children (in contrast with the model of natural and logical consequences found in the public agency training sessions), hoping to become the child's best friend as well as parent and encouraging independent action. While spongy boundaries between parents and children are a common problem in professional class families, they are especially ineffectual for children who have had chaotic histories, who need clear structure and predictable consequences for behaviors in order to feel safe and connected. Moreover, while independence is not a problem in general and, indeed, is typically seen as a virtue in capitalist societies in particular, children coming from institutional settings such as orphanages often have difficulty trusting others. Adopters untrained in the parenting required for children with such attachment problems can mistake their behaviors, at least in the early years, as showing precocious signs of independence.

SIX

INCLUSIVE, EXCLUSIVE, AND CONTRACTUAL FAMILIES

What Adoption Can Tell Us about Kinship Today

Our birth children, our "biological" offspring, rarely question their security. Adopted kids don't have that luxury; the promise has already been broken, at least once.

— JUDY ASHKENAZ, "INDIANS" (1995: 148)

The adopters in this study varied widely in how closely they adhered to dominant cultural "kinscripts" regarding what family is supposed to be (see Stack and Burton, 1993). The approaches adoptive parents took to issues of their children's origins, sense of belonging, socialization, and learning styles or perceived capacities reflected class, ethno-racial, and gender configurations as well as the parents' own upbringing and willingness to engage or change such received patterns. Class, gender, and race all provided the framework in which kinship of some sort developed.

SUBSTANTIATION: KINSHIP AS PROCESS

Substantiation is what I call the process through which people enter and are embraced in a web of sharing, obligation, reciprocal claiming, and emotional and material support that is considered the most sustaining kind of kinship or family. It is a process of naming, asserting connection, and pooling material and non-material resources that, depending on its intensity, can carve out what Richard Lee terms a "safety net" for participants, the closest degree of kinship, regardless of state definitions of "family" (see Lee, 1992).

Kinship may be enduring or contingent, inclusive or exclusive. In this study, we have seen that class, gender, and race articulations in a particular social formation frame the conduct of substantiation. The term *substantiation* focuses attention on the fact that there is no connection among people who consider themselves to be kin that is not built or believed. Shared genetic material may exist, but it is only a ground for kinship formation if people think it is. Birth or adoptive kinship must be constructed and acknowledged with the ideological and material resources available. Calling the process *substantiation* emphasizes the absence of naturalness in all kinship. For the United States, the term also prevents collapsing all kinds of families and their accompanying ideologies into a variation of what Schneider (1984) called the primary belief in American kinship: "Blood is thicker than water."

Certain anthropological theories of giving enter into substantiation, notably the concepts of generalized, balanced, and negative reciprocity (see Sahlins, 1972). Generalized reciprocity involves giving or pooling resources and services without expectation of return in any but the most abstract sense. It is the closest to the communist maxim "From each according to his ability, to each according to his need." Balanced reciprocity is the exchange of work or goods in a manner that anticipates a comparable return: social distance is indicated by what is considered an appropriate return and the timing of the return. The more the kind of return is subject to negotiation rather than trust and the less time between the initial and return gift or service, the more distant the relationship. Negative reciprocity follows the logic of the marketplace: the greatest return for the least expenditure. The relationships are contingent on the perception of adequacy rather than comparability; cheating and theft mark the extreme of the form.

The adoptive parents in this study engaged in generalized reciprocity when their children were very young: giving the adoptees material and non-material goods and services simply because the children needed the effort at the time. Not all the adopters continued this pattern indefinitely. The wealthier the sector, the more the parents moved toward a more balanced form of reciprocity as children grew into adolescence. In many cases, emotional distancing accompanied the move away from generalized reciprocity toward a balanced form. In the few cases where negative reciprocity set in — the child stealing or otherwise denying connection, the parents withholding displays of affection — substantiation became more of a memory or a failed attempt at family formation, often attributed to the child. Class issues seemed accentuated in the degree and type of return expectations parents had of their adopted children, whether "unconditional love" was demonstrated or became a rhetorical device, and what parents would do when children, particularly adolescents, were in crisis. The degree or intensity of substantiation shifted among adopters when some of the children showed signs of developmental delays, cognitive impairments, or emotional difficulties.

In the abstract, adoption would seem to subvert any ideology of "shared substance" as the basis of strong bonding and familial identification. In practice, most of the families in the study did so. But some parents, especially within the wealthier group of independent and international adopters, recreated the belief that "real" kinship is genetic connection and adoption is second-best. They did so in two ways: first, when they transformed the condition of infertility that led them to adopt into an enduring tragedy; second, when the child they brought into their lives did not exemplify what they thought a child appropriate to their circle should. These adopters attributed the gap between the child's behavior and their own performance expectations to innate qualities in the child, even as many did not call into question parenting practices typical of their own configurations of class, ethnicity, and gender. These parents expressed either a deep belief in genetic causation of many social and behavioral traits, or a kind of conversion to that position because of the difficulties they encountered in rearing their adopted child.

In general, the more economically stable the adopters, the more likely they were to define kinship as *exclusive,* that is, they saw their families as bounded entities, marked by both law and social distance from others. These bounded entities might overlap to form networks, but the participants had a sense of "the family" being fairly fixed at any one time and centered on a marriage. Most of the white middle-class adopters operated on this basis, with the notable exception of middle-income single mothers. The wealthier single-mother adopters saw themselves as heading a family that also was bounded, or as part of a geographically dispersed family entity with a grandparent couple at the center. By way of contrast, middle-income and working-class single mothers could not rely on a consistent flow of material resources that permitted creating kinship as a fairly impervious group.

Some adoptive parents practiced what I call *contractual kinship.* Alongside a belief that the strongest bonds of kinship were determined by birth or genetic connection, these parents believed family life should be grounded in clearly ordained, exclusive legal rights. The business/professional independent and international adopters were committed to this sort of family formation. Adoption as legal contract, the transfer of exclusive rights to a child, was a way to redress the failure of the kinscript they believed—"shared substance" or genetic connection—due to fertility impairment. Adoption, thus, carried with it an implicit fragility or potential for dissolution, just as marriage carried with it the implicit potential of divorce. These parents tended to see the strength or weakness of family ties as rooted in a set of mutually understood performance expectations: about half the couples had had prenuptial contracts, for instance. This group viewed nurturance as the provision of caregiving and educational services and opportunities; most hired nannies, tutors, and other supportive specialists throughout the children's preadolescent years.

Other adopters constructed what I call *inclusive kinship:* apart from fixed patrilineal or matrilineal surnames, their families were a contextually defined set of overlapping networks based on exchanging skills and sharing goods. The networks included a number of family names, often in the same household. Similar to the working-class African American families described by Stack, boundaries were fluid, merging with other networks and sometimes with community-wide relationships (Stack, 1974). These families might express a belief in marriage at the core of kin formation, but in practice the core could be a married couple, a mother and children, a group of adult siblings, or a grandmother who orchestrated the activities of other members. Most of the working-class and single-mother adopters had constructed families in this manner.

In general among the couples in the sample, wives were more willing to adapt or at times abandon received models of child rearing if the guidelines did not seem to be working with the children. The only mothers who did not engage in such critical self-reflection were among the business/professional international adopters. The mothers in this group demonstrated impressive resourcefulness toward finding professionals to mediate the parent-child connection or address the perceived needs of the children; few, however, redefined their modes of mothering.

GENDER AND CLASS DYNAMICS IN ADOPTION

Adoption remains primarily a domain defined by a gender division of labor that makes women primarily responsible for kinship creation and maintenance. Except in surrogacy or embryo adoption,[1] the ideological adoption triad is a birth mother, an infertile woman, and a child. In almost all situations involving an adoptive mother, it was she who initiated the process. If married, she must also convince her husband to adopt: in my study most of the husbands agreed because, as one man said, it "was so important to her and I wanted to keep her happy."

Generally, the working-class and middle-class adoptive fathers actively engaged with their children. For the wealthier adoptive fathers, engagement was more likely to involve being an occasional spectator at weekend children's sports activities, rather than sustained interactive activities (such as fishing trips, bowling, or intergenerational backyard or neighborhood festivities). Across class, the bulk of child rearing remained in the women's hands. The working-class mothers shared child tending with other women—sisters, mothers, grandmothers, neighbors, and sometimes child-care workers. The middle-class women generally used day care when their children were small and after-school care later on. The single mothers rarely could afford much babysitting in addition to these services, but these women often had arranged exchange care with other single mothers in their apartment building, neighborhood, or friendship networks to permit a rather minimal degree of child-free social life. For the business/professional adopters, child care remained the responsibility of the mothers to arrange. Mothers conducted searches, interviewed workers, contracted for, supervised, and terminated the generally combined child-care services they used: nannies, babysitters, and day-care centers. The business/professional mothers varied in the degree of involvement they had in their children's lives, but in my observation, whether they were stay-at-home or employed, these women had far more outside assistance than did the other mothers in the study.

Working-class adopters constructed kinship as a net of obligations and entitlements based on work and demonstrated loyalty. The adoptee was expected to help out with household maintenance tasks and ceremonial preparations, and to contribute toward the celebration of life transitions and holidays that marked the passage of time and boundaries of kinship and community for these families. Mothers required their daughters to do more of these tasks than their sons. Although these gendered disparities were more onerous for girls than boys, it also provided more occasions for bonding, identifying with the family, and imagining a parallel future family life for daughters rather than sons.

Loyalty was conceived as sticking up for other members of the family and showing family pride in conduct around others. In some of the families it also included keeping family secrets, which could and did in three families in the sample lead to denial of major problems, such as alcoholism, drug abuse, or beatings. In the extended working-class families, fostering and adoption tended to occur with some regularity, oftentimes on an informal basis. While women kept the kin networks operating, men were active in community-based networks related to work and the maintenance activities and sports that brought neighbors together on the weekends.

Working-class adopters' descriptions of their children's shift from foster care to permanent family life contrasted with the middle-income and wealthier parents' descriptions of "adoption transition." While the period in question was never easy, the narratives indicated less disruption, adjustment, and confusion on the part of the adoptees in the working-class families.

Taking the parenting narratives at face value, I think the significance of class mobility in adoption has received short shrift in the adoption literature. The older the child, the more likely "adoption transition" becomes a gloss for sudden class change. Parenting approaches in working-class families tended to be less permissive and lines of authority clearer than those in more prosperous groups. As such, adoptees in working-class families are more likely to recognize the rules, whether or not they abide by them. For better or worse, working-class adopters were more likely to practice the kind of parenting approaches and discipline found in the child's experience of foster care. The familiarity of rules and disciplinary practices, even if punitive, made adoption transition easier for these children.

For adoptees who shifted as young children to middle-income and professional-class families, there was far more confusion about boundaries and consequences. Parents in this group described more instances in which the child would test boundaries in an effort to provoke a clear message, even if a negative one. Such continued behavior tended to wear on parents' patience and sometimes, in the few narratives that admitted such, to physical punishment, especially slapping.

Although not all the working-class parents used physical discipline and not all the middle-income parents refrained from it, the difference between the two groups in adoption transition poses a conundrum. Is it better for the child to have an easier transition and be somewhat less safe? Is it better to have a period of considerable upheaval in a relatively safer environment? What seems clear is that whatever the manner, children who felt utterly claimed by their adoptive parents fared well.

In the middle-class families there was a great difference between the couples and the single mothers in how family was constructed. The married couples maintained connections to grandparents and adult siblings for the most part; even when the links were to the husband's family, the wife remained the primary agent of maintaining relations. More so than the working-class families, these couples lived in relative isolation from their extended kin, who often resided beyond commuting distance. While this was true for the single-mother adopters, too, the single mothers had transformed friendships or brought fellow adopters into kin networks that approximated on some levels the kind of community that working-class families had.

The focus of activity for the middle-class couples was more or less nucleated. The couples had assumed prior to adopting that their children would become college educated; for some, the prospects had dimmed as their children showed persistent difficulties in school. These middle-income professionals attributed their position to education as a vehicle for upward mobility; accordingly, they saw a lack of educational attainment as a major threat to their children's prospects for maintaining middle-class status. One mother sighed, "My son may not ever go to college, but whatever he does do, he'll have our values. Culturally he'll be middle-class, even if he's working-class." When I asked her what "middle-class" meant, she answered, "Valuing education, sharing the workload with his wife, being there as a father for his kids, not being 'macho' or violent." Then she laughed a bit self-consciously and said, "OK, so it's not a very accurate view of the middle class—I guess it's more of what I want our family to be." Kinship in this group was based on a belief in choice and feelings of family love, and much effort was spent to encourage the development of these feelings and clusters of values in the children. There were educational performance expectations, too, but in most cases, the values and feelings had priority. Claiming behaviors by the parents included the kinds of material displays and ritual activities (birthdays, "Coming Home Day," and holidays) found in the working-class families, but involved fewer participants. Processing feelings was a major part of the mother's efforts in child socialization—and in the marriage for the mothers who had husbands.

The wealthy adoptive families showed the greatest discrepancy between the parents' views of their own achievements and what they thought their adopted children could achieve; viewed over five years, I found that the longer the child was home, the greater the discrepancy. This clearly caused distress for the mothers particularly, since they bore family accountability for children's educational performance. Both mothers and fathers viewed kinship as a combination of genetic connection and feelings for one another, more than a process structured in everyday practices of claiming and sharing, as among the other groups. This group had the least community involvement of any of the adopters; their children had the fewest sleepovers and attended the smallest day-care centers. Opportunities for the children to mingle with other children were almost always adult-managed, in a continuum of minimal adult supervision among the working-class children through adult-supervised groups in the middle-income sector, to the dyads and triads with adult oversight that were typical of this group. Parental claiming of the adoptee centered on public display—announcing that the child was theirs in adult groups—and the provision of special, historically meaningful objects to decorate the child's room or to give directly to the adoptee. One father had given his adopted son a stuffed dog he had when he was a child, and one of the mothers had given her five-year-old a bracelet that the mother's grandmother had given her when she was five.

Parents in this wealthy group viewed their primary role as providing quality care, an atmosphere of physical safety, top-quality educational opportunities, and tutelage in appropriate behavior. The parents expected children to give outsiders a good impression of the family, which meant using proper etiquette and "being well turned out," as one mother put it. The mothers of this group seemed the most disturbed by children's misbehavior or violent outbursts and tended to consider deviations from their view of normal activity as indications of something more serious or innately problematic. While the medicalization of children's—especially boys'—behavior anomalies is rampant in the United States and among the adoptees in the sample, the children of the wealthiest sector showed the most medical intervention.

Often subsumed in parenting practices by class differences, race emerged as significant in familial discourses of justice, integrity, personal agency, and other core values among black adopter families and the white adopters of black children in the sample. One major distinction associated with African American adopters, and constructed by the white adopters of black children, was in the way parents and other relatives and neighbors situated the child in a community that all the participants viewed as being historically oppressed. Race and racism were frequent topics of discussion and strategizing in the African American and transracial adoptive families. This was not the case in any of the other groups, including the white adopters of Asian or Latino children. Parents enlisted older relatives or, as often was the case among white adopters, friends they had worked to develop into kin, as tutors in survival strategies for their children. The most supportive of these kin bolstered the children's ways of viewing themselves and their own strengths in the face of societal devaluation. One father said,

> I tell him, don't fall into the traps "the man" sets for our young men. The drugs, the gang fighting, the crime. I tell him, I know it's rough out there. I know the temptations. But you think about your mother, your sisters, and me and how we believe in you, and you'll be a man and stay out of that mess.

One of the mothers told me,

> We *talk,* girl. I let her stay sometimes and listen when I talk with my girl-friends. She needs to hear how we deal with the racism—at work, in the stores, on the T [Boston's subway system] or wherever. . . . When I braid her hair, we talk about womanhood, about boys, about the problems we face in this place. . . . I try to give her a sense of dignity, confidence, you know, so she can hold her head up no matter what.

This entwining of child socialization with community-wide dilemmas stood out among these adopter narratives. As we saw earlier, working-class black parents said explicitly that the outcome for their adopted children was not entirely in their control: gang violence, paramilitary policing, or predatory behavior by criminals could obliterate their best efforts; racism in the form of discrimination or structural barriers could limit their children's future success. White working-class adopters and middle-class black and white adopters were more apt to claim responsibility for their children's outcomes, for better or worse. The black working-class adopters expressed keen responsibility for shaping their children's characters, resourcefulness, and ability to get along with others, but they seemed more aware of the limits of personal agency than other groups.

CONTINGENT VERSUS CONTINUOUS CLAIMING

Verbal claiming of the child reflected the parents' relative commitment to blood connection as the genesis of kinship and family. The working-class and middle-class adopters never said anything along the lines of "We love him like our own," as did several of the business/professional adopters. Avoidance of this phrase is telling, since the words intrinsically convey the sense that the adopted child is not "our own." Working-class adopters instead used claiming phrases such as "He reminds me a lot of his uncle, my brother," or "I feel like we were meant to be family." One of the middle-class domestic adopters told her daughter, "I didn't give birth to you, but you're part of my heart and my soul." Indeed, a number of the mothers had developed similar ways of expressing the closeness they felt to their children. The following interchange reflects the claiming issues between a middle-class single mother and her adolescent daughter, adopted from foster care seven years earlier:

Mother: When I looked in your eyes the day we met—remember?—I could tell you were trying to decide whether or not I'd be an OK mom for you, whether I was the one.

Daughter: Well, yeah, of course I was. I didn't know who you were. I wanted to know if you'd be mean. I was scared.

Mother: You had every right to be. . . . I was a stranger and strangers had hurt you. That's why we visited for so long.

Daughter: Oh, *that's* why! I always wondered why we went back and forth so much. At first I thought it was 'cause you weren't sure you wanted me.

Mother: Oh, Honey! I just wanted you to move in when *you* were ready. Otherwise I'd have taken you home the minute I set eyes on you!

Absent from discussions of adoptive parenting is the role played by the demands of class reproduction. The expectations made of children, the tolerance or intolerance for given types of behavior, and the gendered scripts resonated with the ways parents consciously or unconsciously sought to ensure an acceptable position for the child in later life. The extent to which children were supposed to have agency, or supposed to show agency, varied as much as the interpretations of the children's actions. Even among the most ambitious of the parents, the ideas for how one was supposed to act or to relate to others were deeply influenced by what was imagined to be the "right" way. These imagined ways were themselves shaped by media representations of class, race, and gender as well as by the parents' more immediate social milieu.

Many of the business/professional adopters in the sample had come from business and professional families. The difference between generations was that these couples generally were dual-income earners while their mothers had not had careers outside the home. In keeping with the increasing concentration of wealth in the United States over the past thirty years, these couples had accumulated greater wealth than had their parents. The satisfaction they expressed related to this prosperity centered on their pride in the "hard work" and "disciplined intelligence" involved in the accumulation process.

Three of the couples represented a marital pattern that is common in this class fraction: the older executive who divorced his first wife and mother of his adult or near-adult children and then married a woman ten years or more his junior, often referred to as a "trophy wife" who physically is the reflection of the husband's success and power. The younger wife may or may not have a career, but if she does her position is decidedly less powerful than her husband's. In all three cases in the study (about one-fourth of the married couples at this income level), the marriage was the first for the wife, she was the infertile partner, and she initiated the adoption process. In two cases the husband had been reluctant to adopt, but was persuaded by his wife's expressed need to be a mother. Two of these couples had been rejected by a private agency before one couple located an agency that would work with them; the other couple decided to work through lawyers as independent international adopters. These three couples had the most accentuated concern that the child match them physically and have a predictable, high "potential for success," as one of the wives put it. It is tempting to call their adoption process a search for a "trophy child." I asked the mother of a toddler adopted from Ecuador why she thought more girls than boys were adopted:

[My husband] would never have gone for a boy. It's, like, a man has to have a son that carries his sperm in him. It's a male bonding thing, I think. It doesn't seem to matter so much with girls. But don't tell him I said so [giggling]. . . . I'm just glad he agreed to adopt.

Another wife commented,

We wanted an infant as close to birth as possible, because, well, that way you don't have a whole lot of historical baggage to deal with. It's like he was really born to us. [Do people ever think he is your birth child?] Oh, yes. I don't think I need to explain it, to go into it. Actually, it makes me feel good. Don't get me wrong, I know it's just a fantasy, but sometimes fantasies can make you feel great, can't they?

The business/professional international adopters considered their children as virtually kinless prior to placement and, after the adoption, as treasured possessions. Almost all these adopters considered themselves entitled to adopt because they believed their prosperity and social position would guarantee a child a better life. This assumption parallels the tone of Elizabeth Bartholet's treatise on transracial and international adoption (Bartholet, 1993). Almost all chafed at the intrusiveness of home studies and other credentialing processes. The couples could list the advantages they offered to a child: an "ethic of productivity," "good values," "educational opportunities," "a stable home life," and high-quality child care by both parents and hired professionals. Their focus in the adoption process was on making sure they received a very young, healthy child. Most of the parental narratives revealed an underlying belief in genetics as the basis of "real" kinship and, therefore, a certain discomfort with their status as adoptive parents. Among these international and independent domestic adopters were the only cases in the study of those who wished for some degree of secrecy surrounding the adoption itself. Even in this group, however, most parents had either read or been told in training sessions that telling the child about adoption was better for their emotional development and self-identity.

One of the major reasons for the shift in U.S. adoption practices away from secrecy, which was pervasive until the 1960s, is the demonstrably negative effects of pretending to the child that he or she was not adopted (see Herman, 1998). Yet among the independent and international adopters, fully half said this issue was not discussed in the agency parental training sessions they attended during their home studies. The couples who were most involved in finding a child who matched them physically and was as young as possible were the most reluctant to reveal the adoption to the child. One of these mothers told me she intended to tell her son that he was adopted, but she was not clear when they would do so:

> The timing has to be right, you know. We want him to feel very secure before we do that. [How will you know when the time is right?] When . . . well, I don't really know, but definitely before he goes to school, or, well, kids can be so mean if they know someone's different, so, well, maybe not. Richard [her husband] and I haven't really discussed it.

This couple had no plans to join a post-adoption support group in their area or otherwise to consort with other adopters and their children. Another of the mothers explained,

> I mean, we don't know the ones [adoptive families] around here. None of the people I met in the hotel [in the sending country] live that near us. They were nice people and all, and we got pretty close during the waiting period. We all said we'd stay in touch after we got back to the States, but it just hasn't panned out.

Most of the parents seemed to assume that, because in most cases they received their children as infants, they were as close to being like a birth child as adoption would allow. They did not entertain the possibility that their infant could have experienced psychological distress or emotional trauma due to the shift in caregivers or other early disruptions (van der Kolk, 1994). None had had the degree of training, as public agency adopters typically had in their mandatory sessions, that would have informed them that unattachment can occur even in very young infants, depending on how they have been treated prior to disruption (through institutionalized care, hospitalization, foster care, or adoption) and whether the adopters address the consequences of early lack of nurturance (Cline, 1979; Jewett, 1978).

The love offered by the international adopters appeared to be caring and encouraged independence, learning, and negotiating skills. This was demonstrated through the provision of opportunities, quality services, and a generally safe family atmosphere. Several of the couples seemed to have notions of love that were performance based, subject to evaluation and possible rejection. This seemed in keeping with the ways they spoke of their marital relationships or relationships with their own parents. I did not get the sense that, once scrutinized and accepted, their expectations of adopted children were qualitatively different than those for birth children in their families of origin.

Certainly these adopters spoke of love between married couples and between parents and children as unconditional, but in discussing their own infertility and their children's problems, the bonds were premised on acceptable performance in both behavioral and achievement terms. These parents gave every indication, at times explicitly, that in the face of persistent problems shown by their children they practiced a form of emotional abandonment that I call "professional distancing." These parents inserted a range of hired professionals between themselves and the child unless or until the behaviors or academic performance became more acceptable. While this shielded the child from parental anger in terms of face-to-face confrontation, any attachment issues would likely be exacerbated.

In the cases where children seemed to show attachment problems—one little girl ran over to me and called me "Mommy" when she met me, for instance—the situation was viewed as intrinsic to the child, rather than attributed to her early history (see Bagley, Young, and Scully, 1993). One father half-jokingly expressed his concern about his four-year-old daughter, adopted in infancy from Korea:

> Our daughter is overly friendly, even seductive, if you want my opinion, and I don't appreciate the way she tries to manipulate my wife. When she acts that way, she reminds me of an old movie from the fifties—maybe you saw it if you're my age—*The Bad Seed*.[2] But then, I've always seen the nature-nurture bit as more weighted toward the nature end of things.

When I asked him later why he thought more girls than boys were adopted, he joked, "Well, if they don't turn out right, at least they change their names when they marry." This father and mother had not considered that their daughter might have experienced the kind of trauma that can lead to such self-protective and "survivalist" behaviors in a relatively powerless person, even an infant. Because they had not considered historical reasons, they considered her behavior to derive from her "inborn personality," as her mother put it.

For children who have experienced early disruption and may have attachment or post-traumatic stress as a result of conditions in institutional or foster care, emotional distancing can reinforce the very self-isolating or manipulative behaviors, submerged rage at abandonment, and profound mistrust of caregivers that are problematic in the first place. One of the business/professional group mothers appeared emotionally exhausted when she told me,

> I didn't really sign on for this, but well, you make the best of it is all I can say. . . . Hugging her is like hugging a board. There just isn't the response you expect: it's depressing sometimes. I don't know what to do, really. She's just so withdrawn. [Have you looked into therapies for unattachment?] Oh, yes, but they ask you to be so structured, so *rigid,* and I'm just not that kind of person. It's not how I was brought up. I don't think I could be that way.

Withdrawal of parental affection and reluctance to change approaches to meet the needs of the child are two of the symptoms of what has been termed "adoption breakdown" (Zwimpfer, 1983). Maternal depression was reported by a wide range of adopters, particularly the single mothers, while emotional estrangement such as the narrative above indicates was rare (see Wadia-Ells, 1995). More commonly, mothers acknowledged emotional exhaustion and depression; especially but not exclusively the white mothers sought professional help or medication when they felt this became unbearable. Alongside addressing and thereby trying to stretch their own limitations, these mothers' narratives revealed flexibility and emotional engagement with their children. One of the NGO international adopters, a single mother, described the major problem in her relationship with her six-year-old daughter:

> My kid has a real hard time trusting, but, hey, look what she's been through! I asked friends who'd adopted older kids who'd been through a lot and they told me about the need to create clear boundaries so the kid will feel safe. I put the boundaries right here [puts flat hand an inch away from her nose] and it's really helped. I've noticed that on the occasions when she collapses (it's so emotionally draining for her to keep up her guard day in and day out) I can reach her, hug her, rock her. She softens then. It's working, even if my neighbors sometimes see me as the "nightmare mother from hell" for how closely I have to watch her. Hey, some day she'll feel secure enough that I can be my old loose self again.

In addition to the three children who might be considered to have attachment problems, five of the internationally adopted children over the age of four at the time of the interviews were considered by their parents to have some kind of learning or emotional difficulties. What was remarkable about the way the business/professional international adopters discussed these issues was the clinical detachment with which they spoke, in stark contrast to the ways the NGO/academics and the public agency adopters spoke of whatever issues their children had. One of the academic international adopters expressed her view of her son's diagnosis of attention deficit disorder (ADD):

> Maybe he has it and maybe he doesn't. Even if he does, it's not the end of the world. I know a lot of artists who flit from one project to the next, who are real space cadets. There are lots of ways to make a decent living. He has good friends even now, so I'm sure he'll find his way all right.

One of the business/professional international adoptive fathers said,

> We think he has ADD. The doctor put him on Ritalin and that helps, but half the time he's so wired he's out of control. He has a very short attention span. We put him in a special pre-school and I suppose he'll have to have special schooling all the way through. . . . Fortunately we have the means to be sure he'll be able to live comfortably even if he isn't capable of living independently.

Another indication of adoption breakdown is isolation of the child from family gatherings. One of the independent adoptive couples and two of the international adopter couples in the study had done this. One mother said,

> One of my fantasies was that we'd give these big family get-togethers and everyone would be here with their kids, and we'd be there with our son, and everything would be great. But it's just out of the question: He's too unpredictable. . . . No, I don't take him to family occasions anymore. It puts too much stress on me, waiting for when he'll start to act out. I have to watch him too closely. It's just a lot easier on everyone if he stays here with [the nanny]. . . . At first my parents were upset when we didn't bring him, but after a couple of utter disasters, I know they're relieved when we don't.

Another mother commented,

> I try to spend quality time with her. I try to read to her, or do 'girl' things with her. . . . I can't take her anywhere; it's just too embarrassing to have your kid act out in public or in front of your in-laws. . . . Her mood swings really disturb me and when she flies into a tantrum, I can't really

calm her down. I don't think anyone could. She's in therapy, of course, and I do what I can. I just hope she doesn't get unmanageable before she gets better.

Again, this isolation contrasted with the inclusive approaches of the other adopters. One unmarried, public agency white adopter said of her five-year-old, whose birth mother had scalded her as discipline:

Hey, she acts out: on the subway, in the park, at Thanksgiving, at the birthday parties. I last as long as I can, or as long as I think the company can, and then whisk her away. I think it's important for everyone that she be included, even if it's only for two minutes—and believe me, it is sometimes! I mean, I think it's important that her grandparents and our friends see that she's not a monster, she's just a kid who's been through a lot and is finally in a safe space. She'll learn that she won't die if she has a good time, but in the meantime I've had to shed my middle-class baggage. Like, "What will the neighbors say?" or thinking her behavior is some kind of reflection of me, the ego thing in parenting, that kind of stuff.

One of the working-class African American adopters said of her eleven-year-old daughter, who had been in five foster homes after having been removed from her crack-addicted mother for severe abuse and neglect:

Well, let me tell you, I don't need to go to no health club for a workout! She used to thrash about and try to hit her head, bite me, kick me, whatever. I had to restrain her, but I didn't want to hurt her, you know, 'cause that'd just be the wrong message, right, so I'd use a bear hug. Once I sat on her—not all the way, not hard, but enough so's she couldn't hurt herself or me. All the while I'd be talkin' quietly, soothing. It worked. Not right away, but slowly, slowly they [the episodes] came less and less. Now, praise Jesus, they're in the past! I been through hell and back again *twice over* with that girl, but let me tell you, by now she is *my* daughter.

The tentative quality of the business/professional adopters' acceptance of their children stands in contrast to the commitment that is the undertone of the other adopters. The business/professional adopters whose children showed signs of emotional distress or learning difficulties seemed from their narratives to be somewhat embarrassed, perhaps even ashamed if their children didn't perform up to expectations. These narratives revealed a degree of narcissism that did not appear in other groups; the most obvious manifestation was the parents' emotional distance from children if they did not fulfill parental images of what they should be like, that is, more or less like themselves. Certainly the public adopters quoted above assumed that others would see the child as a reflection of themselves as parents, but the white single mother rejected sole accountability and the black single mother took pride in her child-rearing efforts, whether or not the child's public behavior always reflected her aims.

Among the independent domestic and international adoptions, children who experienced difficulties were dealt with sympathetically at the outset. If the problems persisted beyond the parent's capacity to see them as at a stage, or if they worsened through time, later interviews with these parents found them attributing the problems either to an indelible early history or innate qualities of the child: what one father called "hard wiring." While this may indeed be the case, it is notable that with perhaps one exception, the problems shown by the children in this group were less severe than those of the public agency adoptees.

In fact, virtually all the public agency adoptees were considered to have learning or emotional problems at the time of placement. But because of more extensive pre-adoptive training and the parents' receptivity to such training, the public agency adopters recognized the impact of early histories and the possibility of intrinsic problems and had learned some techniques for therapeutic parenting. In part because of the training seminars and in part because of class-based kinship patterns, a broader notion of what constitutes success, or feminist networking, the public adopters understood the need for broader, community-based support, including but not restricted to professional help. The business/professional adopters were more private in their struggles with their children and more apt to avail themselves exclusively of professional help or seek support through anonymous vehicles, such as internet support groups.

Other differences related to class, ethno-racial, and gender configurations affected kinship formation among these adopters. The public agency adopters were predominantly working class, with the exception of the single mothers, who were almost all middle-class professionals. The working-class couples were already embedded in networks of kin, neighbors, and work-friends who exchanged labor on a number of levels, including child care and advice on parenting. The middle-class single mothers were keenly aware of the need for such networks of support and developed them if they did not already have them; the difference was that the middle-class adopters had more friends and fewer birth relatives in the effective sphere of generalized exchange. Both groups showed far more willingness to examine critically their own parenting techniques to develop more effective means of meeting their children's needs.

The degree of personal engagement with the child was decidedly different between the two groups. The middle-class single mothers read voraciously in the child development, adoption, and parenting literatures, as did some of the business/professional adopter mothers—especially the single mothers and the part-time worker mothers. But the business/professional adopters seemed less apt than the public agency adopters to alter their parenting styles or lifeways to adapt to the child, other than by providing professional services. Most of the other parents whose children had problems spoke of adjustments they made to meet the needs of the child and the ways their interactions with the child at the height of the child's turmoil were designed to help the child. That the reluctance to "get into the trenches with the kid," as one public agency father put it, may be an artifact of the class/race configuration of this population can be glimpsed in the sympathetic news coverage of other international adopters who have encountered difficulties.

A national conference in 1997 that focused on "hidden problems" in international adoption drew hundreds of adoptive parents. A reporter covering the conference writes that one woman "adopted a boy and his two sisters from Russia in 1993 . . . [and] the adoption destroyed [her] marriage" (Hart, 1997: B3). The son was then in a home for troubled adolescents; the ten-year-old daughter "killed farm animals," "rocks violently and sucks her thumb," and had been hospitalized for psychiatric problems. The mother thought the brother had sexually abused his sisters (Hart, 1997: B3).

Husbands threatening to leave because of the child's problems are by no means limited to international adoptions: any special-needs adoption, whether or not it is recognized as such at the time, entails a high risk of separation or divorce within five years. Only one of the adopters in my sample had moved their son, then age eight, out of their home for most of the time because of the threat of marital breakup. The mother said,

> I was really afraid [my husband] would leave if we didn't do something to take care of Mikey outside our home. He just couldn't deal with the day-in, day-out stress. He's a real over-achiever—I am, too—and it just killed him to see how far behind Mike Jr. was from where he thought he should be. I tried to teach Mikey but it was pretty hopeless. He'd get frustrated and so would I. . . . I don't think it bothered me as much as it did [my husband], but I could see what it was doing to our relationship. So, hard as it was, we decided that moving Mike Jr. from [a private day school for children

with special needs] to [a boarding school for children with severe learning disabilities] was better for both of us. It definitely saved our marriage and I think it's better for Mike Jr., too. We visit every weekend and he comes home for vacations.

Other parents opt for medicalization (of the child, themselves, or both) or, generally as a last resort, institutionalization. Institutionalization does not necessarily indicate emotional distancing. One case in the public agency adopter group showed continued close ties despite a period the child spent in an in-patient psychiatric hospital:

I had him committed [at age twelve] when he punched me and threatened me with a knife and then tried to cut his wrists. I was not able to deal with that. I told him as I was doing the arrangements that it wasn't going to be forever, that I loved him and would miss him very much while he was away and hoped he could come home again soon. But I also told him that [as] much as I love him, I cannot live with anyone who is violent: it's not what our family is about, and that he is part of our family and we all have had to learn how to manage our anger differently. I told him that right then he needed more help than I was able to give him. He was in for six weeks and I visited him three times a week. We do family counseling now and things are much better. He's told me that I was the first person who ever stood by him when he was acting crazy. He'll be OK: I really have faith in him. It's just so hard to see your kid suffering like that.

In the two cases among the public adopters where an adolescent child had been institutionalized, the parents treated it as a temporary situation that their child would overcome and come back home to them. In the child's absence, each of the couples had sought counseling and additional training and support around the child's issues. Most of the public agency adopters who said they had at one time or another become too stressed to cope with the behavioral and emotional demands of their children had requested respite care from friends, relatives, or, in one case, from the state. It should be noted that few states provide post-adoption respite care.

Parents from the business/professional international adopter group, particularly the fathers, seemed reluctant to seek additional post-adoptive training for themselves. The mothers, akin to the middle-class adoptive mothers, readily sought psychotherapy for themselves and their children. Indeed, the business/professional adopter group mothers were experts in locating professional services for their children: specialists in learning disabilities, specialized day and summer camps and programs, and neuropsychological assessments.

For the parents most committed to biological determinism, whether in the form of gender stereotyping, ethnic stereotyping, or genetic causation of intelligence or other social characteristics, emotional closeness or distance rested on how well the child measured up to parental expectations. The greater the discrepancy in terms of behavior or educational attainment, the greater the emotional distance became, to the extent that two of the children in the business/professional group were so mediated by professional help that they were virtually estranged from the father and only in contact with the mother for about an hour a day. Yet in the absence of post-adopting monitoring and because the relative wealth of the parents provided professional layers between parents and children that signaled care, this was not considered to be neglect or emotional abuse as it might have been in more scrutinized sectors (see Sack and Dale, 1982).

There were distinct class-associated patterns among the adopters that reflected how deeply committed they were to the notion of immutable or genetically given personality, temperament, or intelligence. The wealthier adopters were the most apt to attribute problems their children had to immutable causes, thereby relieving them of any sense of responsibility for the worsening of the children's conditions through time. Although the children having emotional or learning difficulties who were placed with working-class parents risked being hit on occasion, they did not risk emotional neglect or social isolation to the extent that the children in the business/professional group did. Similarly, the abused girls and boys placed with the single working- or middle-class mothers did not receive the quality of professional therapy that the children placed with wealthier parents did, but they did gain a sense of inclusion and acceptance that the other children could expect only if they performed in accordance with the parents' desires or only if they became attached to long-term nannies.

At the beginning of the adoptions all of the parents in the study spoke of the unconditional love they had for their children. But after five years it was clear from the parent's commentaries about their children that, among the wealthier adopters particularly, their love was deeply conditional and that "family bonds" were contingent upon performance that approached parental expectations. The single mothers, although they were under the most duress in terms of their children's histories, the financial straits many of them were experiencing, and the need to work harder than most to create support networks and still maintain careers, were the most consistently appreciative of the strides their children had made and how close they felt to their children.

PROBLEMS WITH CHILDREN OR "PROBLEM CHILDREN": STRUGGLING, COPING, OR GIVING UP

"Adoption disruption" is the term used for relinquishing parental claims to the child or otherwise turning them over to state care. In some states, "disruption" is used prior to finalizing the adoption while "failure" is used afterward. By using such a term as "disruption," rather than, for instance, "child rejection," the intention is to relieve feelings of guilt, blame, or shame on the part of adoptees or adopters. The term, however, has an unfortunate implication for anyone familiar with school lingo, as any school-age child is: children who are "disruptive" are removed from regular classrooms, slated for disciplinary procedures or special education classes. In other words, "disruptive" is an adjective rarely used to describe adults. By implication, then, at least for school-age children, adoption "disruption" shifts the potential for blame from the parents for rejecting the child to the child. Again, the invention of a supposedly neutral term disguises a judgment that verges on blaming the victim.

States record rejections of children adopted from foster care, but no database exists for independent or private agency adoptions. I have heard of cases anecdotally, but it is extremely difficult to get any firm sense of how often it occurs. Newspapers occasionally cover a story that involves international adopters attempting to return a child to a private adoption agency, but the "disruption" is rarely the focus of the story. More often the parents are depicted as victims of the absence of information or lack of complete disclosure by agencies or local officials. One reporter writes:

> Cane and other [international] adoptive parents said they get little sympathy from others, some of whom even blame them for the children's behavior. . . . "I thought there would be help and understanding, but no one believes you when you describe what is happening and there is no help," said an anguished Beck. . . . And there is no going back. Families can give up their troubled children only if they find another family to adopt them or if they place them in rehabilitative homes or hospitals. (Hart, 1997: B3)

The reporter had quoted one of these mothers as saying of her adoption of two boys from Ukraine, one of whom she and her husband had placed in "state custody," "I would rather be dead than do this again" (Hart, 1997: B3). Without minimizing the trauma these parents experience in confronting special needs of an order of magnitude far beyond their imagining—particularly when their imagining was getting a healthy white infant—it is still unusual to find adopters saying they would not do it again. And only in the business/professional group did I encounter this sentiment. The father of the child in the boarding school said,

> Don't tell her [his wife], but I think we should have left well enough alone. OK, so my wife wasn't able to have a kid. So what? We had a good life. I let myself be persuaded: You do a lot of things out of love, right? It hasn't worked out the way we hoped. I mean, it's hard not to be disappointed after we had our hopes and dreams of what this kid would be like. Sometimes I think I made a bad call going ahead with it.

The mother of a child adopted as a newborn from Latin America, who at three showed significant developmental delays, sighed:

> If I'd known then what I know now, I truly don't think I would have done it. Sometimes I feel like such a fool: I spent so long working on my husband to adopt and then, this. It's like we were betrayed.

One of the public adopters became a single mother after her husband divorced her four years after they adopted a three-year-old boy. At the age of nine her son still had tremendous difficulty reading and writing. She reflected on what had happened:

> I have a very different life now than the one I planned. I had a good marriage to a good man and I wanted the child to make things even better. Well, now I'm single, work like a dog to pay the bills, and my kid is not going to have a career in the usual sense. [Would you do it again, knowing what it would be like?] Yeah, I would, because he's brought so much into my life. I see him struggle and I see the world differently. He's made me a better person. I'm so much more patient now, and I think I'm more tolerant of more different kinds of people than I used to be. I wanted a kid who would make me proud with his accomplishments and . . . well, he has, but they're the accomplishments I'd always taken for granted. . . . Sometimes I wish Dave was still around, but it's actually easier making the decisions about Chad without his ego in the way.

When domestic adoptions are depicted as nightmares in the press, the theme is almost always a birth parent attempting to reclaim the child. In such cases, as in the Baby Richard and Baby Jessica cases, the print media agonize between class sympathy for the adoptive parents and ideologies of birth-bonding. But the press is uniformly on the side of the adoptive parents unless a birth parent's claims or accusations of physical or sexual abuse are involved. For example, in a Florida case, an adoptive couple had their five-year-old adoption legally annulled; the judge assigned the boy to a county group home. In the media coverage, the son, then age fifteen, was described as "a troublemaker" (see Associated Press, 1981: May 10: A8). When the media address international adoptions turning into a nightmares, the adopters are shown as victims of unscrupulous adoption agencies or local orphanages or officials, regardless of the outcome for the child.

One case is particularly vivid in this regard. The *Boston Globe* reported the death of a toddler in a Ukrainian orphanage (Sennott, 1996: 27ff). He had been adopted as an infant by an American couple, both lawyers who, years earlier, had adopted a daughter from the United States as an infant through a private agency. After they brought the baby boy back to the United States, it became clear that he had severe mental retardation and, upon medical examination, they discovered that a large part of his brain had not developed. Over the course of two years the couple spent $30,000 in treating the infant and arranging for home care, but, it was reported, they came to the conclusion that the attention the baby demanded was causing problems for their relationship with their daughter, "the joy of my life," according to her mother. They looked into private institutionalization in the United States and found it prohibitively expensive. So, on the advice of medical personnel, they traveled back to Ukraine and left the boy in the same institution where he had lived before. "I decided to keep this family together, to do what's right for our daughter and us. It's made us terribly sad," the mother told the reporter. When he died two years later, they tried to claim the body, but Ukrainian officials refused to respond to their request.

This case was written in a tone that was decidedly sympathetic to the adoptive parents. It was clear from the mother's comments that the boy's medical condition made him unacceptable as a family member: the phrase "this family" clearly excluded him. No mention was made in the article about what impact giving away a little brother might have had on his sister, especially when it is presented as having been done for her sake. The position of the Ukrainian officials was portrayed as an unreasonable response to the parents' wish to bury the child in the United States, despite their having abandoned him. The article was neither an indictment of the horrendous expense of decent institutional care in the United States nor a call for national health care reform. Rather, it was an indictment of adoption agencies and Ukrainian officials and a warning to other potential adopters. The mother explained,

We are lawyers . . . and we still got scammed. . . . Bringing a child from a poor country here is a beautiful thing. We don't want to discourage that. I think this whole thing went way beyond anything you could foresee. Maybe that is what makes it so tragic. (Sennott, 1996: 32)

In the same vein, the father of one of the children who showed cognitive impairments after the foreign adoption had been finalized was unusually forthcoming:

It's not politically correct to say this, I know, but really, they ought to have a "lemon law"[3] for these kinds of adoptions. You pay an agency a lot of money and you ought to be able to get the kind of kid you want—anybody wants. Bright, normal.

The international adopter couples also spoke of their children's strengths in addition to their problems, but the positive comments about the children tended to center on appearances rather than personality, behaviors, or talents. Some of these business/professional couples were unique in the sample in the ways they withdrew emotionally from the adoptees they came to see as "problem" children, or responded to their children as if they were unmanageable. One of the mothers appeared intimidated by her six-year-old son's screaming tantrum, which occurred while I was visiting (by no means the only child to have done so during the project). She acceded to his demands for a new set of Pokemon cards to "get him to calm down." She turned to me in front of the child and explained,

I know I shouldn't give in to his demands, but what can you do? When he goes off I have trouble managing him. The nanny is better at it, actually, but she's off today with the flu.

While this instance was a tantrum, I observed other mothers and fathers in this business/professional group refuse to set boundaries for their adopted children; their lack of engagement stood in contrast to the interactions I witnessed with other groups of adopters. If adoptees have come from institutionalized settings, as most of these international adoptees had, unattachment is a genuine risk, and when adopters do not become actively involved in showing the child that they are safe and predictable, with demonstrated and consistent expectations, the child can experience the kind of panic and anxiety (being alone in an unsafe place) that signal mistrust of others. Unaddressed if parents interpret the behaviors as signs of desired independence or if parents are intimidated by their children's behavior at earlier ages, attachment disorder does not just go away. Some older child adoptees can require temporary institutionalization or medication coupled with intensive outpatient psychotherapy.

PARENTING AND CLASS REPRODUCTION

The stakes of class reproduction loom in the background here. For working-class families, educational attainment is not as crucial for obtaining and retaining employment as it is for other social classes. To ensure security where not everyone working full-time has medical benefits or where the amount one can expect to receive in retirement is not adequate to sustain a standard of living, kinship provides a safety net. As such, the emphasis in child rearing for the working class is on expectations and obligations defined by kinship and kin-like connections, such as caregiving, inclusion, loyalty, and reciprocity. In short, the child's needs for socialization within a setting where kinship is so important is consistent with the parents' and other relatives' reliance on kin networks throughout life. Inclusion of new members is one of the necessary markers of the existence and continuity of the entire network.

For the middle-class single mother adopters, making community and neighborhood linkages became important for addressing everyday child-rearing demands. For the women who adopted through public agencies, the prospect of their children attaining the same educational level they had was not at all certain. However, because of their experiences juggling motherhood with their careers, these women were less committed to class reproduction than the married middle-class adopters who tended to adopt through private agencies or independently. As is typical of their social class, these single mothers read to their children, encouraged them in school, and were vigilant in resisting school officials' attempts to treat their children with lower expectations or, particularly in the case of black children (adopted or not), to assign them to special education, as is common throughout the country (see Goldberg et al., 1992; Eisenman, 1992). One mother in particular resisted special education placement for her son, who was abused by his birth mother's boyfriend and later in foster care. She explained,

> Before I adopted my son, I used to work in a shelter for battered women with children and then in a transitional housing project for women and

children getting back on their feet after escaping abuse. The kids when they first arrived acted out like crazy: They had no idea what "safe" was! For weeks they'd bounce off the walls. Real short attention spans, hyper-vigilance, some aggression. Once the moms were safe and the kids realized what that meant, they gradually calmed down. I wasn't going to have the school label him when he was still transitioning from an unsafe foster care situation to our family. Especially not when the guidance counselor knew nothing about adoption or recovery from trauma. I did, so I fought it. Two years later, they admitted I was right.

These single-mother, public agency adopters altered their lifestyles more than any other group in the study to accommodate their children's needs. In some ways they became less middle class in practice as they became more embedded in community-level support groups, enmeshed in the exchange labor that neighborly relations entail, and more involved in constructing kin networks when natal ones failed to provide the support they needed. In doing so, however, they used the skills they had developed in networking through their careers. Most were feminists by their own account and attributed their ability to develop new strategies and linkages to their feminism.

The single mothers in general deployed their educations as a means of assessing how their children were being treated in community institutions and to reflect on the effectiveness of their own and alternative parenting practices. If their children did not perform as well in school as they had, most of the mothers had wrestled with their disappointment. One mother echoed the sentiments of most of these adopters when she said,

> I had to realize that school is not her "safe place"—home is; for me, school was my "safe place." She feels more judged at school and more accepted at home, and I was the opposite. It's actually a compliment to how we've made family happen. I've had to come to grips with the fact that she's not going to be an academic. At first I was really frustrated by her crummy grades, but then I realized how much else she has to sort out: she's using her intelligence in other ways. I mean, we're all "emotional learners," aren't we? I've come to realize how intelligent she really is, putting her priorities where they belong—making herself whole again.

The middle-class single mothers were aware of how dependent their class position was on their salaries; most had a goal of being able to pass on a condo or house to their adopted son or daughter so their child would have "a cheap place to live" in the future:

It gives her more options. That way she won't necessarily have to go to college to support herself well. Of course, I hope she will and I'll do all I can to encourage her, but I want her to have the option, too, if that doesn't work out.

These mothers were less into class reproduction than they were committed to rearing children who "have a good sense of who they are and who'll be good parents when they grow up," as one put it. An African American father, a bus driver whose wife was a school teacher, said of their daughter, whom they had adopted at the age of nine after years of being shifted from one foster home to another,

> Maybe our daughter won't go to college—maybe the rough time she's had will make it hard for her to apply herself in school. But my wife and I know that even if she doesn't, her kids will. . . . Sometimes it takes a generation to heal the wounds, you know, to pave the way for the ones coming up.

One of the middle-class single mothers, whose daughter had been sexually abused in foster care, echoed this sense of adoption as extending generationally when she spoke of her daughter:

> Sometimes when it gets really hard—when her pain is just so overwhelming and I'm on the edge of a nervous breakdown—I tell myself, "You're in this for the long haul, woman! You're doing this for those grandchildren!" It helps.

For the wealthier adopters, the networks and business ties forged through fraternities and sororities in college and the associations formed in postgraduate professional schools were extremely important in maintaining and augmenting social position. Moreover, their professional friendships were more important on a daily basis than were their neighbors, community ties, or most relatives. Since much of the sense of accomplishment these people felt derived from success in their careers, the prospect of a child who might not attend an Ivy League university—or any university—was alarming and profoundly disappointing, particularly to the fathers. Moreover, they saw the time and effort they put into the adoption process, though no lengthier than that of the public adopters, as subverted by the problems they perceived in their child.

A number of these parents expressed anger at the adoption process itself: their child was not the "blue-ribbon baby" they had sought. Faced with a child they viewed as "starting off with two strikes against him," as one father put it, what began as a two-parent child-rearing project rapidly devolved upon the mother and whatever professional caregivers could be hired. The mothers did not express anger toward their husbands in this transformation, which often entailed cutting back on the mother's work hours or, in one case, quitting her job entirely. Her husband put it quite bluntly: "She was the one who wanted to adopt. It's her baby, so to speak. Don't get me wrong—I'm as good a dad as the next guy, but she has primary responsibility and she calls the shots, too." It is hard not to think that the widespread depression and anti-depressant consumption I found in this group of adoptive mothers was related to placing the burden of child rearing on the wives and the women they hired as nannies.

Public agency adopters tended not to blame the children themselves for whatever problems they exhibited. Rather, these parents expressed the most anger at the conditions the children had faced before adoption, and felt that any lingering behavioral or psychological issues could still be ameliorated. In contrast, both middle-class single mothers in the study, who agreed with the opinion of medical professionals that the children's problems were congenital, had known some of the issues prior to the adoption. They had been told by the social workers that a particular condition was "suspected" or "likely," and so they were able to make an informed decision about whether their material and emotional resources were good matches for the needs of the child. Thus, these adopters were not unduly disturbed or disappointed by their children's imperfections.

Would they do it all again? Among the adopters in the sample, the public agency adopters, the middle-class private agency adopters, and the independent domestic adopters were the most likely to agree or strongly agree with the statement that "adoption has brought about very important, positive changes in my life." All these adopters, including those whose children had the most severe problems, said that they would adopt the same child again knowing the difficulties involved. Many said they did not plan to adopt again in the future, mostly because they felt they were "too old now" or because "our family is the right size now." The single-mother adopters who said they did not plan to adopt another child mentioned an additional reason: "I don't have the energy to take on another child"; "one is my emotional limit." About a quarter of these parents were in the process of adopting another child or planned to do so.

Among the business/professional adopters, both domestic and international, the responses were mixed. About three-fourths said they would adopt again, knowing the difficulties involved; one-fourth said they would not.

One-fourth also said they would not adopt the same child if they had it to do all over again. Half of these business/professional adopters strongly agreed with the statement, "Adoption has brought major changes to my life, some positive, some negative." None of the international adopters planned to adopt another child, although about a fourth of the wives said they would but their husbands were opposed. Among the business/professional adopters, men were far more likely than women to express ambivalence or negativity toward the adoption experience.

OPENNESS, SEARCHING, AND QUESTIONS OF ORIGINS

Whatever cultural and racial issues the business/professional international and independent domestic adopters considered were addressed at the selection point. Among these international adopters, with the exception of one couple and one single-parent adopter, cultural heritage and identity issues were acknowledged as serious issues, though they rarely influenced family activities. The parents talked about providing human and material resources to give the child a sense of his/her heritage: books, dolls, nannies, and tutors. They clearly privileged their own cultural background over that of the child's, which they seemed to conflate with the child's social class or an image of underdevelopment from the child's country of origin. One mother noted:

> Of course, we intend to bring up our daughter with a sense of her cultural heritage. [How so?] Oh, books and music, special foods, that sort of thing.

I asked if they planned to visit the child's country of origin. She said she had considered that carefully:

> It really depends of the child, doesn't it? Some might need to [find birth families], some might not. We'd do it if it really mattered to her.

Indeed, analytical literature on international adoption points out that for some (but by no means all) foreign adoptees, visiting and searching are very important as an affirmation of worth and sometimes as a kind of resolution to a range of anxieties. But whether or not they want to visit, children harboring deeply negative imagery of their country of origin may disguise a serious sense of personal devaluation (see Simon and Altstein, 1992; Bagley, 1993).

Few of the business/professional adopters mentioned ways they had changed their social involvements to reflect or accommodate the addition of someone from another country into their families. One mother addressed the issue of providing her child with a sense of her natal country and its diverse cultures this way:

> We hired a gem of a nanny from the same country as our daughter. Catherine [the daughter] gets to play with her [the nanny's] little nephew once a week, too. This way she feels connected to her heritage. We're hoping she grows up bilingual.

When I asked if she or the father spoke to the child in that language, she said, "Not really. We just don't have the time to take the courses." I asked an international adoption lawyer how he and his wife—they also had adopted internationally and were partners in the agency—were addressing the cultural issues for the children adopted through their auspices. He responded:

> We started a support group . . . for people who've adopted kids . . . through us. We have parties a few times a year. We celebrate these kids' heritages. It's fun and it's a service.

As for trying to locate and possibly develop a relationship with their children's birth relatives, private agency and independent adopters, whether international or domestic, found the idea unsettling. The two domestic independent adopters had met the birth mothers prior to the adoption and realized that some day their children might want to meet them, too. They assumed that they would help their child do this search, but they did not seem to welcome it. The domestic public agency adopters were very mixed on this subject as well, depending on what they knew of the circumstances surrounding the child's relinquishment. The adoptive mothers of children whose birth mothers had not been responsible for any abuse welcomed a possible search as "a chance to say thank you for my child," while those whose children had suffered at the hands of birth relatives vehemently opposed searching.

Among the international adopters, the NGO/academic adopters were for the most part already in contact with birth relatives or, if not, were committed to helping the child search when it was legally or financially possible to do so. The other international adopters in the study seemed receptive to visiting the child's country, including the orphanage, but were more reticent about searches for birth relatives. Many believed that their children were actually orphans, accepting the legal definition to mean that a child has no living parents. The idea that, whether or not the birth parents were living, the child might want to find other birth relatives had not occurred to the business/professional couples. Still others seemed aware that their children had living birth mothers and seemed skittish about a possible search. "You don't know what you'll find, and it might be too traumatic for her," one of these mothers said. Most understood that the chances were slight of locating birth relatives in countries where records are spotty at best. One father admitted, "It's easy for us to be open to it, because there's almost no way that they [birth relatives] could be found."

Of those business/professional international adopters that realized their children were not orphans, none mentioned a desire to thank the birth mothers. Among domestic adopters, only the single-mother transracial adopters expressed anything beyond a wish to thank the birth mother: these women wanted to show the birth mothers that their joint children were sound and reared in a way that the birth mothers would approve.

INCLUSIVE KINSHIP AND
COMMUNITIES OF RESISTANCE

Ambivalence toward dominant kinship ideologies permeates the adoption literature. Authors unwittingly underscore the dominant ideology of kinship in declaring that it is strongest when "natural," in emphasizing adoptive kinship as overcoming the "birthbond" (Gediman and Brown, 1989) or as "shared fate" (Kirk, 1982) or as dramatically different from blood relation and implicitly more difficult because of its difference. This problem exists in part because the authors on some level believe the dominant ideology.

I suggest that "blood is thicker than water" as an ideology is inherently linked with patriarchal notions of exclusive possession and lineage. Kinship becomes a state of connection, not a process of connecting. To move beyond, and to normalize adoption at the same time, we need to acknowledge the gendering of kinship in the United States. Stack's and di Leonardo's research emphasizes the effort, largely accomplished by women, of creating and maintaining all forms of sustaining connections (Stack, 1974; di Leonardo, 1987). I would add that because it is largely done by women, the work is rendered invisible and undervalued. Adoption provides a lens onto kinship formation merely because it is more obviously constructed.

My contention is that adoption is not necessarily different: it becomes different only to the degree that the families consider "real" kinship to be genetically based. Cutting across birth and adoption, genetic and legal connection, is the substantiation that forges a sense of belonging, mutual obligation, and whatever security that sustaining connections can provide.

Looking at how different adopters talk about their children, birth mothers, adoption as a process, and their own relationships gives us a far better sense of the arenas where adoption is not an alien or fragile form of connection and those where it is. The more that adoptive families eschewed the dominant ideologies of kinship in favor of substantiation, inclusive family formation, and generalized reciprocity, the more resistant they tended to be in the face of social messages that made their connections appear inferior. As one public adopter expressed about her rather difficult position as a single mother,

> Adoption makes you appreciate diversity. . . . You get to see differences because you can't sweep them under the rug. [Sweep them under the rug?] The "blood is thicker than water" thing: It blinds you to differences, to the ways kids are *always* different from their parents. Adoption lets you see the individual. And you know you have to make family; you get to appreciate the work involved. *All* families have to be made. Adoption just lets you see it.

For the African American public agency adopters, building and relying on communities in resistance is hardy novel (see Stack, 1974). The adopters were well aware that they were helping to redress the fallout from problems that were largely not the making of the birth mothers, unless they had abused their children (see Erdrich, 1995). Few were involved in blaming the birth relatives for neglect, choosing to view it as a consequence of poverty. As a group these adopters had a heightened sense both of the influence of the past on the present and of personal agency in the face of a troubled past. Many of the adopters had themselves suffered as children: in foster care or having lost relatives to violence, abandonment, incarceration, or the streets. The impact of this shared condition was not necessarily compassion: most were in fact very compassionate, but a few expected the children to be able to surmount their own suffering with as little parental investment in recovery as they had had. Fortunately for the children in the sample, the individuals who took this approach were offset by their spouses, who were more attentive to the specific emotional needs of the children.

Many of the middle-class adopters were deeply ambivalent about innate versus environmental influences. In general, their adherence to the notion of dominant innate influences grew the longer their children's problems persisted. Some expressed the sense that relinquishing their belief in environmental causation was liberating. Others acknowledged that some of their children's issues probably were congenital or due to prenatal exposure to alcohol or drugs, but refused to see that innate causation as "an excuse to turn your kid over to the experts." One mother explained,

> There's still so much you can do if your kid has FAS [fetal alcohol syndrome]. First, you need to read up on it—there's all different levels of the thing and some are far less severe than others. Second, you can provide outlets for your kid's anger, like drumming "punch a pillow" into his head. Third, there are support groups, which can give you ideas and strategies you wouldn't have thought of. There's a lot. It's not a fast ticket to alcoholism or prison. You just can't give up on the kid, even if he does get into trouble.

As a group, these middle-class parents, particularly the mothers, seemed to worry more about their children than did other parents, even as the mothers were quite resourceful when an issue arose that they were ill equipped to handle on their own. In general, the middle-class adoptive mothers, married and single, had become strong advocates for adoption and were actively involved in community groups that brought together not only adoptive families in general, but families with children from particular countries or regions, single-parent families, families with post-institutionalized children, or families with children having specific mental or physical challenges. These support groups provided the adopters with contacts, information, and a sense of shared experience; the participants referred to them as "a lifeline," "my reality check," or "the only place we go where we feel normal." One mother said, "It's so good for both of us [her and her daughter] to see other families like ours, to be able to talk about our adoption without feeling like you have to defend it constantly." One of the transracial adopters explained,

> Imagine what it's like to always be stared at, everywhere you go. Then imagine how wonderful it feels to go to a place where you don't stand out at all! What a blessed relief! We can relax and just have a good time . . . be ourselves instead of an example!

Another example of public involvement came from a mother whose adoption agency recruited her to act as a volunteer lobbyist in her state. She and her daughter would visit legislative offices whenever adoption-related bills were being considered. Over two years, these efforts became increasingly effective, because the local legislators could see how her daughter was changing. When a law was passed that provided for greater post-adoption support for public adopters, her daughter was invited to attend the signing. Other mothers and daughters joined marches and fundraising events, especially those aimed at domestic violence:

> I can't tell you how much it meant to both of us to be there, walking next to each other, each in our own thoughts, knowing that we were doing something about the situation that [had] caused her problems. It really brought us closer together.

Other forms of public involvement did not necessarily relate to adoption. For example, the African American adopters and their families were deeply engaged in community service. One of the African American single mothers explained:

> Every Thanksgiving we cook an extra turkey and go down to our church and serve supper for the homeless. It's so important for my girl to see how others have so much less and how in our family if God has given you enough, it's your responsibility to share with those who don't.

Overall, middle-income adopters tended to be the most active in officially designated organizations related to their family types or children's issues. Parents engaged in such activities primarily to help develop a sense of community for their children and for themselves.

The most radical departures from the dominant "family values" agenda could be found among the single-mother adopters, whether lesbian or heterosexual. These women had fulfilled a gender script that views women as predestined for maternity, and thus by adopting they had joined the sorority of motherhood, normalizing them to an extent (see Lewin, 1993). Yet they had subverted both the nuclear family paradigm and the unacceptability of being an "unwed" mother. The more political of the mothers saw themselves as helping to legitimate a wider range of families than the dominant script permitted. Although some regretted not having a partner to help with the child rearing, most saw this as unrealistic and in some cases (generally divorcées) as an impediment to effective parenting. The longer the adoptions had been in place, the more likely the mothers were to see themselves as doing as good a job as anyone in rearing their children. Others felt pride in their accomplishments when their children, daughters for the most part, said they would like to adopt some day. One of the academic single mothers said,

I have this vision now of a long line of mothers and daughters, all adopted, all strong in their sense of belonging to each other and to the women who bore them. Women whose men are different, better.

This kind of feminist dream was related by several of the adopters. Perhaps the most subversive statement was made by one of the public adopter single mothers:

I feel like I'm doing something for me and we're doing something together for ourselves. Being the family we are, we're also doing something, well, *political,* although not really on purpose political. . . . I think we're the healthiest family I know and who are we? A single mom who survived an alcoholic family, an adopted kid who's been through the wringer, friends who are family, lesbians with birth kids and adopted kids, a few relatives who really act like family, gays, blacks, whites, Asians, Latinos, a straight guy or two (but nice). I mean, we're the real America, aren't we?

CONCLUSION

The differences adopted children are made to feel are largely the result of media representations that portray adoption as an inferior, second-best connection and adoptees as problem children. Certainly these children experience early disruption. So do many birth children, because of poverty, war, dislocation, migration, chronic or acute illness, or domestic violence. The early loss of security cited by Ashkenaz is common to all adoptees (Ashkenaz, 1995), but it is a shared condition with millions of children throughout the world. Adoptive kinship has everything in common with the making of kinship in the wake of such trauma.

What makes adoptive kinship different in practice, then, is not a lack of "shared substance," but a call to address, validate, and integrate unshared histories as they affect relationships and human potentiality in the present. Substantiation may be delayed or truncated by post-partum depression or a number of other conditions. Substantiation is central to feelings of security and belonging, and it must occur for anyone to develop a healthy sense of being in the world. By emphasizing substantiation as a process common to all kinship formation, but conducted in a context of class, race, and gender hierarchies, we can focus on children's particular needs. Normalizing adoption is not denying that disruption occurs or that adoptees encounter identity issues or that adoptive families are made to feel different. It merely places the difference in a context that challenges a dominant ideology. The effects of violence—whether interpersonal or structural in the sense of conditions forcing women to give birth or being unable to care for a desired child—shape adoptees' entry into social personhood.

The fact of adoption does not make adoptive children different from birth children, unless parents believe that only birth children experience a shared history with their kin. If one permits birth children autonomous existence from birth onward, there always is an unshared history. Again, the adoption difference either fades or is heightened. The vicissitudes of history, political economy, class, race, and gender hierarchies mark all children. From the ways class, race, and gender hierarchies shape ideologies of kinship we can learn how adoption can become difference. From the class, race, and gender concerns of adoptive parents we can learn the ways they can make kinship key to class reproduction, to construct a porous set of connections that either buoy participants and routinely include others, or to create an impervious shield around select members.

Adoption allows us better understanding of kinship as a process. The adoptive parents in this study tell us about the process of kinship formation and the consequences of inclusion, exclusion, or contingent/performance-dependent membership for children whose histories are always lived but not always known. Whatever their parents label them, adoptees are not "blue-ribbon babies" nor are they "labors of love." Love is indeed work, but the phrase "labor of love" connotes an endeavor undertaken because of a deep affection on one person's part, with the work in the relationship being mostly one-way and an uphill struggle at that. Missing from both formulations is the person that is the personhood and agency of the child and the potential in adoption, as in all kinship, for transforming all the participants through the dynamic of substantiating their histories together. The adoptees are children caught in the cross-hairs of political and economic forces beyond their control. Some are adopted by parents who will always claim them; others are not so fortunate, although they may be wealthier. The adoptive parents' practices tell us of patterns of kinship that articulate social hierarchies and, depending on their stances, reinscribe, accommodate, or subvert them. They tell us of people, usually mothers, who sometimes shed their class aspirations to help children become themselves and in the process help build communities that sustain their members.

NOTES

CHAPTER ONE

1. In addition, I interviewed one white woman who had adopted a young boy from a country in southern Africa where she had worked with an NGO for years. The boy's mother, who had been a co-worker and close friend, had contracted AIDS from her husband and been rejected by both her family and his before her death. The woman I interviewed had adopted the son as an international adoption through an agency that normally only did adoptions for the state, but where one of the social workers was a good friend. Because of the highly unusual circumstances, I did not count her in either the public adopter or international adopter groups, but I did include her in the discussions of transracial adoption.

2. All quotes are from interviews conducted during the field research. I assured anonymity for all those interviewed, including name, exact age of the adopter, and city of residence. Names, where given, are invented but consistent throughout the manuscript. Adopters agreed for themselves and their children to be identified by the racial or ethnic category they ascribed to themselves or their children.

CHAPTER TWO

1. Some of the quotes and materials on single-mother adopters also appear in my essay "'Whatever They Think of Us, We're a Family': Single Mother Adopters," in *Adoptive Families in a Diverse Society,* ed. Katarina Wegar (New Brunswick, NJ: Rutgers University Press, 2006), 162–174.

CHAPTER THREE

1. Such race and class hierarchies have operated to privilege whites in other countries as well. Recently, protest from Aboriginal groups in Australia have called attention to "the stolen generation." From 1918 until the 1970s, lighter-colored aboriginal children or

those assumed to be mixed-race were taken from their communities—literally seized, as were Native American children in some localities in this country—and given by the state to white couples for adoption. Depending on the location, between 10 and 47 percent of Aboriginal people over the age of twenty-five had been taken from their birth parents (see Thornhill, 1997: A4). Half of the five hundred Aboriginal people who testified for a state human rights inquiry said they had been beaten and "excessively punished" and a fifth had been sexually abused in foster homes, orphanages, or youth work places; fully half had been separated from their parents between the ages of one and five (see Creed, 2001: 218–221; see also Bird, 1998).

In Israel, ethno-racial divides have created a widespread belief, upheld by some birth mother–adult child reunions, that hundreds of Yemeni infants had been kidnapped for adoption by Israeli couples. Many Yemeni refugee children had been declared dead or disappeared in the refugee camps after the migration of some 50,000 Yemeni Jews to Israel in 1949–1950. It appears from a national inquiry in the late 1990s that a network of doctors and clinics were involved in the adoptions (Greenberg, 1997: A4).

CHAPTER FOUR

1. Until the 1980s in U.S. adoption social work, "older child" meant anyone age two years and up. The 1996 national adoption law streamlines termination of parental rights and speeds up what is called "permanency planning" in a child's foster care career. Reflecting agency wishes to solicit adopters for children already in foster care, the term "older child" has become less clear. Depending on the degree of individual state efforts to attract permanent families for foster children, the term may now refer to anyone of school age.

2. This chapter is a revised and expanded version of an article written for a special issue of *Identities: Studies in Global Power and Culture,* edited by Mary Anglin, on surviving gendered violence (see Gailey, 1998b).

3. I did not interview the adoptees. I realize that their participation would have given a valuable depth to the research, but while parents sometimes offered me permission to do limited interviewing with their daughters, I found it very difficult to conceive of "informed consent" where children are involved in such a sensitive research topic.

4. The implication in some of the social work literature that somehow women working are at least partially the cause of declining numbers of foster families must be rejected. It would be better to focus instead on why long-term foster care providers in the United States are not accorded medical or pension benefits or evaluated, as regular government employees are. Foster care is not a civil service occupation, but it could be. Instead, the full-time therapeutic child rearing involved is poorly compensated, placing additional pressure on families in an economic climate where dual incomes in a household are needed to maintain an adequate standard of living.

CHAPTER FIVE

1. This chapter is a significantly revised and expanded version of two chapters published in Norway and the United Kingdom (Gailey, 1999; Gailey, 2000).

2. While the landmark *Brown v. Board of Education* desegregation case was decided in 1954 and 1955, changes were not implemented in many regions of the country for over a decade.

3. Melvin Oliver and Thomas Shapiro have analyzed the growing wealth differentials in the United States, and how difficult it is to assess wealth rather than income differences (Oliver and Shapiro, 1995). I gauged wealth by asking adopters about their educational attainment and income range, whether trust funds had been set up for the adopted children, the kind of day care the family had, whether they had babysitters or nannies, which public or private schools the children attended, and whether the family spent summers in a vacation home and, if so, where. I also looked up the average market price for homes in their neighborhood and the average income per household for their town. In some cases, the adopters provided more information than I requested, but generally they answered only the questions posed. In keeping with Pierre Bourdieu, perusing family photograph albums and the placement of photographs of family around the home provided a rough indication of class status and, along the lines of Mary Bouquet's argument, ways that kinship was marked (Bourdieu, 1984; Bouquet, 2001).

4. Until *Parade* magazine ran a lead article on the phenomenon, few Americans knew that African American infants and toddlers, often from the South, were being adopted by middle-class European couples, particularly in Great Britain and Germany (Mason, 1999; Selman, 1999). Although the numbers are not large, the situation has arisen due largely to four factors. First, the 1990s adoption reforms in this country facilitated early termination of birth-parent rights. Second, independent or lawyer- and broker-mediated adoptions are legal in the United States but illegal throughout Western Europe (see Zelizer, 1992), meaning that U.S. adoptions enable Europeans to avoid the long waits typical there. Third, the United States does not bar single-mother adoptions as some European countries still do. Finally, the wait for preschool-age children arranged through private, non-independent channels is shorter in the United States than in Europe. Of the business/professional adopters I interviewed, none could conceive that U.S. children of color placed for adoption might be desirable or even preferred by other adopters.

5. No studies have shown that secrecy helps children feel they belong. Indeed, all have shown that cloaking the child's history damages the parent-child relationship and that sharing information lets children feel connected both to adoptive family members and to the birth parent(s). Acknowledging a separate origin does not ask the child to choose between the past and the present.

6. The Baby M case in New Jersey in the late 1980s pitted a working-class surrogate mother's claim of prenatal bonding against the contractors, the sperm donor and his wife, both professionals. The court eventually gave the custody to the prospective adopters, but with the birth mother having visiting rights (see Pollitt, 1987; Ragoné, 1996).

CHAPTER SIX

1. Anthropologist Risa Cromer is examining the dynamics of embryo adoption in the United States, which draws a distinction between genetic parenthood and birth parenthood. In this practice a donated fertilized ovum is implanted in a woman who has "adopted" the embryo. Since she is also the birth mother, using the term "adoption" to describe the practice can be seen as an assertion that the embryo is a person. Legally this has not been established, although organizations orchestrating this exchange have received federal funding under the rubric of adoption services.

2. This movie was frequently cited by the adoptive parents in my study. The father quoted here, like so many other adopters of the baby-boom generation, assumed the adoptee in the movie was the murderous child, when the only adoptee in the film was that child's devoted birth mother.

3. In Massachusetts, a "lemon law" gives the buyer of an automobile the right to return a car that turns out not to be in good working order within a specified time and have the purchase price refunded.

REFERENCES

ADOPTALK

1990   Bibliography of Adoption Disruption. Spring Issue: 4.

ALLEN, D.

2002   The Adoption Option. *The Advocate* 42 (May 28): 7.

ALTSTEIN, HOWARD, AND RUTH MCROY

2000   *Does Family Preservation Serve a Child's Best Interests?* Washington, DC: Georgetown University Press.

ALTSTEIN, HOWARD, AND RITA J. SIMON

2000   *Intercountry Adoption: A Multinational Perspective.* New York: Praeger.

AMES, ELINOR

1995   Orphanage Experiences Play a Key Role in Adopted Romanian Children's Development. *Adoptalk* (Fall): 1–2.

ANAGNOST, ANN

2000   Scenes of Misrecognition: Maternal Citizenship in the Age of Transnational Adoption. *Positions: East Asian Culture Critique* 18(2): 389–421.

ANDERSON, DAVID

1971   *Children of Special Value: Interracial Adoption in America.* New York: St. Martin's Press.

ANONYMOUS

1989   *Quotable Women: A Collection of Shared Thoughts.* Philadelphia: Running Press.

ASHKENAZ, JUDY

1995   Indians. In *The Adoption Reader.* Susan Wadia-Ells, ed. Pp. 141–149. Seattle: Seal Press.

ASSOCIATED PRESS

1981   Miami Couple Unadopts 15-Year-Old Boy. *Boston Globe* (May 10): A8.

BACHRACH, C., K. STOLLEY, AND K. LONDON

1992   Relinquishment of Premarital Births: Evidence from the National Survey Data. *Family Planning Perspectives* 24: 27–32, 48.

BAGLEY, CHRISTOPHER

1993   Transracial Adoption in Britain. *Child Welfare League of America* 15: 285–299.

BAGLEY, CHRISTOPHER, AND LORETTA YOUNG

1979   The Identity, Adjustment, and Achievement of Transracially Adopted Children: A Review and Empirical Report. In *Race, Education, and Identity.* Gajendra Verma and Christopher Bagley, eds. Pp. 129–219. New York: St. Martin's Press.

BAGLEY, CHRISTOPHER, AND LORETTA YOUNG, WITH ANNE SCULLY

1993   *International and Transracial Adoptions: A Mental Health Perspective.* Brookfield, VT: Avebury Press.

BAKER, LEE D.

1998   *From Savage to Negro: Anthropology and the Construction of Race, 1896–1954.* Berkeley: University of California Press.

BANKS, SANDY

2002   An Unlikely, but Loving, Father-Daughter Bond. *Los Angeles Times* (May 5): E1, E4.

BARON, A., AND R. PANNOR

1993   Perspectives on Open Adoption. *The Future of Children: Adoption* 3(1): 119–124.

BARTH, RICHARD

1988   Disruption in Older Child Adoptions. *Public Welfare* (Winter): 323–329.

BARTH, RICHARD, AND MARIANNE BERRY

1988   *Adoption and Disruption: Rates, Risks, and Response.* New York: Aldine de Gruyter.

BARTH, RICHARD, DEVON BROOKS, AND SEEMA IYER

1995   Adoptions in California: Current Demographic Profiles and Projections through the End of the Century. Executive Summary. Berkeley, CA: Child Welfare Research Center.

BARTHOLET, ELIZABETH

1993   *Family Bonds: Adoption and the Politics of Parenting.* Boston: Houghton-Mifflin.

BATES, J. DOUGLAS

1993   *Gift Children: A Story of Race, Family, and Adoption in a Divided America.* New York: Ticknor and Fields.

BEASLEY, MAURINE

1973   A Look at Transracial Adoption in D.C. Area. *Washington Post* (April 30): C1.

BECK, SAM

1992   Persona Non Grata: Ethnicity and Romanian Nationalism. In *The Politics of Culture and Creativity.* Christine Ward Gailey, ed. Pp. 119–145. Gainesville: University Press of Florida.

BEITCHMAN, J. H., K. J. ZUCKER, J. E. HOOD,
G. A. DACOSTA, D. AKMAN, AND E. CASSAVIA

1992   A Review of the Long-Term Effects of Child Sexual Abuse. *Child Abuse and Neglect* 16: 101–118.

BEREBITSKY, JULIE

2001   Redefining "Real" Motherhood: Representations of Adoptive Mothers, 1900–1950. In *Imagining Adoption: Essays on Literature and Culture.* Marianne Novy, ed. Pp. 83–96. Ann Arbor: University of Michigan Press.

BERMAN, CLAIRE

1974   *We Take This Child.* Garden City, NY: Doubleday.

BERQUIST, KATHLEEN JA SOOK, M. ELIZABETH VONK,
DONG SOO KIM, AND MARVIN FEIT, EDS.

2007   *International Korean Adoption: A Fifty Year History of Policy and Practice.* New York: Routledge.

BERRY, M.

1992   Adoptive Parents' Perceptions of, and Comfort with, Open Adoption. *Child Welfare* 77(3): 231–253.

BIRD, CARMEL, ED.

1998   *The Stolen Generation: Their Stories.* Sydney, Australia: Random House.

BOHLEN, CELESTINE

1990   Bucharest Journal: The Hurdles Are Many, but Reward Is a Child. *New York Times* (November 15): A4.

BOUQUET, MARY

2001   Visualizing Kinship: Family Photography as Technically Assisted Shared Substance. In *Relative Values: Reconfiguring Kinship Studies.* Sarah Franklin and Susan McKinnon, eds. Durham, NC: Duke University Press.

BOURDIEU, PIERRE

1984   *Distinction: A Social Critique of the Judgment of Taste.* Cambridge, MA: Harvard University Press.

BOYNE, J., L. DENBY, J. R. KETTENING, AND W. WHEELER

1984   *The Shadow of Success: A Statistical Analysis of Outcomes of Adoptions of Hard-to-Place Children.* Westfield, CT: Spaulding for Children.

BRADLEY, TRUDY

1967   *An Exploration of Caseworkers' Perceptions of Adoptive Applicants.* New York: Child Welfare League of America.

BRANHAM, ETHEL

1970   One-Parent Adoptions. *Children* 17(3): 103–107.

BRIAN, KRISTI

2004   "This is not a civic duty": Racial Selection, Consumer Choice and the "Multiculturalist" Bind in the Production of Korean-American Adoption. Ph.D. dissertation, Temple University.

BRIERE, J.

1989   *Therapy for Adults Molested as Children: Beyond Survival.* New York: Springer.

BRIGGS, JEAN

1970   *Never in Anger; Portrait of an Eskimo Family.* Cambridge, MA: Harvard University Press.

BRODKIN, KAREN

2000   Global Capitalism: What's Race Got to Do With It? *American Ethnologist* 27(2): 237–256.

1998   *How Jews Became White Folks and What That Says about Race in America.* New Brunswick, NJ: Rutgers University Press.

BROOKE, E. H.

1994   Adoption Saga of Rio's Streets. *New York Times* (December 29): C1.

BROWN, LAURA, AND MARY BALLOU, EDS.

1992   *Personality and Psychopathology: Feminist Reappraisals.* New York: Guilford Press.

BURLINGHAM-BROWN, BARBARA

1994   *"Why Didn't She Keep Me?" Answers to the Question Every Adopted Child Asks.* South Bend, IN: Langford Books.

CAHN, KATHERINE, AND PAUL JOHNSON, EDS.

1993   *Children Can't Wait: Reducing Delays for Children in Foster Care.* New York: Child Welfare League of America.

CARNEY, ANN

1976   *No More Here and There: Adopting the Older Child.* Chapel Hill: University of North Carolina Press.

CHANG, IRIS

1997   *The Rape of Nanking.* New York: Penguin Books.

CHESTANG, LEON

1972   The Dilemma of Biracial Adoption. *Social Work* 17: 100–115.

CHILD WELFARE

1996   Kinship Care (Special Issue). September/October.

CHILD WELFARE INFORMATION GATEWAY

2009   Intercountry Adoption. Washington, DC: U.S. Department of Health and Human Services. http://www.childwelfare.gov/pubs/f_inter/

2004   How Many Children Were Adopted in 2000 and 2001. Washington, DC: U.S. Department of Health and Human Services. http://childwelfare.gov/systemwide/statistics/adoption.cfm#dom

CHIMEZIE, A.

1975   Transracial Adoption of Black Children. *Social Work* 20: 296–301.

CHRISTY, MARIAN

1990   Adoption: The Qualms and Quirks. *Boston Globe* (December 2): A30ff.

CLINE, FOSTER W.

1979   *Understanding and Treating the Severely Disturbed Child.* Evergreen, CO: Evergreen Consultants in Human Behavior.

COLLARD, CHANTAL

2000   Stratified Reproduction: The Politics of Fosterage and International Adoption in Haiti. Paper presented in the session "Stratified Reproduction: The Politics of Fosterage and Adoption" at the annual meeting of the American Anthropological Association, San Francisco, November 15.

1991   Les Orphelins Propres et les Autres. *Culture* 11(1/2): 135–149.

COLLIER, JANE, MICHELLE ROSALDO, AND SYLVIA YANIGASAKO
1997   Is There a Family? In *The Gender/Sexuality Reader: Culture, History, Political Economy.* Roger Lancaster and Micaela di Leonardo, eds. Pp. 71–81. New York: Routledge.

COLLINS, PATRICIA HILL
1990   *Black Feminist Thought: Knowledge, Consciousness, and the Politics of Empowerment.* New York: Routledge.

COOK, WENDY
1995   The Use of Adoption as an Expedient Foster Care Permanency Plan. *Adoptalk* (Fall): 13–17.

COSTIN, LELA, AND SHIRLEY WATTENBERG
1979   Identity in Transracial Adoption: A Study of Parental Dilemmas and Family Experiences. In *Race, Education, and Identity.* Gajendra Verma and Christopher Bagley, eds. Pp. 220–235. New York: St. Martin's Press.

COX, SUSAN SOON-KEUM, ED.
1998   *Voices from Another Place: A Collection of Works from a Generation Born in Korea and Adopted to Other Countries.* St. Paul, MN: Yeong and Yeong.

CREED, BARBARA
2001   Breeding Out the Black: Jedda and the Stolen Generations in Australia. In *Body Trade.* Barbara Creed and Jeanette Hoorn, eds. Pp. 208–230. Sydney, Australia: Pluto Press.

CUMMINGS, JUDITH
1983   Homosexual Views Adoption Approval as Victory. *New York Times* (January 10): B5.

CUNNINGHAM, LAURA
1997   Mother in a Strange Land. *New York Times* (August 17): A29.

DALEN, MONICA
1999a   *The Status of Knowledge of Foreign Adoptions.* Oslo: University of Oslo Department of Special Needs.
1999b   Interaction in Adoptive Families. In *Mine—Yours—Ours and Theirs: Adoption, Changing Kinship and Family Patterns.* Anne-Lise Rygvold, Monica Dalen, and Barbro Saetersdal, eds. Pp. 82–100. Oslo: University of Oslo/GCS.

DALMAGE, HEATHER
2006   Interracial Couples, Multiracial People, and the Color Line in Adoption. In *Adoptive Families in a Diverse Society.* Katarina Wegar, ed. Pp. 210–224. New Brunswick, NJ: Rutgers University Press.

DANIELS, BERNICE
1950   Significant Considerations in Placing Negro Infants for Adoption. *Child Welfare* (January).

DAY, DAWN
1979   *The Adoption of Black Children: Counteracting Institutional Discrimination.* Lexington, MA: Lexington Books.

DEANS, JILL

2001   "File It under 'L' for Love Child": Adoptive Policies and Practices in the Erdrich Tetralogy. In *Imagining Adoption: Essays on Literature and Culture*. Marianne Novy, ed. Pp. 231–250. Ann Arbor: University of Michigan Press.

DI LEONARDO, MICAELA

1987   The Female World of Cards and Holidays: Women, Families, and the Work of Kinship. *Signs* 12(3): 340–350.

DODDS, P. F.

1997   *Outer Search, Inner Journey: An Orphan and Adoptee's Quest*. Puyallup, WA: Aphrodite Press.

DOROW, SARA

2006   *Transnational Adoption: A Cultural Economy of Race, Gender, and Kinship*. New York: New York University Press.

2002   "China R Us"?: Care, Consumption, and Transnationally Adopted Children. In *Symbolic Childhood*. Daniel Thomas Cook, ed. Pp. 149–168. New York: Peter Lang.

2001   Adoptive Families of Chinese Girls: Negotiating Cultural Difference and Degrees of Immersion. Paper presented at the Conference on International Adoption, Hamilton College, May 11–13.

DOROW, SARA, ED.

1999   *I Wish for You a Beautiful Life: Letters from the Korean Birth Mothers of Ae Ran Won to Their Children*. St. Paul, MN: Yeong and Yeong.

DORRIS, MICHAEL

1989   *The Broken Cord*. New York: Harper and Row.

DRYFOOS, P.

1993   Risks. *Adoptalk* (Fall): 13.

DUNNE, PHYLLIS

1958   Placing Children of Minority Groups for Adoption. *Children* (March–April): 43–48.

EISENMAN, RUSSELL

1992   The Assignment of Black Children to Special Education Classes. *Mankind Quarterly* 23(2): 227–236.

ELBOW, M.

1986   From Caregiving to Parenting: Family Formation with Adopted Older Children. *Social Work* (September–October): 366–370.

ERDRICH, LOUISE

1995   The Broken Cord. In *The Adoption Reader*. Susan Wadia-Ells, ed. Pp. 97–104. Seattle: Seal Press.

ETIENNE, MONA

1979   The Case for Social Maternity: Adoption of Children by Urban Baulé Women. *Dialectical Anthropology* 4: 237–242.

EWICK, PATRICIA, AND SUSAN SIBLEY

1995   Subversive Stories and Hegemonic Tales: Toward a Sociology of Narrative. *Law and Society Review* 29(2): 197–226.

FALK, LAURENCE

1970   A Comparative Study of Transracial and Inracial Adoptions. *Child Welfare* 49 (February): 82–88.

FANSHEL, DAVID

1972   *Far from the Reservation: The Transracial Adoption of American Indian Children.* New York: Scarecrow Books.

1957   *A Study of Negro Adoption.* New York: Child Welfare League of America.

FEIGELMAN, WILLIAM

1997   Adopted Adults: Comparisons with Persons Raised in Conventional Families. *Marriage and Family Review* 25(3/4): 199–223.

FEIGELMAN, WILLIAM, AND ARNOLD SILVERMAN

1997   Single Parent Adoption. In *The Handbook for Single Adoptive Parents.* Pp. 123–129. Chevy Chase, MD: National Council for Single Adoptive Parents.

1983   *Chosen Children: New Patterns of Adoptive Relationships.* New York: Praeger.

FIGLEY, C. R., ED.

1985   *Trauma and Its Wake: The Study and Treatment of Post-Traumatic Stress Disorder.* New York: Brunner/Mazel.

FINGERHUT, LOIS, AND JOEL KLEINMAN

1990   International and Interstate Comparisons of Homicide Among Young Males. *Journal of the American Medical Association* 263: 3292–3295.

FISHER, CLARENCE D.

1971   Homes for Black Children. *Child Welfare* (February): 108–111.

FLANGO, VICTOR, AND CAROL FLANGO

1995   How Many Children Were Adopted in 1992. *Child Welfare* 74: 1018–1031.

1994   *The Flow of Adoption Information from the States.* Williamsburg, VA: National Center for State Courts.

FOLBRE, NANCY

1994   *Who Pays for the Kids? Gender and the Structures of Constraint.* New York: Routledge.

FONSECA, CLAUDIA

2001   The Circulation of Children in a Brazilian Working-Class Neighborhood: A Local Practice in a Globalized World. Paper presented at the Conference on International Adoption, Hamilton College, May 11–13.

1986   Orphanages, Foundlings, and Foster Mothers: The System of Child Circulation in a Brazilian Squatter Settlement. *Anthropological Quarterly* 59(1): 15–27.

FRANKLIN, SARAH, AND HELÉNA RAGONÉ, EDS.

1998   *Reproducing Reproduction: Kinship, Power, and Technological Innovation.* Philadelphia: University of Pennsylvania Press.

FREDRICKSON, GEORGE

1971   *The Black Image in the White Mind.* Middletown, CT: Wesleyan University Press.

GABER, IVOR, AND JANE ALDRIDGE, EDS.

1994   *In the Best Interests of the Child: Culture, Identity, and Transracial Adoption.* London: Free Association Books.

GAILEY, CHRISTINE WARD

2006   "Whatever They Think of Us, We're a Family": Single Mother Adopters. In *Adoptive Families in a Diverse Society.* Katarina Wegar, ed. Pp. 162–174. New Brunswick, NJ: Rutgers University Press.

2004   Adoptive Families in the United States. In *Families and Society: Classic and Contemporary Readings.* Scott Coltrane, ed. Pp. 377–389. Belmont, CA: Thomson/Wadsworth.

2000a   Race, Class, and Gender in Intercountry Adoption in the USA. In *Intercountry Adoption: Developments, Trends, and Perspectives.* Peter Selman, ed. Pp. 315–345. London: British Agencies for Adoption and Fostering.

2000b   Ideologies of Motherhood in Adoption. In *Ideologies and Technologies of Motherhood: Race, Class, Sexuality, Nationalism.* Heléna Ragoné and France Winddance Twine, eds. Pp. 11–55. New York: Routledge.

1999   Seeking "Baby Right": Race, Class, and Gender in U.S. International Adoption. In *Mine—Yours—Ours and Theirs: Adoption, Changing Kinship and Family Patterns.* Anne-Lise Rygvold, Monica Dalen, and Barbro Saetersdal, eds. Pp. 52–81. Oslo: University of Oslo/GCS.

1998a   Feminist Methods. In *Handbook of Methods in Cultural Anthropology.* H. Russell Bernard, ed. Pp. 203–233. Walnut Creek, CA: Altamira/Sage.

1998b   Making Kinship in the Wake of History: Gendered Violence in Older Child Adoption. *Identities* 5(2): 249–292.

1988   Evolutionary Perspectives on Gender Hierarchy. In *Analyzing Gender.* Beth Hess and Myra Ferree, eds. Pp. 32–67. Newbury Park, CA: Sage Publications.

GALTON, SIR FRANCIS

1925 [1869]   *Hereditary Genius: An Inquiry into Its Laws and Consequences.* London: Macmillan.

GEDIMAN, JUDITH, AND LINDA BROWN

1989   *Birthbond: Reunions between Birthparents and Adoptees—What Happens After . . .* Far Hills, NJ: New Horizon Press.

GIBBS, JEWELLE

1988   *Young, Black, and Male in America.* Dover, MA: Auburn House.

GILL, OWEN, AND BARBARA JACKSON

1983   *Adoption and Race: Black, Asian, and Mixed Race Children in White Families.* New York: St. Martin's Press.

GILLIES, VAL

2007   *Marginalised Mothers: Exploring Working-Class Experiences of Parenting.* New York: Routledge.

GOLDBERG, D., M. MCLAUGHLIN, M. GROSSI, A. TYTUN, AND S. BLUM

1992   Which Newborns in New York City Are at Risk for Special Education Placement? *American Journal of Public Health* 82: 438–440.

GOLDBERG, ROBERTA

1997   Adopting Romanian Children: Making Choices, Taking Risks. *Marriage and Family Review* 25(1,2): 79–99.

GORDIMER, NADINE

1988   The Essential Gesture: Writers and Responsibility. In *The Essential Gesture: Writing, Politics, and Places.* Stephen Clingman, ed. Pp. 285–300. New York: Alfred A. Knopf.

GORELICK, SHERRY

1991   Contradictions of Feminist Methodology. *Gender and Society* 5: 459–477.

GRANELLI, J., AND D. REYES

1984   Court Orders Girl's Return from Mexico: Charges "Appalling Breach" of Duty in International Adoption Case. *Los Angeles Times* (February 11): 5.

GREENBERG, JOEL

1997   The Babies from Yemen: An Enduring Mystery. *New York Times* (September 2): A4.

GREGORY, STEVEN, AND ROGER SANJEK, EDS.

1994   *Race.* New Brunswick, NJ: Rutgers University Press.

GRIFFIN, BARBARA, AND MARVIN ARFFA

1970   Recruiting Adoptive Homes for Minority Children—One Approach. *Child Welfare* (February): 105–107.

GROTEVANT, HAROLD

1999   Adoptive Identity Development: New Kinship Patterns, New Issues. In *Mine—Yours—Ours and Theirs: Adoption, Changing Kinship and Family Patterns.* Anne-Lise Rygvold, Monica Dalen, and Barbro Saetersdal, eds. Pp. 101–117. Oslo: University of Oslo/GCS.

GROTEVANT, HAROLD, AND RUTH MCROY

1998   *Openness in Adoption: Exploring Family Connections.* Thousand Oaks, CA: Sage Publications.

GROW, LUCILLE, AND DEBORAH SHAPIRO

1975   *Black Child—White Parents.* New York: Child Welfare League of America.

GROZE, VICTOR

1996   *Successful Adoptive Families: A Longitudinal Study of Special Needs Adoption.* Westport, CT: Praeger.

1986   Special Needs Adoption. *Children and Youth Services Review* 8(4): 363–373.

GROZE, VICTOR, AND JAMES A. ROSENTHAL

1991   Single Parents and Their Adopted Children: A Psychosocial Analysis. *Journal of Contemporary Human Services* (1991): 130–139.

HABERMAN, C.

1990   Court Aborts Adoption and Tugs at Child. *New York Times* (March 1): A4.

HALDANE, DAVID

2003   Adoption Agency Says It Didn't Reject Lesbians. *Los Angeles Times* (June 11): B8.

HALL, CARL T.

2002   Pediatricians Endorse Gay, Lesbian Adoption: "Children Deserve to Know Their Relationships with Both Parents Are Stable, Legally Recognized." *San Francisco Chronicle* (February 4): A1.

HARDING, SANDRA

1987   Introduction: Is There a Feminist Method? In *Feminism and Methodology*. Sandra Harding, ed. Pp. 1–14. Bloomington: Indiana University Press.

HARRISON, FAYE

1995   The Persistent Power of "Race" in the Cultural and Political Economy of Racism. *Annual Review of Anthropology* 24: 47–74.

HART, JORDANA

1997   Forum Explores Hidden Problems in Overseas Adoption. *Boston Globe* (September 29): B3.

HARTMANN, HEIDI, ROBERTA SPALTER-ROTH, AND JACQUELINE CHU

1996   Poverty Alleviation and Single-Mother Families. *National Forum* (Summer): 25ff.

HENRY, JULES

1963   *Culture against Man*. New York: Vintage Books.

HERMAN, ELLEN

1998   Family Matters: Secrecy and Disclosure in the History of Adoption. *Reviews in American History* 26(4): 751–759.

HERMAN, JUDITH

1981   *Father-Daughter Incest*. Cambridge, MA: Harvard University Press.

HERZOG, ELIZABETH, CECILIA SUDIA, JANE HARWOOD, AND CAROL NEWCOMB

1971   *Families for Black Children: The Search for Adoptive Parents—An Experience Survey.* Washington, DC: Government Printing Office.

HOELGAARD, SUZANNE

1998   Cultural Determinants of Adoption Policy: A Columbian Case Study. *International Journal of Law, Policy and the Family* 12: 202–241.

HOFF, LEE ANN

1990   *Battered Women as Survivors*. New York: Routledge.

HOOKS, BELL

1995   *Killing Rage: Ending Racism*. New York: Henry Holt.

HOPSON, DARLENE POWELL, AND DEREK S. HOPSON

1990   *Different and Wonderful: Raising Black Children in a Race-Conscious Society.* New York: Simon and Schuster.

HOUSTON, PAUL

1992   Romania's Experience Spurs Adoption Treaty. *Los Angeles Times* (February 12): A5.

HOWARD, ALICIA, DAVID ROYSE, AND JOHN SKERL

1977　　　Transracial Adoption: The Black Community Perspective. *Social Work* 22: 184–189.

HOWE, RUTH-ARLENE

1997　　　Transracial Adoption: Old Prejudices and Discrimination Float under a New Halo. *Boston University Public Interest Law Journal* 6(2): 409–430.

1995　　　Redefining the Transracial Adoption Controversy. *Duke Journal of Gender Law and Policy* 2(1): 131–150.

HUNT, KATHLEEN

1991　　　The Romanian Baby Bazaar. *New York Times Magazine* (March 24): 24ff.

JAFFE, BENSON, AND DAVID FANSHEL

1970　　　*How They Fared in Adoption: A Follow-Up Study.* New York: Columbia University Press.

JAFFE, E., ED.

1995　　　*Intercountry Adoptions: Laws and Perspectives of Sending Countries.* London: Martinus Nijhoff.

JAGGAR, ALISON

1992　　　Love and Knowledge: Emotion in Feminist Epistemology. In *Gender/Body/ Knowledge.* Alison Jaggar and Susan Bordo, eds. Pp. 145–171. New Brunswick, NJ: Rutgers University Press.

JARDINE, SUE

2000　　　In Whose Interests? Reflections on Openness, Cultural Roots, and Loss. In *Intercountry Adoption: Developments, Trends, and Perspectives.* Pp. 484–491. London: British Agencies for Adoption and Fostering.

JEWETT, CLAUDIA

1982　　　*Helping Children Cope with Grief and Loss.* Cambridge, MA: Harvard Common Press.

1978　　　*Adopting the Older Child.* Cambridge, MA: Harvard Common Press.

JOHNSON, A., AND VICTOR GROZE

1993　　　The Orphaned and Institutionalized Children of Romania. *Journal of Emotional and Behavioral Problems* 2(4): 49–52.

JOHNSON, DANA, LAURIE MILLER, AND SANDRA IVERSON, ET AL.

1992　　　The Health of Children Adopted from Romania. *Journal of the American Medical Association* 228(24): 3446–3452.

JOHNSON, DIANE J., ED.

1995　　　*Proud Sisters.* White Plains, NY: Peter Pauper Press.

JOHNSON, KAY, HUANG BANGHAN, AND WANG LIYAO

1998　　　Infant Abandonment and Adoption in China. *Population and Development Review* 24(3): 469ff.

JORDAN, VELMA, AND WILLIAM LITTLE

1966　　　Early Comments on Single Parent Adoptive Homes. *Child Welfare* 45: 536–538.

KADUSHIN, ALFRED

1970   Single Parent Adoptions: An Overview and Some Relevant Research. *Social Science Review* 44: 263–274.

KASSIOLA, BETH

1999   National Adoptions a Priority. *Court* (November–December): 1, 4–5. Judicial Council of California.

KATZ, L.

1986   Parental Stress and Factors for Success in Older-Child Adoption. *Child Welfare* 65(6): 569–578.

KIM, DONG SOO

1978   Issues in Transracial and Transcultural Adoption. *Social Casework* 59: 477–486.

KIM, ELEANA

2001   The Gathering as Secular Ritual: The "Koreanness" of Korean Transnational Adoptees. Paper presented at the Conference on International Adoption, Hamilton College, May 11–13.

KIRK, H. DAVID

1985   *Adoptive Kinship: A Modern Institution in Need of Reform.* Port Angeles, WA: Ben-Simon Publications.

1982   *Shared Fate: A Theory and Method of Adoptive Relationships.* Port Angeles, WA: Ben-Simon Publications.

KIRSCH, GESA

1999   *Ethical Dilemmas in Feminist Research.* Albany: State University of New York Press.

KLEIN, CAROLE

1973   *The Single Parent Experience.* New York: Walker and Company.

KREIDER, ROSE M.

2003   *Adopted Children and Stepchildren: Census 2000 Special Reports.* Washington, DC: U.S. Census Bureau.

KROLL, JOE

1993   The Role of Race in Child Welfare. *Adoptalk* (Summer): 1.

1991   Barriers to Same Race Placement. *Adoptalk* (Spring): 1–3.

LADNER, JOYCE

1977   *Mixed Families: Adopting across Racial Boundaries.* Garden City, NY: Doubleday/Anchor.

LAMAS, CARDARELLO, AND ANDREA DANIELLA

2000   Du mineur a l'enfant-citoyen: drois des enfants et droits des familles au Brésil. *Lien Social et Politiques/RIAC* 44: 155–166.

LEACOCK, ELEANOR BURKE

1980   Montagnais Women and the Jesuit Program for Colonization. In *Women and Colonization.* Mona Etienne and Eleanor Leacock, eds. Pp. 25–42. New York: Praeger.

LEE, RICHARD B.

1992   Demystifying Primitive Communism. In *Civilization in Crisis.* Christine W. Gailey, ed. Pp. 73–94. Gainesville: University Press of Florida.

LEE, ROBERT, AND RUTH HULL

1983   Legal, Casework, and Ethical Issues in "Risk Adoption." *Child Welfare* 62 (September–October): 450–454.

LEWIN, ELLEN

1993   *Lesbian Mothers: Accounts of Gender in American Culture.* Ithaca, NY: Cornell University Press.

LEWIN, TAMAR

1997   The U.S. Is Divided on Adoption, Survey of Attitudes Asserts. *New York Times* (November 9): 16.

LOEHLIN, J. C., L. WILLERMAN, AND J. M. HORN

1987   Personality Resemblances in Adoptive Families: A 10-year Follow-Up. *Journal of Personality and Social Psychology* 53(5): 961–969.

LORDE, AUDRE

1995 [1980]   Age, Race, Class, and Sex: Women Redefining Difference. In *Race, Class, and Gender in the United States.* Paula Rothenberg, ed. Pp. 445–451. New York: St. Martin's Press.

LOS ANGELES TIMES

2001   Adopted Kids May Face Higher Suicide Risk. (August 7): A7.

MALLON, GERALD

2000   Gay Men and Lesbians as Adoptive Parents. *Journal of Gay and Lesbian Social Services* 11(4): 1–20.

MCMURTRY, S. L., AND G. W. LIE

1992   Differential Exit Rates of Minority Children in Foster Care. *Social Work Research and Abstracts* 28(1): 42–48.

MCNAMARA, J., AND B. H. MCNAMARA

1990   *Adoption and the Sexually Abused Child.* New York: Human Services Development Institute.

MCROY, RUTH, HAROLD GROTEVANT, AND KERRY WHITE

1988   *Openness in Adoption: New Practices, New Issues.* New York: Praeger.

MCROY, RUTH, AND C. HALL

1995   Transracial Adoptions: In Whose Best Interest? In *Multiracial People in the New Millennium.* M. Root, ed. Pp. 63–78. Newbury Park, CA: Sage Publications.

MCROY, RUTH, ZENA OGLESBY, AND HELEN GRAPE

1997   Specialized Minority Adoption Programs. *Adoptalk* (Summer): 7–8, 10–11.

MCROY, RUTH, AND L. A. ZURCHER

1983   *Transracial Adoptees: The Adolescent Years.* Springfield, IL: Thomas Publishers.

MCROY, RUTH, L. A. ZURCHER, M. LAUDERDALE, AND R. ANDERSON

1982   Self-Esteem and Racial Identity in Transracial and Inracial Adoptees. *Social Work* 27(6): 522–526.

MALONEY, MICHAEL

1994   Baby Jessica. *Journal of the American Academy of Child and Adolescent Psychiatry* 33: 430–431.

MANDELL, BETTY REID

1973   *Where Are the Children? A Class Analysis of Foster Care and Adoption.* Lexington, MA: Lexington Books.

MANSFIELD, LYNDA GIANFORTE, AND CHRISTOPHER WALDMANN

1994   *Don't Touch My Heart: Healing the Pain of an Unattached Child.* Colorado Springs: Piñon Press.

MARCH, KAREN

1995a   Perception of Adoption as Social Stigma: Motivation for Search and Reunion. *Journal of Marriage and the Family* 57: 653–660.

1995b   *The Stranger Who Bore Me: Adoptee-Birth Mother Interactions.* Toronto: University of Toronto Press.

MARKS, JONATHAN

1995   *Human Biodiversity: Genes, Race, and History.* New York: Aldine de Gruyter.

MARTINSON, BECCA, ED.

1993   Special Issue on Adoption and Adoptism. *Pact Press* (Spring). San Francisco.

MASON, KATHY

1999   Intercountry Adoption in the UK: Families' Experiences of the Adoption Process. In *Mine—Yours—Ours and Theirs: Adoption, Changing Kinship and Family Patterns.* Anne-Lise Rygvold, Monica Dalen, and Barbro Saetersdal, eds. Pp. 205–220. Oslo: University of Oslo/GCS.

MEEZAN, WILLIAM

1997   *Adoptions without Agencies: A Study of Independent Adoptions.* New York: Child Welfare League of America.

MEEZAN, WILLIAM, AND JOAN SHIREMAN

1985   *Care and Commitment: Foster Parent Adoption Decisions.* Albany: State University of New York Press.

MINK, GWENDOLYN

1998   *Welfare's End.* Ithaca, NY: Cornell University Press.

MITFORD, NANCY, ET AL.

1974 [1956]   *Noblesse Oblige: An Enquiry into the Identifiable Characteristics of the English Aristocracy.* Westport, CT: Greenwood Press.

MODELL, JUDITH SCHACHTER

2001   Natural Bonds, Legal Boundaries: Modes of Persuasion in Adoption Rhetoric. In *Imagining Adoption: Essays on Literature and Culture.* Marianne Novy, ed. Pp. 207–230. Ann Arbor: University of Michigan Press.

1997   Where Do We Go Next? Long Term Reunion Relationships Between Adoptees and Birth Parents. *Marriage and Family Review* 25(1,2): 43–67.

1995   "Nowadays Everyone Is Hanai": Child Exchange in the Cultural Construction of Hawaiian Urban Culture. *Journal, Société des océanistes* (100–101): 201–219.

1994   *Kinship with Strangers: Adoption and Interpretations of Kinship in American Culture.* Berkeley: University of California Press.

MOSHER, W. D., AND C. A. BACHRACH

1994   Understanding U.S. Fertility: Continuity and Change in the National Survey of Family Growth, 1988–1995. *Family Planning Perspectives* 28(1): 4–12.

NADER, LAURA

1982   Up the Anthropologist: Perspectives Gained from Studying Up. In *Anthropology for the Eighties.* Johnnetta Cole, ed. Pp. 456–470. New York: Free Press.

NAKASHIMA, ELLEN

1996   Untold Disabilities: U.S. Parents Encounter New Problems After Adoptions in Russia, Romania. *Washington Post* (June 18): A1.

NASH, M.

1991   Ordeal in Peru: Cuddling a Baby, Clinging to Hope—Americans Encounter Problems Attempting to Adopt Children in Peru. *New York Times* (June 9): A4, A7.

NATIONAL ADOPTION INFORMATION CLEARINGHOUSE (NAIC)

2002a   Cost of Adopting. http://www.calib.com/naic/pubs/s_cost.htm

2002b   Finalized Adoptions from Foster Care. http://www.calib.com/naic/pubs/s_final.htm

2002c   Infertility/Impaired Fecundity. http://www.calib.com/naic/pubs/s_infer.htm

2002d   Persons Seeking to Adopt. http://www.calib.com/naic/pubs/s_seek.htm

2002e   Single Adoptive Parents. http://www.calib.com/naic/pubs/s_single.htm

2002f   Transracial Adoption. http://www.calib.com/naic/pubs/s_trans.htm

NATIONAL ASSOCIATION OF BLACK SOCIAL WORKERS (NABSW)

1972   Position Statement on Transracial Adoptions. Presented at the NABSW Conference, Nashville, TN, April.

NATIONAL PUBLIC RADIO

2001   Transracial Adoption. *Justice Talking.* Margot Adler, host. (June 17).

NEW YORK TIMES

1995   Ukraine Arrests Two in Baby-Selling Case: Doctors Detained by Police Officials. (March 3): A8.

1990   Romania Is Prohibiting Adoption by Foreigners. (February 9): A8, A11.

NINIVAGGI, CYNTHIA

1996   The Traffic in Children: Adoption and Child Relinquishment in the U.S. Ph.D. dissertation, Temple University.

O'BRIEN, PAT

1993   Youth Homelessness and the Lack of Adoption Planning for Older Foster Children: Are They Related? *Adoptalk* (Spring): 5–7.

OLIVER, MELVIN, AND THOMAS SHAPIRO

1995   *Black Wealth/White Wealth: A New Perspective on Racial Inequality.* New York: Routledge.

OUELLETTE, FRANÇOISE-ROMAINE

1999   Gift-Giving in Legal Adoption. Paper presented at the annual meeting of the American Anthropological Association, San Francisco, November 15.

OUELLETTE, FRANÇOISE-ROMAINE, AND HÉLÈNE BELLEAU,
WITH THE COLLABORATION OF CAROLINE PATENAUDE

2001   Family and Social Integration of Children Adopted Internationally: A Review of the Literature. Paper presented at the Conference on International Adoption, Hamilton College, May 11–13.

PATTERSON, THOMAS C., AND FRANK SPENCER

1994   Racial Hierarchies and Buffer Races. *Race, Racism, and the History of U.S. Anthropology* (Special Issue). Lee D. Baker and Thomas C. Patterson, eds. *Transforming Anthropology* 5(1,2): 20–27.

PATTON, SANDRA LEE

2000   *BirthMarks: Transracial Adoption in Contemporary America.* New York: New York University Press.

PERLEZ, J.

1994   Britons Sentenced in Romania in Baby Case. *New York Times* (October 19): A4, A6.

PERRY, BRUCE, RONNIE POLLARD, TOI BLAKLEY,
WILLIAM BAKER, AND DOMENICO VIGILANTE

1997   Childhood Trauma, the Neurobiology of Adaptation and Use-Dependent Development of the Brain: How States Become Traits. *Infant Mental Health Journal* 16(4): 271–291.

PERTMAN, ADAM

2000   *Adoption Nation: How the Adoption Revolution Is Transforming America.* New York: Basic Books.

1998a   Detectives Offer Searchers Professional Help. *Boston Globe* (March 10): A16.

1998b   Adoptees Not Deterred by Uncertainty of Searches. *Boston Globe* (March 10): A17.

1998c   Request Sparks Historic Change. *Boston Globe* (March 10): A16.

PIANTANIDA, MARIA

1993   Children at Risk. *Adoptalk* (Spring): 13.

POHL, CONSTANCE, AND KATHY HARRIS

1993   *Transracial Adoption: Children and Parents Speak Out.* New York: Franklin Watts.

POLLITT, KATHA

1987   The Strange Case of Baby M. *The Nation* (May 23): 681–686, 688.

RAGONÉ, HELÉNA

1996   Chasing the Blood Tie: Surrogate Mothers, Adoptive Mothers and Fathers. *American Ethnologist* 23(3): 327–345.

REGISTER, CHERI

1991   *"Are Those Kids Yours?" American Families with Children Adopted from Other Countries.* New York: Free Press.

ROLES, PATRICIA

1989   *Saying Goodbye to a Baby.* Washington, DC: Child Welfare League.

ROOT, MARIA

1992   Reconstructing the Impact of Trauma on Personality. In *Personality and Psychopathology: Feminist Reappraisals.* Laura Brown and Mary Ballou, eds. Pp. 229–265. New York: Guilford Press.

ROSENTHAL, JAMES A., AND VICTOR GROZE

1992   *Special-Needs Adoption: A Study of Intact Families.* New York: Praeger.

ROSENTHAL, JAMES A., VICTOR GROZE, AND H. CURIEL

1990   Race, Social Class, and Special Needs Adoption. *Social Work* 35(6): 532–539.

RUBIN, LILLIAN

1995   *Families on the Fault Line: America's Working Class Speaks Out about the Family, the Economy, Race, and Ethnicity.* New York: Harper Perennial.

1976   *Worlds of Pain: Life in the Working Class Family.* New York: Basic Books.

RUTTER, MICHAEL, THOMAS O'CONNOR, CELIA BECKETT, JENNY CASTLE, CARLA CROFT, JUDY DUNN, CHRISTINE GROOTHUES, AND JAYNA KREPPNER

2000   Recovery and Deficit following Profound Early Deprivation. In *Intercountry Adoption: Developments, Trends, and Perspectives.* Pp. 107–125. London: British Agencies for Adoption and Fostering.

SACK, W. H., AND D. DALE

1982   Abuse and Deprivation in Failing Adoptions. *Child Abuse and Neglect* 6: 443–451.

SAHLINS, MARSHALL

1972   *Stone Age Economics.* Chicago: Aldine.

SALTUS, RICHARD

2000   DNA Tests Cast Shadow on Adoption. *Boston Globe* (March 27): A1.

SATZ, MARTHA

2001   Should Whites Adopt African American Children? One Family's Phenomenological Response. In *Imagining Adoption: Essays on Literature and Culture.* Marianne Novy, ed. Pp. 267–276. Ann Arbor: University of Michigan Press.

SCHEPER-HUGHES, NANCY

1993   Lifeboat Ethics: Mother Love and Child Death in Northeast Brazil. In *Gender in Cross-Cultural Perspective.* Caroline Brettel and Carolyn Sargent, eds. Pp. 36–41. Upper Saddle River, NJ: Prentice-Hall.

SCHNEIDER, DAVID

1984   The Fundamental Assumption in the Study of Kinship: "Blood Is Thicker than Water." In *A Critique of the Study of Kinship.* Pp. 165–177. Ann Arbor: University of Michigan Press.

1968   *American Kinship: A Cultural Account.* Englewood Cliffs, NJ: Prentice-Hall.

SCHUERMAN, JOHN, TINA RZEPNICKI, AND JULIA LITTELL

1994   *Putting Families First: An Experiment in Family Preservation.* Hawthorne, NY: Aldine de Gruyter.

SELMAN, PETER

1999   The Demography of Intercountry Adoption. In *Mine—Yours—Ours and Theirs: Adoption, Changing Kinship and Family Patterns.* Anne-Lise Rygvold, Monica Dalen, and Barbro Saetersdal, eds. Pp. 230–246. Oslo: University of Oslo/GCS.

SELMAN, PETER, ED.

2000   *Intercountry Adoption: Developments, Trends, and Perspectives.* London: British Agencies for Adoption and Fostering.

SENNOTT, CHARLES

1996   Adoption Joy Turns to Nightmare. *Boston Globe* (June 16): 27, 32.

SHARKEY, NORA CLARE

1971   White Parents, Black Children: Transracial Adoption. *Time* (August 16): 42–45.

SHARP, C., AND S. PUNNETT

1982   On Baby Selling: Columbian Children. *Christian Science Monitor* 74 (October 28): 22.

SHIREMAN, JOAN, AND PENNY JOHNSON

1986   A Longitudinal Study of Black Adoptions: Single-Parent, Transracial, and Traditional. *Social Work* (May–June): 172–176.

1985   Single-Parent Adoptions: A Longitudinal Study. *Children and Youth Services Review* 7: 321–334.

SILBER, KATHLEEN, AND PHYLLIS SPEEDLIN

1991   *Dear Birthmother: Thank You for Our Baby.* San Antonio: Corona Publishing.

SILVERMAN, ARNOLD, AND WILLIAM FEIGELMAN

1981   The Adjustment of Black Children Adopted by White Families. *Social Casework* 62(9): 529–536.

SIMON, RITA JAMES

1992   *Adoption, Race, and Identity: From Infancy through Adolescence.* New York: Praeger.

1987   *Transracial Adoptees and Their Families: A Study of Identity and Commitment.* New York: Praeger.

1975   An Assessment of Racial Awareness, Preference, and Self-Identity among White and Adopted Non-white Children. *Social Problems* 34: 43–57.

SIMON, RITA, AND HOWARD ALTSTEIN

2000   *Adoption Across Borders: Serving the Children in Transracial and Intercountry Adoptions.* Lanham, MD: Rowman and Littlefield.

1992   *Adoption, Race, and Identity: From Infancy through Adolescence.* New York: Praeger.

1987   *Transracial Adoptees and Their Families: A Study of Identity and Commitment.* New York: Praeger.

1977   *Transracial Adoption.* New York: John Wiley and Son.

SIMON, RITA, HOWARD ALTSTEIN, AND MARYGOLD MELLI

1994   *The Case for Transracial Adoption.* Washington, DC: American University Press.

SIMON, RITA JAMES, AND RHONDA ROORDA

2000   *In Their Own Voices: Transracial Adoptees Tell Their Stories.* New York: Columbia University Press.

SMITH, DOROTHY, AND LAURIE NEHIS SHERWEN

1988   *Mothers and Their Adoptive Children: The Bonding Process.* New York: Tiresias Press.

SMITH, JANET FARRELL

2006   Identity, Race, and Culture in Adoption: Ethical Values in the Power of Language. In *Adoptive Families in a Diverse Society.* Katarina Wegar, ed. Pp. 243–258. New Brunswick, NJ: Rutgers University Press.

SMITH, S. L., AND J. A. HOWARD

1991   A Comparative Study of Successful and Disrupted Adoptions. *Journal of Social Service Review* 65: 248–265.

SPERRY, SHELLEY

2008   The Politics of Adoption. *National Geographic* (January).

STACK, CAROL

1974   *All Our Kin.* New York: Harper and Row.

STACK, CAROL, AND LINDA BURTON

1993   Kinscripts. *Journal of Comparative Family Studies* 24(2): 157–170.

STANLEY, A.

1997   U.S. Adoption Agencies Fear Tightening of Russian Law. *New York Times* (December 4): A5.

STOLLEY, K. S.

1993   Statistics on Adoption in the United States. In *The Future of Children.* I. Schulman, ed. Pp. 26–42. Los Altos, CA: Center for the Future of Children.

STRONG, PAULINE TURNER

2002   To Forget Their Tongue, Their Name, and Their Whole Relation: Captivity, Extra-Tribal Adoption, and the American Indian Welfare Act. In *Relative Values: Reconfiguring Kinship Studies.* Sarah Franklin and Susan McKinnon, eds. Pp. 468–493. Durham, NC: Duke University Press.

SUSSER, IDA

1996   The Construction of Poverty and Homelessness in U.S. Cities. *Annual Reviews in Anthropology* 25: 411–435.

SUTPHEN, JUDITH

1995   Alex Has Two Mothers. In *The Adoption Reader: Birth Mothers, Adoptive Mothers, and Adopted Daughters Tell Their Stories.* Susan Wadia-Ells, ed. Pp. 76–84. Seattle: Seal Press.

SUZUKI, PETER T.

1980   A Retrospective Analysis of a Wartime "National Character" Study. *Dialectical Anthropology* 5(1): 33–46.

TALBOT, MARGARET

1998   Attachment Theory: The Ultimate Experiment. *New York Times Magazine* (May 24): 24–30, 38, 46, 50.

TELFER, JONATHAN

2000   Partial to Completeness: Gender, Peril and Agency in Australian Adoption. Paper presented at the European Association of Social Anthropologists, Krakow, July 2000.

1999   Relationships with No Body? "Adoption" Photographs, Intuition, and Emotion. *Social Analysis* 43(3): 144–158.

TERRELL, JOHN, AND JUDITH MODELL

1994   Anthropology and Adoption. *American Anthropologist* 96(1): 155–161.

THIEMAN, A. A., R. FUQUA, AND K. LINNAN

1990   *Iowa Family Preservation Three Year Pilot Project: Final Evaluation Report.* Ames: Iowa State University.

THOMPSON, ERA BELL

1974   The Adoption Controversy: Blacks Who Grew Up in White Homes. *Ebony* (June): 84–94.

THORNHILL, ALAN

1997   Australia Rues Removal of Aboriginal Children: Defunct Policy Is Likened to Genocide. *Boston Globe* (May 21): A4.

TIZARD, B., AND A. PHOENIX

1989   Black Identity and Transracial Adoption. *New Community* 15 (3): 427–437.

TOUSIGNANT, MARYLOU

1994   Bogged Down in Bucharest. *Washington Post* (October 26): B1.

TOWNSEND, RITA, AND ANN PERKINS

1992   *Bitter Fruit: Women's Experiences of Unplanned Pregnancy, Abortion, and Adoption.* Alameda, CA: Hunter House.

TRIMBORN, H.

1983   U.S. Couple Fights for Polish Child: Adoption Saga. *Los Angeles Times* (August 21): 1.

TRISELIOTIS, JOHN

1999   Inter-Country Adoption: Global Trade or Global Gift? In *Mine—Yours—Ours and Theirs: Adoption, Changing Kinship and Family Patterns.* Anne-Lise Rygvold, Monica Dalen, and Barbro Saetersdal, eds. Pp. 14–31. Oslo: University of Oslo/GCS.

1992   Inter-Country Adoption: In Whose Best Interest? In *Inter-Country Adoption: Practical Experiences.* Michael Humphrey and Heather Humphrey, eds. Pp. 119–137. London Tavistock/Routledge.

TRUDGE, JONATHAN

2008   *The Everyday Lives of Young Children: Culture, Class, and Child Rearing in Diverse Societies.* Cambridge: Cambridge University Press.

UNITED STATES CENSUS BUREAU

2000   Census 2000 (Special Tabulation). Washington, DC: Government Printing Office.

UNITED STATES DEPARTMENT OF HEALTH AND HUMAN SERVICES (USDHHS), ADMINISTRATION FOR CHILDREN AND FAMILIES

2003   Single Adoptive Parents. National Adoption Information Clearinghouse. http://www.calib.com/naic/pubs/s_single.cfm

1996   Statistical Tables on Foster Care and Adoption. http://www.acf.dhhs.gov/programs/cb/stats/afcars/reed96b.htm

UNITED STATES FEDERAL RESERVE

2004   Survey of Consumer Finances. Washington, DC: U.S. Government Printing Office.

VAN DER KOLK, BESSEL

1994   The Body Keeps the Score: Memory and the Evolving Psychobiology of Post Traumatic Stress. *Harvard Review of Psychiatry* 1: 253–265.

VAN DER KOLK, BESSEL, AND RITA FISLER

1994   Childhood Abuse and Neglect and Loss of Self-Regulation. *Bulletin of the Menninger Clinic* 58(2): 145–168.

VERHULST, F., M. ALTHAUS, AND H. VERLUISDEN BIERMAN

1990   Problem Behaviour in International Adoptees. *Journal of the American Academy of Child and Adolescent Psychiatry* 29: 94–103.

VERMA, GAJENDRA, AND CHRISTOPHER BAGLEY, EDS.

1979   *Race, Education, and Identity.* New York: St. Martin's Press.

WADIA-ELLS, SUSAN, ED.

1995   *The Adoption Reader: Birth Mothers, Adoptive Mothers, and Adopted Daughters Tell Their Stories.* Seattle: Seal Press.

WALDRON, JAN

1995   *Giving Away Simone: A Memoir.* New York: Times Books.

WATSON, MARLENE FAYE

1999   Confronting the Secret: Skin Tone Is the Hardest Issue for African American Families to Face. *Family Therapy Networker* (September/October): 50–57.

WEGAR, KATARINA

1997   *Adoption, Identity, and Kinship: The Debate over Birth Records.* New Haven, CT: Yale University Press.

WEINRICH, PAUL

1979   Cross-Ethnic Identification and Self-Rejection in a Black Adolescent. In *Race, Education, and Identity.* Gajendra Verma and Christopher Bagley, eds. Pp. 157–175. New York: St. Martin's Press.

WGBH

1994a   *Adoption: In Whose Interest?* "Say Brother." Video.

1994b   *Adoption: Which Home?* "Say Brother." Video.

WILLIAMS, CAROL

1994   Baby Smuggling Trial Underway in Romania. *Los Angeles Times* (September 15): A4.

WILLIS, MADGE GILL

1996   The Real Issues in Transracial Adoption: A Response. *Journal of Black Psychology* 223: 250–251.

WILSON, WILLIAM JULIUS

1990   *The Truly Disadvantaged.* Chicago: University of Chicago Press.

WINIK, LYRIC

1998   It's About Love. *Parade Magazine* (August 2): 4–7.

WOLLSTONECRAFT, MARY

1975 [1798]   *Maria, or The Wrongs of Woman.* New York: W. W. Norton.

WOOD, FRANCIS J., AND ALICE LANCASTER

1962   Cultural Factors in Negro Adoptive Parenthood. *Social Work* (October): 14–21.

YASSEN, JANET

1995   Preventing Secondary Traumatic Stress Disorder. In *Compassion Fatigue: Coping with Secondary Traumatic Stress Disorder in Those Who Treat the Traumatized.* C. Figley, ed. Pp. 178–207. New York: Brunner/Mazel.

YNGVESSON, BARBARA

2001   National Bodies and the Body of the Child: "Completing" Families through International Adoption. Paper presented at the Conference on International Adoption, Hamilton College, May 11–13.

2000   "Un Niño De Cualquier Color": Race and Nation in Intercountry Adoption. In *Globalizing Institutions: Case Studies in Regulation and Innovation.* Jane Jenson and Boaventura de Sousa Santos, eds. Pp. 145–168. Burlington, VT: Ashgate.

1997   Negotiating Motherhood: Identity and Difference in Open Adoptions. *Law and Society Review* 31(1): 31–80.

YORKSHIRE PUBLIC TELEVISION

1998   *International Dispatch* (documentary).

YOSHINO, KIMI

2002   Families Bear Adoption Hoax Pain. *Los Angeles Times* (May 5): B1, B18.

YUAN, YING-YING, WALTER MCDONALD, CHARLES WHEELER, DAVID STRUCKMAN-JOHNSON, AND MICHELE RIVEST

1990   Evaluation of AB 1562 In-Home Care Demonstration Projects. Sacramento: Walter R. McDonald Associates.

ZACK, NAOMI

1993   *Race and Mixed Race.* Philadelphia: Temple University Press.

ZELIZER, VIVIANA

1992   Repenser le marché. La construction sociale du marché des enfants aux Etats-Unis. *Actes de la recherche en sciences sociales* 94: 3–26.

1985   *Pricing the Priceless Child: The Changing Social Value of Children.* New York: Basic Books.

ZIBART, ROSEMARY

2002   Welcome Home, My Daughter. *Parade Magazine* (January 20): 4–6.

ZWIMPFER, D. M.

1983   Indicators of Adoption Breakdown. *Social Casework* 64: 169–177.

INDEX

abortion, 9, 41, 83, 93, 97, 108

abuse, child. *See* child abuse

adolescence: identity in, 32, 48, 50–51, 77; race in, 48, 50–52; risks for abuse survivors in, 26–27, 58–59

adoption: as a gendered phenomenon, 1, 120–121, 126; media imagery of, 9, 30, 33–34, 38, 41, 90–93, 98–101, 113, 138–139, 151 (*see also* international adoption: in the media); myths about, 80, 98–116; older child, 6, 9, 19, 56–57, 61–65, 75–77; plenary, 91–92, 107, 119; scandals, 89, 91, 93–95, 98

adoption agencies: private, 1–2, 4, 6–8, 11–14, 16, 18–19, 24–26, 28, 30, 40, 45, 59, 75, 79, 81, 83, 86, 88, 92, 101, 111, 113–115, 126, 137, 139, 141, 144–146 (*see also* facilitators; private adoption); public, 1, 6, 8, 11–13, 18, 22, 24, 29–30, 40, 45, 48, 53–54, 59, 88, 112–113, 115–116, 141 (*see also* public adoption); variable practices in, 11, 13–14, 24, 29–30, 40, 62, 85, 88, 106, 112–116

adoption failure. *See* disruption

adoption policies, 33–34, 40, 49, 52–55, 61, 77, 113, 156

adoption statistics, 1–2, 5, 8–9, 14, 79, 95, 103, 108

adoption transition, 10, 20–21, 27, 43–45, 47, 67–69, 72, 75, 87, 121–123, 125–126, 131–132, 134, 142–143

African American adopters, 6–8, 11, 13, 19–22, 26, 29, 38–42, 45–46, 52–53, 66, 81, 120, 124–125, 132, 143, 148, 150

attachment: as a process, 10, 12, 43, 63, 65, 72–73, 77–78, 111–112, 114, 128; disorder, 41, 56, 63, 65, 67, 72, 78, 94, 112, 116, 128–130, 140–141. *See also* adoption transition; substantiation

biracial identity, 12, 26, 33–34, 48–49

birth mothers: attitudes toward, 3, 24–25, 33, 52–53, 61–62, 97, 100–102, 107–110, 146–148; and drug or alcohol addiction, 54, 61–62, 132; and loss of children to foster care, 9, 54–55, 76, 107, 132, 141 (*see also* foster care); in open adoption, 9, 33, 53–54, 86, 146, 155; in private adoption, 3, 7, 9, 13, 86, 104, 146 (*see also* private adoption); relinquishment by, 1, 80, 86, 92, 97, 107, 109–110; socioeconomic conditions of, 2, 13, 24–25, 33, 52, 54–55, 62, 76, 97, 100–101, 108–109, 132, 147–148. *See also* parental rights: termination of

"blue-ribbon baby," 79, 88–89, 103–104, 143

Brazil, 14, 88–90, 99, 101–102, 104

Bulgaria. *See* Eastern European adoptions

business/professional adopters, 13, 84–86, 90, 97, 100–106, 108, 110–111, 114–116, 119–121, 125–127, 130–137, 140, 143–147, 155